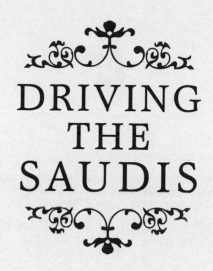

DRIVING
THE
SAUDIS

*A Chauffeur's Tale of Life, Liberty,
and the Pursuit of Happiness on Rodeo Drive*

Jayne Amelia Larson

Simon & Schuster Paperbacks

New York   London   Toronto   Sydney   New Delhi

Simon & Schuster Paperbacks
A Division of Simon & Schuster, Inc.
1230 Avenue of the Americas
New York, NY 10020

First Simon & Schuster trade paperback edition October 2013

SIMON & SCHUSTER PAPERBACKS and colophon are registered trademarks of Simon & Schuster, Inc.

For information about special discounts for bulk purchases, please contact Simon & Schuster Special Sales at 1-866-506-1949 or business@simonandschuster.com.

The Simon & Schuster Speakers Bureau can bring authors to your live event. For more information or to book an event contact the Simon & Schuster Speakers Bureau at 1-866-248-3049 or visit our website at www.simonspeakers.com.

Excerpt from *The Once and Future King* by T. H. White, copyright 1938, 1939, 1940, © 1958 by T. H. White, renewed. Used by permission of G. P. Putnam's Sons, a division of Penguin Group (USA) Inc.

Manufactured in the United States of America

1   3   5   7   9   10   8   6   4   2

The Library of Congress has cataloged the Free Press hardcover edition as follows:

Larson, Jayne Amelia
Driving the Saudis: a chauffeur's tale of the world's richest princesses
(plus their servants, nannies, and one royal hairdresser) /
Jayne Amelia Larson.
p.   cm.

1. Al Sa'ud, House of—Anecdotes. 2. Saudi Arabians—California—
Los Angeles—Anecdotes. 3. Los Angeles (Calif.)—Social life and
customs—Anecdotes. 4. Chauffeurs—California—Los Angeles—
Biography—Anecdotes. 5. Larson, Jayne A.—Anecdotes. I. Title.
DS244.525.L37 2012
953.805'40922794—dc23   2012005133

ISBN 978-1-4516-4001-4
ISBN 978-1-4516-4003-8 (pbk)
ISBN 978-1-4516-4004-5 (ebook)

Author's Note

This book is based on my real-life experiences while working as a chauffeur in Los Angeles over a period of several years. For narrative purposes, I have merged or compressed many of those experiences and have also changed somewhat the timeline of their occurrences.

The names and identifying characteristics of many of the individuals whom I met and with whom I worked have been changed, as well as some of the settings in which I encountered them. In some cases, I have created composite characters in order to portray the spirit of the people concerned while sparing the reader an overwhelming onslaught of characters.

I have worked hard to convey the essential truth of my experience, and have re-created events, locales, and conversations based on notes I took at the time as well as my memories of them. I believe I have a careful memory, or at least I've happily convinced myself that I do. Ultimately, though, human memory is flawed and it is likely that I haven't gotten every last detail just exactly right.

This is, in the end, my own interpretation of events of my own witnessing and my own participation.

For Chris
wherever you are, I hope you are happy

"The best thing for being sad," replied Merlin, beginning to puff and blow, "is to learn something. That's the only thing that never fails. You may grow old and trembling in your anatomies, you may lie awake at night listening to the disorder of your veins, you may miss your only love, you may see the world about you devastated by evil lunatics, or know your honour trampled in the sewers of baser minds. There is only one thing for it then—to learn. Learn why the world wags and what wags it. That is the only thing which the mind can never exhaust, never alienate, never be tortured by, never fear or distrust, and never dream of regretting. Learning is the only thing for you. Look what a lot of things there are to learn."

—T. H. White, *The Once and Future King*

Contents

DRIVING THE SAUDIS

1

The $100 Million Pickup

The drivers were sent to pick up the family and the entourage in the middle of the night. No one was there. Los Angeles International Airport (LAX) was hushed, practically shut down. I'd been there dozens of times before, but I'd never seen it like that; it was spooky. Even the light seemed different, as if all the exterior fixtures had been gelled and dimmed to create an ominous orange haze.

Everything was quiet but I was not. I was way revved up, like a Ferrari at a race start. I felt as if I was in the middle of a $100 million movie set filming an international thriller. Just as on a movie set, our instructions had been minimal and information was scarce, as well as constantly changing. Everybody was silent as if cameras were rolling, but this wasn't a film shoot. This was real.

The head security officer said the Saudi royal family wanted their arrival at the airport to be low key, but we had pulled into the airport with at least forty vehicles—Lincoln Navigators, Cadillac Escalades, Porsche Cayennes, bulletproof armored Mercedes-Benz S600s (the big boys), and even a couple of $300,000 Bentleys—all black, with full-on black tinted windows, and we snaked through the horseshoe-shaped airport in a tight convoy as if we owned the place. I'd never driven before in a caravan of so many cars and it was forceful. We had several LAX police escorts, but they didn't have their bubbles flashing. Even so, we were not low key. We were impressive.

Fausto, the lead driver, waved at us to park along the curb, put our flashers on, and wait. Our windows were open and I could see that many of the other drivers looked as nervous as I felt, their foreheads glistening with beads of perspiration. Our eyes darted about maniacally, trying to follow the torrent of commotion around us; every now and then a driver would wipe sweat off his brow or pull at his collar.

We drivers were told that the Saudi consul and his staff were in attendance to usher the passengers through customs. Since no one spoke to us, we had no idea who was who, but I presumed that the group of men in sharp suits, talking in low tones among themselves just ahead of the convoy at the entrance to the Bradley International Terminal, were from the consul's office. A cadre of serious-looking Saudi Army officers in khakis came out first and conferred with the consulate staff assigned to greet the family. Several linebacker-sized men in civvies strutted about, stepping away from the gathered men to bark instructions on Nextel radios.

As I looked down our line of sedans, SUVs, and luxury vehicles, my eyes tracked the large assembly of black-suited drivers and armed security personnel attending the family. *I was the only woman.*

We had started work at noon and then waited around for several hours for the cars to be made available from various Beverly Hills rental agencies. We then made sure they were carefully detailed, inside and out, and provisioned with water—Fiji water only—and assorted snacks and goodies that the Saudis might request. Some of us had a prior list of what we should be buying for the family member we'd be driving, such as Mentos or Ritz crackers, but we had all stocked up on breath mints and tissues.

Most of us had been working nonstop all day prepping the cars and running errands for the family's security; it didn't look as if we'd be getting a meal break anytime soon, and it was now late evening. I hadn't eaten anything since the morning, and hopped-up nerves had made my throat sandy from thirst. I had stocked my car with the required designer water, placing the pint-sized bottles in each of the cup holders and several more in the pockets behind the front seats along with crisp current copies of *LA Confidential, 90210,* and *Angeleno* magazines. When I saw that most of the other drivers had gotten out of their cars and were making cell phone calls, tugging at their pants, and lighting cigarettes, I retrieved one of the extra bottles from the trunk of my car and choked down a few sips of the fancy water. It was hot, car hot. It tasted like it could be LA River water. I made a mental note to start carrying an iced cooler in the trunk as I'd seen other drivers do.

My stomach churned from hunger. I took another sip of the car-hot water and popped a few Altoids.

I'd never met any members of a royal family before, so I was keen to know what they might be like and to see if they were really all that different from me. Were they smarter? Were they prettier? Were they happier? Would they like me?

It was an unusually warm July evening, and by this time we had been waiting several hours for the family to arrive. I felt as if I was burning up and clammy at the same time. I had so wanted to make a good impression on the royals, and now that seemed lost for good. As I picked up the acrid scent of wet wool wafting up from the inside of my jacket, it was apparent that the eau de toilette I had spritzed on in the morning was now gone, long gone. I had chewed all my lipstick off hours ago, my feet were pink and screaming in the stiff new stacked heels I had just bought for the job, and the silk lining of my black suit was sticking to me like a wet bathing suit. I wriggled around and shook out my legs. I felt like a snake trying to shed its old skin. Every now and then I'd surreptitiously pluck at my suit to put some air between my skin and the lining. I hoped no one noticed.

The drivers had been told to wear black suits to the airport but thereafter could dress in more casual clothes. I was instructed to make sure that my arms and legs were completely covered at all times and that my neckline was never low cut or revealing, but the male drivers could dress more freely and were permitted to wear polo shirts and shorts. I did not have to cover my hair. I was relieved when I was told that; I have copious amounts of curly dark-blond hair, and wrestling it into some kind of contained state can be something akin to an extreme sport, especially in the blazing California summer weather, when it's particularly unruly. Fingers, toes, even a champagne cork or two have been known to get stuck in it. Tearing a rotator cuff trying to get it under control after a wild night is not out of the question.

The family had actually arrived a short while before at a fixed base operation (FBO), a half-mile south of LAX, in their private plane. *FBO* is aviation parlance for a private airport. If you're Oprah in her Gulfstream G500 that seats eight, then you land at one of the FBOs operating out of the cozy Santa Monica private airport 10 miles north up the road. If you're John Travolta in his Boeing 707, or a head of state, or members of the Saudi royal family, then you must land at FBOs such as the ones near LAX, where the big jet planes come in on the 2- and 3-mile-long runways that can accommodate them. Jets cover a lot of distance taking off and even more on landing.

I'd been inside this FBO's plush reception area before on several past jobs when waiting for clients. It was a first-class lounge, and I knew it offered warm saucer-sized chocolate chip cookies, cool drinks, and refreshing ionized conditioned air, but it was off-limits on this pickup. Clearly no one wanted us to be comfortable.

All the drivers had waited in the heavily secured FBO parking lot lined up at attention and watched through a 16-foot-high chain-link and barbed-wired fence as the Saudi royal family's plane descended. The jet's tail had the distinctive gold and blue logo—crossed scimitars above a date palm tree—that I knew to belong to Saudi Arabian Airlines, owned by the Kingdom of Saudi Arabia. Just as the jet's engines shut down, several luxury coach buses pulled up and parked at the base of the air stairs truck on the tarmac. The passengers exiting the plane piled in them and then drove off across the airport tarmac in the direction of the Bradley International Terminal at LAX within view of us one-half mile northwest of the FBO.

We drivers looked at each other in confusion, then we looked around for Fausto to tell us what to do but he had disappeared with the family in the first coach. We didn't know whether we should wait or follow him and the passengers to the Bradley Terminal via surface streets. We thought that we'd be picking up the Saudis at the FBO and driving them back to the hotel, but they had taken off in the buses instead of in our cars. No one had said that this might be a possibility. We had no idea what to do.

After a few tense moments, one of the royal family's security personnel shouted at us to get moving. We jumped in our cars and took off, jockeying to get in position to exit as quickly as we could, but we didn't know where we were supposed to go. Just as we were leaving the gated parking lot, another security guy pulled us back. "No! Wait here! Stay in your cars! Just be ready!" he said. So we waited, engines running. Several of the first cars out had to be tracked down and brought back in line. Everyone was rattled.

Ten minutes later we were told to get on the move again and then abruptly stopped a second time. Now we were totally confused. We were supposed to be a smooth, efficient, and highly professional group, but this pickup was completely disorganized and chaotic; it was a mess. I chewed at a hangnail on my thumb until it bled and then sat on my hands to stop the carnage. I haven't chewed on my nails since I was nine, and I didn't want to start again.

I come from a big family—my immediate circle includes ten children, fifteen grandchildren, with perhaps more on the way, and two great-grandchildren with the statistical probability of at least ten more—and I am accustomed to chaos. Thanksgiving is bedlam, Christmas is pandemonium, weddings are free-for-alls and funerals are a bust, especially if there's a dispute about how or where cremated ashes are to be scattered. I grew up in a cacophony of passionate voices demanding this, commandeering that, negotiating whatever and everything—all at top volume and top speed, often in the middle of the night and through the night. One of my brothers built a 16-foot canoe by hand in his bedroom when he was sixteen, realized it wouldn't fit through the door, hauled it out the window after removing the window frame, and then had the balls to take it down the Raritan River in New Jersey—so I've had a deep and lasting relationship with chaos. Even so, this was unsettling.

Finally, I released my hands and called my chauffeur friend Sami on my cell phone. He was driving one of the Lincoln Navigators in the line ahead of me. "What's going on?" I asked.

"They're going through customs at Bradley," he said. "It never takes long."

"Are you kidding? That could take hours," I said.

"Not for them, *chica*," he said.

Just then, another security guy came tearing out of the FBO waving his arms frantically like a semaphore signalman on an acid trip. "Go! Go! Go to Bradley!" he yelled. After a few unsure moments, we gunned our cars and raced to LAX up the road.

2

How Did I Get Here?

*P*eople always ask me how I ended up being a chauffeur, and there's no rhyme or reason to it. It wasn't a childhood aspiration; I didn't spend hours daydreaming about getting behind the wheel of a large automobile.

I was a multi-hyphenate like everybody else in Hollywood— a stage and film actress who also did voice-overs who also developed movie scripts who had also been the vice president of development at a film company who was scrambling to make it as an independent movie producer on her own. Everybody had warned me about going into the entertainment business. It's so risky, so unreliable, so random. But I was undaunted by the possible perils.

When I was a little girl, I saw one of my older sisters in a play at her all-girls high school. My sister portrayed one of the male characters. She was curvy and very feminine, but with the right costuming, makeup, and attitude, she transformed before my eyes into an astonishingly handsome dude. At first, I didn't even know who she was. She had an exotic accent and movements I didn't recognize as her own, and she was talented too. Yes, I could still see that she was a girl underneath her pinstriped suit and slicked-back hair, but she deftly and poignantly portrayed the emotional truth that could belong to a young man. It was she, but not she. I was thunderstruck.

That's what I want to do! I said to myself. *I want to transform myself like that, all the time, in all different ways. That's what I want to do!* And in spite of the constant admonitions, I thought I would make it as an actress, that I would be the exception to the rule, and I was determined to make it happen at any price—if I could. But of course at the time I had no idea what that might mean.

One of my sisters is a painter who is so focused on her work that one afternoon she burned a hole in her Jean Paul Gautier faux fur coat when she stood for too many hours contemplating one of her paintings while simultaneously warming herself in front of a wall heater. She was so immersed in her process that she didn't notice that she was literally on fire. I paid attention to her, because I knew that she had the goods to be a real artist.

She informed me early on that to be an artist, it was important to have a well-rounded and diverse education, so I spent my undergraduate years at a school in upstate New York, where I developed friendships with talented overachievers who were studying to be physicists, engineers, and architects, while I explored a freer and broader education. I muddled through NeoRealism in Italian Cinema, Acoustical Physics, Mahayana Buddhism, and other essential disciplines. My first two years at school, I didn't have a class before noon because my nights were long and full of other imperative social investigation for my creative and spiritual growth. I learned how to think critically and heard the word *intelligentsia* for the first time, understanding it to mean a class of people actively engaged in the pursuit of knowledge. I liked the sound of that, and I aspired to be part of that group. It didn't trouble me that the intelligentsia didn't concern themselves with acquiring the necessary skills to make a living. They were *thinkers.* Amazingly, I graduated, and even made the dean's list once or twice. Okay, maybe once.

But I received very little dramatic training. I failed the first exercise in my Acting 101 class when I balked at pretending that I was a slice of bacon having an orgasm in the shower, and things went downhill from there. It seemed highly dubious to me that a slice of bacon would be taking a shower in the first place, much less having an orgasm. *So why did I have to do it?* I demanded to know. The instructor muttered something about learning how to use my imaginative powers to stimulate sense memory, but I didn't like the sound of it. It seemed fishy. Graduate school was an absolute necessity if I wanted to develop my acting chops.

I chose, or rather was *chosen by* because the competition for admittance was fierce, a conservatory graduate acting program that was reputed to be one of the best in the world and was also conveniently proximate to my sister's celebrated Cambridge restaurant, where I ensconced myself as a well-fed regular. My figure was never better. I focused on quality, not quantity. If I wasn't dining on insalata caprese, osso buco, and panna cotta, then I didn't eat. Occasionally, before a rehearsal or performance, I would infuriate the restaurant's celebrated chef by ordering a double salad only, but neither my sister nor she held it against me, at least not for long. On special nights, I'd order the pizza, which was so delectable that I still dream about it. It was a happy time.

I performed in over twenty shows; worked with world-renowned directors, designers, and playwrights; and began to understand what it meant to be an artist. I learned about stagecraft, dialects, and sword fighting. I learned how to move, sound, and act like an actor. I played myriad roles: a scatterbrained 1940s film studio secretary costumed in a black velvet gown with a 6-foot train; Hippolyta, the warring queen of the Amazons; and a ninety-year-old Japanese crone transformed into a young woman by the power of love. I even contracted walking pneumonia from riding my bicycle to class in the dead of winter. My freshly washed morning hair would freeze into foot-long icicles—a highly dramatic and also stunning look that I can't really recommend—which afforded me the real sense memories of a real-life Chekhovian heroine with a real cough, and dangerously low blood pressure that gave me a peaked and haunted pallor. I didn't need to pretend that I was a sizzling piece of bacon having an orgasm in the shower. That was for lightweights.

At the graduation ceremony, one of the commencement speakers shared some insight with us regarding our likely future: "I hope you've enjoyed your stay here because it may be the last time you will be acting. From now on, most of you will be bartenders, carpenters, and telemarketers with an Ivy League degree." I paid no attention, because I felt this didn't apply to me. I figured I had a pretty good shot at success since I had paid for part of my graduate training by doing voice-overs in a "Three Musketeers" cartoon, which seemed like a very good omen. Voice-overs are a hoot to do, especially cartoons; you don't have to fix your hair or wear any lipstick because nobody sees you and nobody cares what you look like. It's irrelevant. Voice-over artists just show up at the studio session and have a talent hootenanny portraying characters they might never play if a camera were on them. In one half-day session, I typically recorded a handful of roles: a sexy temptress intent on revenge, a hysterical society matron searching for her stolen pearls, a conniving evil assassin bent on poisoning any and all who got in her way, and even a grieving orphan boy. I had a ball, and I did it all in sweats and my hair pulled back in a ponytail.

I moved to New York City full of confidence to start my theatrical career. The first big gig I landed after graduate school confirmed for me that I had made the absolute right decision. It was a modern adaptation of a Greek tragedy performed outdoors on an abandoned pier in midtown Manhattan. It received great notices in all the papers and was a huge success. My costumes were superb, I performed a romantic dance number with my character's very own Phrygian slave, and I had a love affair with the handsome lighting designer. I was flying high.

Wow! I thought. *I'm working every night in New York with immensely talented people in a hit play—outside under the starry sky, atop a 300-foot steel structure suspended over the Hudson River!*

Wow!

And I'm getting paid to do what I would do for free.

Wow!

How perfect is this?

And the years went by, with a little bit of work here, a little bit of work there, a nice write-up in the paper here, a little Shakespeare there, and then, fifteen years later and after a move to Los Angeles, I was in seriously bad financial straits. I hadn't been on a television show in two years, I hadn't booked a voice-over gig in months, and even then the days of the $20,000 commercial residual paydays were long over.

I'd made a point of learning about the production end of the entertainment business mostly because I loved it, but also because I knew that a way to be part of projects was to create projects. That just made sense.

But I had blown through the $25,000 production bonus I'd received for my work as a producer on an indie film because I had figured that it would last far longer than it did. In the preceding twelve months, every deal I touched, as a producer or as talent, fell through. Every project went south as soon as it looked as if it might be close to taking off. I have a golden-haired brother with the Midas touch—he can just look at something and it makes money. But I was beginning to feel like I had the Dubya touch—one glance from me and everything instantly turned to shit.

In what seemed like overnight, I was $40,000 in debt. It had actually taken quite a while, but it felt that it happened all of a sudden. Bam! It's not that I had lavish lifestyle tastes; in fact, I was agonizingly frugal most of the time, but expenses added up exponentially, especially when I was trying to ignore them. They're sneaky that way: car payments, car registration, car insurance, car servicing, car washing, car parking, car coddling, even car treats. This may seem like overkill, but in LA, your car is vital to your existence because you practically live in it, so you are foolish if you skimp on your vehicle and its needs. Then there were other basics: yoga classes of course, they're a crucial part of the Southern California experience (I went only to the donation-based power yoga— thank you, Bryan Kest—but even so, my downward dogs added up), cell phone bill, cable bill, gas bill, electric bill, and rent, rent, rent, rent!

I'm a banker's daughter, and I've inherited some skills, so I'd spend half the day juggling interest rates on credit cards, making deals with one creditor after another, monitoring the mounting balances with increasing alarm. I even started making deals with myself: *Well, if I don't have any Starbucks for a month, that's at least . . . eighty dollars!!! Holy shit! Okay, I am definitely not buying any Starbucks unless I really, really, really have to have one.* That was hard to live by; desperation deals like that never work.

I became an expert at hiding how truly bad things were; I didn't want people to know, and I was embarrassed that I was failing in my careers— all my careers. I hid from my friends and family. I stopped going out because I was sick of always being somebody's guest, of never being able to pay. That gets tiresome no matter how much your friends like you and want to help you get through tough times.

I needed a regular steady job, even if that meant having to swallow my pride and squelch my soul in work that had nothing to do with my dreams. And then as those dastardly desperation deals are wont to do, they suck you in until hopefully, eventually, you muster up the gumption to say: *I'm not doing this anymore! The money isn't worth it!* But that decision is hard to make when you're trying to figure out how to live or eat or make art.

I knew I had to do something to change things up. I got the idea to work as a chauffeur one night when I was in a limo that my friend Harlow had hired for the evening. We'd been invited to another friend's snazzy party at his penthouse in West Hollywood and didn't want to do any drunk driving like all the Hollywood wannabes who seem to think that a drunk-driving charge and subsequent incarceration is a prerequisite to a movie deal. Harlow arranged a car for us; her friend owns a limo company, and he hooked her up.

I was talking to the chauffeur, Tyrone. He was serene and soft spoken; he told me he loved his job, and he looked sharp in his black Armani suit. He drove us to the party and then read a book in his car while he waited for us. *Hmmmm,* I thought. *Maybe I could do this . . . drive rich people around all day to fancy restaurants and swanky parties. It seems almost glamorous. This might be a perfect temporary solution. It's not as perfect as acting, but maybe it'll be okay for a while until I get things sorted out.*

I started to ask around about the ins and outs of the job. I had a few actor friends who moonlighted in the limo business, and they made it sound pretty tolerable. They said that I'd have a lot of free time to do my own work, that I could take meetings during the day and arrange for time off whenever I booked a job. I could even generate my own A-list clients who would request me and then tip me well for special services. I could be kind of like a concierge in a car. *A concierge in a car . . .* that sounded nice. *I could definitely make that work,* I thought. *In fact, I have to make it work.* I started to think creatively. Perhaps I would pick up some foreign language instruction CDs at the library and brush up on Italian and French on my downtime. Maybe I would even pretend that I was French! I'd treat it as an around-the-clock acting exercise that would also help me pay my rent at the same time. I'd wear deep red lipstick and sheer black silk stockings with a lacy garter belt under my conservative black suit. Even though no one but me would know I was wearing them, my undergarments would imbue me with a secret allure, and no one but me would believe that I was really just a girl from Jersey trying to make ends meet as an artist. It would be me, but not me. Frankly, I had to talk myself into it with that kind of magical thinking because I felt I had few other options. No one from the intelligentsia was helping me get a job in my chosen career, or in any other career for that matter.

When I told my friend Lorelei what I was considering doing to make a living, she was aghast. Lorelei is a gorgeous redhead who had gone to undergraduate school at Columbia and then to acting school with me. Her intelligence and good sense made her sure there had to be better potential revenue streams for me to pursue.

"What the hell? What are you thinking? That's a terrible job for you. Have you lost your mind?"

I ignored her. I decided to force myself to buckle down and make some quick, steady money, and after a few months, I would sell a script I'd been developing or land a great part in a film, and it would all be over. I have a brother who's such a terrific salesman that he can sell the glue off a shoe. It's inspiring to watch and listen to, but more than that, it's empowering. He can get behind anything, full force, if he believes in it, and I knew that that's what I had to do. I was going to get behind it and make it work.

Around this time, a film of mine was finally released in which I played the private nurse of a wealthy man nearing the end of his life. It was a small role, but I had the good fortune to work with Kirk Douglas, and he acted like a doting Jewish grandfather. He was patient, kind, and gracious, and held my arm when we walked to and from the set as if he were escorting me to a ball. My friends on the film said that he made it look as if I was the famous movie star and that he was an ardent older admirer keeping me company.

Before the start of filming, we had a rehearsal with the director in Mr. Douglas's home in Beverly Hills. A small sitting room had been set up with a large bed in which he was lying as if infirm, which he wasn't in the least. In fact, quite the opposite was true. He was in splendid shape, outstanding even, with terrific concentration and focus. Almost ninety years old, he still had regular gym workouts and speech therapy every morning before shooting his scenes to counteract the effects of a recent stroke. We rehearsed with me tending to him as if I were administering medications, making him comfortable by adjusting his pillows, and so on, and he would occasionally wink at me to let me know that it was all a big act—that he could show me a good time the minute I gave him the go-ahead.

At a break in our rehearsal, I looked up at the many beautiful small paintings that covered the walls of the room. I had noticed the art when I'd first come in, but now I really *saw* it, and recognized the artists one after another: Chagall, Miro, Brancusi, and other superb painters whose work I very much admired. The rest of the house was filled with larger pieces that were even more impressive, which he showed me later in the afternoon as if he were a docent at a national museum—strolling from room to room, talking about each painting with great detail. At the end of the day, I thanked him for working with me and for allowing me to see such beautiful art up close in such an intimate setting. He said that he wished he could have shown me his full collection, but that he had already sold most of it. "I wanted to share it," he said, "because it isn't just mine even though I have collected it. It belongs to everyone, and should be enjoyed by everyone." The proceeds of the sales went to the building of hundreds of playgrounds throughout Los Angeles.

On the film shoot, he liked to stay on set to be lit, when most actors would have insisted on a stand-in and retired to their trailers to rest while the camera department did its work. Even though it was very tiring for him, as it would be for any actor much less one his age, Mr. Douglas preferred to help the cinematographer do as good a job as possible by making himself, the star, available. I didn't have a stand-in, so between lighting setups (holding our positions on set as if we were actually filming), we would talk about life and love. He told me that after fifty years of marriage, he was preparing to surprise his wife and ask her to marry him a second time, and he described the elaborate preparations he was undertaking to woo her again as if he were a teenager planning his first date with a major crush. When he discovered that I wasn't married, he shook his head and moaned mournfully.

Each afternoon before his nap, we went through the same routine: he would track through the men he knew, obsessing about which ones he could introduce me to, shaking his head with consternation when he couldn't come up with a satisfactory match. Everyone he knew was married or dead. I had to reassure him over and over again that there was no need for him to worry about it and that everything would be okay. "I just need more time, Mr. Douglas," I said. "I want to find someone special so that I can be as happy as you are with your wife." He'd shake his head and moan a little more. I knew part of him was thinking, in a nice grandfatherly way, *Don't wait too long, bubeleh, because the meter's running.*

My meter was running, and in more ways than one. Deep down, I harbored some last-minute Hail Mary hopes that the release of the movie would catapult me into another phase of financially lucrative work that might save me, but that didn't happen. Movies are a crapshoot, and that one was all snake eyes, as far as box office numbers go.

I had no choice but to continue on with my plan for the fabulous temporary fix. I would be a chauffeur.

In Los Angeles you don't need a special license to drive a limo; you do need a Commercial Class B license if you're hired to drive one of the 30-foot Hummer monstrosities that crowd Sunset Strip on a Saturday night, but a regular eight- or ten-pack stretch limo can be navigated by anybody with a valid driver's license, a small measure of patience, and a willingness to use side mirrors. It would be a long, ugly drive if you didn't use your mirrors. Stretch limos are rarely on the street now; they show up only on prom nights and are usually filled with truculent teenagers wanting to pig out at Taco Bell at midnight. Most people today prefer to be driven in the Lincoln Executive Series Town Car, which has an extended cab and is slightly more luxurious than a regular Lincoln Town Car, and also has more legroom in the back, making it feel like a baby limo. Those are the handsome black sedans you see parked in long lines outside the offices of Wall Street muckety-mucks in all the movies. The car just screams money and power.

I applied to and was immediately hired by an exclusive high-end limo company chauffeuring a lot of movie stars, rock bands, and oh-so-important studio executive types who always seemed to wear size 38 suits when they really needed at least a size 42. I was kept busy with the year-round award shows—the Emmys, Grammys, Golden Globe

15

Awards, MTV Music Awards, People's Choice Awards, BET Awards, Genesis, Nickelodeon—Hollywood bestows a lot of awards on itself to justify the tremendous egomaniacal behavior that runs rampant—and then I was asked to drive for the biggest, baddest night of them all.

The Oscars is not the glamorfest that it appears to be on television. It's a bitch, at least for the chauffeurs. They bring in thousands of town cars and limos from all over the West Coast. Some of the Vegas limos have hot tubs in the back and even a pole in the center for strippers. I've been in a twenty-passenger Hummer limo with a macho chrome exterior and a hot tub that cost a couple of thousand dollars a night to rent. It had a sticky carpet and an assaulting odor (a combination of vomit, sour milk, and chlorine) that no amount of air freshener could fully mask. If something of yours dropped on the floor in that limo, it'd be best to leave it.

My very first Oscars I drove a well-known comedian whose work has an unabashedly political bent. He was unexpectedly well-spoken, but friendly and funny too, as well as tall, and surprisingly good-looking without his moustache. His date was even funnier and so gracious, and delicately pretty, especially up close. She was almost as tall as he was, with long and smooth platinum hair draping over her shoulders in soft waves, and wore an iridescent sea blue and turquoise–colored gown with a sparkly belt and a tremendous train that swished behind her like a long elegant fish tail. She looked like a glittering mermaid with terrific cleavage. Because her gown was so fitted, she could barely sit in the back seat of the car and had to angle herself in a precariously perched position so that her dress wouldn't wrinkle. I was careful not to make any sudden stops so that she didn't slip off the seat and land on the car floor or fly out the window, and I let her borrow my mirrored powder compact when she realized she had forgotten her own.

Our day together started when I staggered to their door in the Hollywood Hills at midday carrying two lavish SWAG bags that were sent along as gifts from the studio, which had also comped the ride. I've been told that SWAG stands for "stuff we all get," but I've never gotten such stuff (I am, however, still hopeful that it's in the offing). Theirs were mammoth baskets, each weighing at least 30 pounds, filled with high-end freebies such as $300 embroidered Italian jeans (size 0 only), caviar firming and bleaching face cream (Can fish eggs really firm and bleach at the same time?), scented soy cruelty-free candles (Who would want to hurt soy, and why?), and a sample selection of reserva tequilas. The hooch was a thoughtful gift because most nominees need a few shots at the beginning, middle, and end of the night.

I dropped off the tall funny guy and the beautiful mermaid at the Kodak red carpet for his photo ops and interviews before I, along with thousands of other limo drivers and their vehicles, was herded a half-mile north into the Hollywood Bowl parking lot, where we were all held hostage for the next six hours as a "security measure." Then the Hollywood parties started and lasted *all night*. I dropped them back at their house after the endless evening of festivities, but I didn't get home until 5:00 A.M. and I had started at noon. That's 17 hours. *Real glamorous.* He graciously tipped me a couple of hundred bucks, but the beautiful mermaid forgot to give back my compact. It was a Christmas gift from my chauffeur friend Sami, with an intricate turquoise enamel inlay, and even though some of the powder had dried out and fallen away in clumps, I loved it. I tried to ask for it at the end of the night, but she dashed out of the car in a flash while he was tipping me, and it seemed small of me to chase her down to try to get it back. I didn't mind, truly, because it did match her dress, but I did miss it, and I wondered if she noticed later that she had forgotten to return it to me.

I didn't realize until I was in the chauffeuring world that it is a man's world and alarmingly lonely when you're a woman. Almost all chauffeurs are men. I'm not sure why I hadn't noticed this before, but it was painfully obvious to me after just one hour of employment. The other women chauffeurs I met were either big and tough, or small and tough, and none of them was gregarious. I am rather medium and not so tough. It would've helped me if I'd been more intimidating.

At times the job was terrifying. One morning at 4:00 A.M., I was pumping gas at a badly lit station on a deserted highway when a drunken bum quietly snuck up and grabbed me from behind. "C'mon baby, you're gonna show me a good time," he slobbered into my neck. I hadn't even heard him coming until he was right there, on me. I shook him off, but I learned from then on to be hypervigilant in order to feel safe. I started carrying around a can of Mace that my dad had given me,

I'd hold my keys strategically placed in my fingers so that I could wield them as a sharp weapon, and I also bought a 2-foot-long Magnum flashlight that could double as a billy club if necessary. I kept it within easy reach just underneath my car seat and practiced whipping it out in the event I ever needed to use it in a hurry.

There were other unexpected perils on the job too. Finding a clean restroom in the middle of the night when I was hours away from home was an all-consuming challenge. I came to truly covet a clean toilet facility and grew to be an expert of the lightning-fast no-part-of-my-body-has-directly-touched-anything-in-here pee. This highly crafty technique employs the use of several disposable paper toilet covers and a stack of paper towels or napkins and, if the facility's paper products are depleted, which is usually the case, some minor acrobatics. In some restrooms, it helps if you have the lung strength to hold your breath for a long time. Years of swimming paid off for me in a big way.

When working late night at one of the hotels, I was often mistaken for a hooker by inebriated Hollywood types tottering out of the lobby bar, even though I am sure I made it clear by my body language—my eyes down, crossing the street ahead of them, and ignoring their catcalls—that I was absolutely not available for hire in that way, ever. Clients regularly propositioned me in the car, even as I was driving them home to be greeted by their wives and kids, and some would become insulting when I refused their advances. "Whaddaya gettin' so high and mighty about? You ain't no Marilyn Monroe anyway," a pockmarked charmer complained to me as I fended him off.

Early one morning, a drunken twenty-something club kid vomited and then passed out in my car, waking up only to try to urinate in it as I was struggling to extricate him from the vehicle. We had driven around for hours with him hanging out of the car window propositioning transvestites on Santa Monica Boulevard. He wanted to hire one as a present for his teenage girlfriend. "I gotta prove my love for her," he cried over and over. How a transvestite would accomplish this I couldn't determine, but thankfully none of them would get in the car. At 4:00 A.M., he couldn't remember the address of his parents' house in Bel Air. When I finally deduced the location and tried to drop him home, he was terrified his parents would awaken and punish him, and he refused to get out of the car, curling into a ball in the backseat. A houseman finally came out of the estate, thanked me for bringing him home, and carried the sobbing, transvestite-less club kid inside to bed.

I hadn't expected this kind of behavior. I had thought the work was going to be classy and maybe even a little bit cool, or at least I had talked myself into thinking that would be true. I had thought I would make a lot of money driving wealthy businessmen on quick trips to the airport who would then ask me to dinner at Nobu when they got back from their conference in Shanghai or Lake Como, possibly bearing gifts for me from duty-free shops. I had thought that I'd decline the invitations and the gifts, thereby gaining a reputation for possessing a high moral character. I had thought that I would be able to pitch movie ideas and field script development offers, but that just wasn't happening. The hours were unbearably long, I was so severely sleep deprived from baby-sitting overly elated tourists on their all-night Sunset Boulevard club-hopping marathons followed by puking binges, that I was useless during the day to do my own work. To top off all the perks, the generous tips were nonexistent or at best disappointedly sporadic, and the job was dishearteningly soul sucking.

As a chauffeur, I began to see behind the Tinseltown curtain in a way I never would have expected or wanted. In my first weeks of employment, I was assigned to drive the courtesy car for a tony Beverly Hills hotel. Most luxury hotels have house cars that drop off and pick up guests within a few miles radius when they want to go shopping or dine at a restaurant in the vicinity. It's a plum job for the chauffeur, and I would have loved doing it routinely. Unfortunately, I was only covering vacation time for the regular senior driver, a permanent fixture who would likely expire on the job before giving it up.

Early one night, the hotel doorman, José, asked me if I would do him a favor by picking up a girlfriend a few blocks away and bringing her back to the hotel. He wrote down a nearby address, and I drove to a condo on Doheny to collect her.

An attractive young woman, simply dressed in a pale pink cotton sheath dress, was waiting outside for me under the portico when I drove up. She was petite and waif-thin, with short blond hair falling in soft curls around her pale face. Without makeup and high heels, she could have passed for a fourteen-year-old girl. She had a slight Russian accent, a bubbly personality, and a whispery voice that was pleasing and refined. I assumed that she was joining José for his dinner break.

"A female chauffeur! I am lucky!" she said as she jumped into the limousine. Her cell phone rang then, and she chattered away on it for the short drive back to the hotel.

"Thank you," the young woman said when we arrived at the hotel. "I am sorry that I have not cash on me to tip you. I have nothing, but perhaps you will be here later and I will see you again? Perhaps at nine o'clock?"

"Don't worry about it," I said. "Have a nice dinner."

A few hours later, I dropped off some guests at the hotel front entrance. José was still on duty, so after he had taken their bags and ushered them inside to the reception desk, I said, "Hey, José, your girlfriend is really pretty and nice," and he grinned.

Just then the hotel lobby elevator doors opened and the young woman stepped out holding the arm of a white-haired older Japanese man in an elegant sharkskin jacket. She kissed him on both cheeks, he got back into the elevator, and then she walked across the lobby alone toward us, smiling. Her high heels clicked loudly on the marble floor, and she swung her beaded handbag playfully as she moved.

"Oh, you are here, this is fantastic!" she said. "Are you perhaps free? I know my apartment is very close, but I am afraid to walk home alone in the dark."

"No, no, I don't blame you," I said. "Of course, I'll take you."

She kissed José and again jumped in the limousine without allowing me to open the door for her. "Please, do not trouble yourself," she said.

She got on her cell phone again right away, so we didn't talk on the way back to her place. In my rearview mirror, I watched her freshen up her lipstick and makeup as she made several calls. When I dropped her off, she handed me a crisp hundred-dollar bill.

"This is for your kindness," she said as she got out of the car.

I tried to give it back. "No, please. You don't need to tip me. I am happy to—"

"I insist," she said. "I appreciate your help very much, and besides the night is just beginning." She winked at me; then instead of walking back into her apartment, she headed across the street to the Four Seasons Hotel. I don't know why it took me so long, but I didn't realize until that moment that she was a prostitute.

I kept the hundred-dollar bill that she had given me for weeks, as long as I could go without spending it, and I thought of her when I finally did. *She was just a baby,* I said to myself.

After a couple of months on the job, I couldn't help but acknowledge that the whole driving thing was not working out on any front. The job was becoming a problem, not a solution. In fact, I was still broke, I hadn't made any movie deals, I spent every evening worrying about where I was going to pee, and I was starting to get depressed about things that I hadn't even thought about before.

Just as I was hitting rock bottom, a new opportunity reared its pretty head. All of the other limousine drivers at the company where I worked were talking about the Saudis: "The Saudis, the Saudis, the Saudis! A family of Saudi royals are coming to Beverly Hills and they need drivers, and they pay top dollar!" Rumors flew about how much money we could make. One driver had a friend who had been invited to travel with a Saudi family after driving them around Los Angeles for only a few weeks. They paid for him to fly with them to London, New York, and Paris for months, all first class. He didn't even have to drive; they just liked his company and wanted him around. They even gave him beaucoup spending money. Charles, an experienced driver friend from the East Coast, said he drove some Saudi royals for only thirty days, and at the end of the job he'd received his pay, a gold Rolex, and a $10,000 tip. Sweet! This group was expected to stay at least fifty days, so there could be some substantial money involved.

The interviewing process for the Saudi job was odd. No one ever asked me about my professional chauffeuring experience. I assumed this was because Fausto, the lead driver running the detail, had recommended me for the job, but to this day I don't know for sure and I can't say it demonstrates very good business practices. Then I received a series of perplexing phone calls over a period of several days. The family's security doing the advance work called me and asked how I had learned about the job, who else I knew on the detail, and who referred me. I knew they knew that Fausto had told me about the job and that he had referred me, and when I reminded them of this, they confirmed that this was so. Okay, so were they testing my memory of the last two days? Were they thinking I might lie about it? It was truly peculiar. And I had no way to know who else was on the job. It hadn't even started yet, and besides it was all too secretive for me to know anything anyway. It was as if the actual job didn't even exist, just the promise of employment, and that was pretty much useless. That's like being told you have the lead in a movie and "principal photography will commence once the funding has been secured." Anybody who has been in the entertainment business for ten minutes knows that that is code for "it's probably not happening."

A couple of more days went by. After several more similarly puzzling calls, I was asked to fax my license to different numbers whose area codes I didn't recognize. I then spent hours in line at the DMV to obtain an H-6 California printout that lists all traffic accidents or infractions incurred in the past ten years. I faxed the H-6 and my license again, this time to other different numbers. I spoke with many people a day about when the family was arriving and when the drivers would be needed. First they needed me, and then they didn't. Then they needed me again, and then the job was off. The details changed on an hourly basis, and the dates were postponed repeatedly. I began to lose hope that the Saudis were coming at all.

Then I had to refax all of my paperwork to still different numbers, but here in Los Angeles. That was encouraging. Fausto finally said it was a go, but first I had to meet with the family's security staff in person. Up until then, it had been a phone romance only. I met a small battalion of superhero action-type figures briefly at a hotel in Beverly Hills. Every now and then one of them squinted at me and asked, "Jew? Are you a Jew?" No one had ever asked me that before, and certainly not repeatedly. Even Fausto asked me this over and over again. "You're not a Jew, you're sure? No Jew in you? You sure? No? Okay! We wouldn't want to find out later. You sure? You sure? You sure?"

"Yeah, I'm sure!" I told them but I thought to myself, *Would they really not hire me if I were?*

22

That was the whole screening process. There were no background checks, no references called, nothing. I did have a clean DMV record, so I am sure that counted for something, but I was surprised at the lack of due diligence given how much rigmarole there had been over basic details. I could have been a Jew in disguise for all they knew.

So I got the job to drive for a family of Saudi royals: Princess Zaahira and her children, the family's security, and their entourage in a large detail of over forty drivers. The chauffeurs were told we'd be required to be on call and available 24/7, seven days a week, for perhaps as long as seven weeks straight. There would be no days off, and we could expect to be fired if we needed one.

It was soon apparent that I was the only female working for the family. I had met two other women whom I rarely saw when the job started, but they didn't last. One was fired after an altercation with the security personnel, and I heard the other one quit almost right away; she didn't like the long hours.

Women aren't allowed to drive in Saudi Arabia, and the Saudis don't really want women driving them here either, but it turned out that I did come in handy in ways that probably no one could have expected.

3

I'm Part of a Special Op!

T hings started off rather nicely. Just before the family arrived, the drivers had a long full-day training session in a Beverly Hills hotel ballroom that was set up as if we were at the Davos World Economic Forum, with rows of tables facing a dais at the front of the room, pads and pencils before each chair, and bouquets of fresh flowers on every table. Several waiters were on hand throughout the day to pour sodas and water, a sumptuous breakfast and lunch were served, and cappuccinos were available whenever we liked. Bowls of chocolates and mints were refreshed throughout the day in case we needed a sugar push. It must have cost $20,000 to rent the room for the occasion. Most of the other chauffeurs looked uncomfortable and lingered near the periphery as if they'd never been in a hotel ballroom before, but I decided to make the best of it and parked myself in the front row of tables. I had three strong double-cappuccinos in a row and followed them with strawberries and pineapple once I was fully awake. This is a high-voltage cleansing regimen that I call the "Hollywood Royal Flush"—massive amounts of caffeine followed by fruit. The lunch later in the day was a selection of grilled salmon or roast beef au jus, with an array of seasonal vegetables. I relaxed in my chair and felt happily feted, like a guest at an expensive all-day wedding waiting for the band to strike up and the dancing to begin.

I saw that two of my driver friends, Sami and Charles, were on the job too. It was nice to see some friendly faces since many of the other drivers seemed to know one another and stood in small groups chatting, and I felt left out. Sami was an unprepossessing Mexican: taciturn, discreet and cautious, sharp as a tack, and fiercely observant. He didn't miss a trick. If I had a SWAT team, I would want him on it.

Charles was a handsome older man filled with an inexhaustible supply of goodwill toward others. He had a calm, friendly manner and was generous with his knowledge and information. He was old school and refused to be easily ruffled; he'd been a chauffeur for nearly thirty years. Nothing surprised him because he'd seen it all and then some, and most likely he had done a considerable amount of it too. He was also accustomed to these long details and said to me early on in the job: "You gots to get your meal, you gots to hydrate whenever you can, you gots to look out for *herself*, girl." It was good advice that I tried to remember as often as I could.

An ex-commando type, Stu, was one of the heads of the security running the detail and conducted most of the instruction. When I say "instruction," what I really mean is that there was a lot of standing around and waiting for somebody to talk to us. It wasn't like an hours-long training class where we had to be responsible for information that was imparted. Mostly we just milled around in a fluid holding pattern that was periodically interrupted by a short lecture on the detail's operation and protocol; overpreparation was not going to be a problem. There were several more imposing jefes who introduced themselves during the afternoon, all bricklike men with monosyllabic names like Buck and Chuck, with short haircuts or closely shaved bald heads. There seemed to be a lot of men in charge, maybe too many, and I never did figure out the chain of command. But they were a surprisingly soft-spoken group; almost no one raised his voice, and never without good reason.

Stu resembled a bizarre cartoon—somewhat like a colossal version of Popeye pumped up on steroids, but dressed in a tight short-sleeved white shirt and sharply creased khaki pants instead of a sailor outfit. He was a huge walking muscle; every part of him was thick and developed and ready to engage. He had a neck as wide as my thigh, solid and pulsing.

Stu was from Mississippi, and he was a nice guy, truly a gentleman, and also a consummate professional. I witnessed this one afternoon when he was on duty covering Princess Zaahira while she was shopping with her friends along Robertson Boulevard. The security guys walked a close parameter around the group, and Stu was covering the rear. I watched him quietly step behind a tree. An instant later he leaned over, hands on knees, and projectile vomited two times in succession, then he wiped his mouth with the back of his hand and got back in step with the group. He told me later that he'd had tooth surgery that morning and was suffering from a bad reaction to the anesthesia. I was the only one who knew what had happened, and Stu worked the detail the rest of the day without missing another beat.

Although he was a genteel southerner, he didn't speak laconically when he was addressing the troops. He was the only member of the security personnel who gave his lungs a workout. He barked loudly in rapid-fire bursts as he patrolled the ballroom in 4-foot strides. "Always say YOUR HIGHNESS. Never look 'em in the eye. Do not speak unless you are spoken to. You are not dismissed until they tell you so. You got that? Always check in to Alpha One Command Post with any unusual situations or difficulties, or Alpha Two Post, or Alpha Three Post, or Alpha Four Post. You got that? The family is staying in many different hotels. All in Beverly Hills. So there are many command posts. There is a security command post in each hotel. Always know your command post leader! You must know where everybody is staying at all times, even if they change hotels every night. Consider yourself warned, because they *will* change hotels!"

I had no idea what he was talking about. I didn't know military speak. Alpha One Post? Command post? I learned later that each command post was a near-empty hotel room with a long rectangular table covered with computers, faxes, and other apparatuses I didn't recognize, which were probably machines used by and to communicate with the Department of Defense. All the artwork was taken down, and the walls were plastered with whiteboards and maps. Along one wall was a bank of monitors with various views of the hotel elevators, hallways, and entrances. Each room had a thick electrical cable snaking out of it that was "Hollywooded," secured with a thick layer of duct tape, along the edge of the hallway, where it disappeared into another room at the far end of the hall that emitted a low hum. The rooms had satellite phones, and there were daily reports from the U.S. State Department regarding risk and travel issues for the family that security monitored. Used room-service trays were often piled high in the corners of the rooms. A thin mattress was placed in the large party bathtub in the Alpha One bathroom, where the security could nap when not on rotational duty. *Wow!* I thought when I saw the room for the first time. *I'm part of a Special Op!*

We were told that everyone in the family and the entourage had his or her own car and driver that was to be available around the clock, and that we should make sure that the cars were clean, stocked, and gassed at all times. That meant that if you had only a quarter tank of gas and your client decided spur of the moment that he wanted to go to San Diego (this happened with surprising frequency), then you had a serious dilemma. You couldn't stop for gas with a client in the car. That's like a waiter taking a restaurant guest into the kitchen and asking him to wait while his cappuccino is made. It is extremely bad form. I had to gas up at least once a day, often in the middle of the night, just to make certain that I was always operating with a half-tank or more.

There's no telling how higher education can pay off. My powers of association and discernment were now defined by a dire and constant need to fill up my vehicle's gas tank. I became an authority on which stations within a 30-mile radius were open after midnight, well lit, and heavily populated. Those with a convenience store attached were the most desirable.

Except for one male, who wasn't a Saudi and didn't mind if a woman drove him, I was permitted to drive only the Saudi women of the group, but I would also occasionally be assigned to drive the servants when the women didn't require my services. Most of the other chauffeurs were assigned to drive only one person and stayed with that one person the duration of the detail.

Stu said the family was here to do some shopping, so I assumed that my missions would be fairly straightforward. I knew all the ins and outs of the Golden Triangle, which encompasses all the best shops and restaurants in Beverly Hills, so I was looking forward to spending time on familiar turf that I'd traversed well and fully while driving the hotel courtesy car. But it turned out that the Saudi women had come to La-La Land for plastic surgery as well as shopping. They did, in fact, shop almost every day, sometimes all day. But if they weren't shopping, they were in surgery. If they weren't in surgery, they were shopping, or enjoying refreshments at a restaurant between shopping and minor surgery. Very rarely, they'd go to the movies and then sit outside to people-watch at a late night café in Westwood. They weren't interested in museums, or the Venice Canals Artwalk, or the Japanese meditation garden at UCLA, or any other cultural activities of any kind, but they really knew and appreciated their high-end goods.

Santiago, a chauffeur originally from Central America, was assigned to drive a teenage prince. The prince and I never formally met (I wasn't introduced to any of the men). I only saw him from a distance occasionally, when he would nod politely to me. He was slender and very tall for his age, dressed neatly and conservatively, and usually all in white. I saw that he paid great attention to everything happening around him without remarking on it, and I could tell that he was very bright.

This young prince always read books in the car. He was taking summer extension school classes at USC from morning until night, and Santiago said he went through a book a day while riding in the car. Besides one other princess, he was the only Saudi I ever met who read books. Some of the royals leafed through magazines, but I never saw anyone from this group with a book in hand or in any of their rooms. Santiago said he heard the young man talking about his great-great-great-grandfather, boasting that he was a noble and valiant warrior and that the Kingdom of Saudi Arabia existed because his family reconquered lands that had been robbed from them. He was very proud of this fact, probably in much the same way that I am proud of my father for being a successful self-made businessman.

The prince had regular assigned security who traveled with him at all times wherever he went, as well as an older Egyptian nanny who doted on him. I wondered why he needed a nanny at that age, but I was told that a nanny often stays until her charge is married in his twenties or even thirties and acts as more of a secretary or handler by that time. Santiago told me that the security and nanny would wait outside in the courtyard at USC with their eyes focused on the classroom door while the prince was in session. They would all have lunch together at midday in the school café. The nanny was always in charge of the money and paid for all of their meals as well as anything the prince might want to purchase on the way home.

"The husband is not traveling with the princess on this trip," Stu told us at the beginning of the training session. "But he will be receiving daily reports from the Saudi Army officers assigned to this very important detail. You got that? So he knows everything that's going on at all times. There are other men traveling with the princess, *sheikhs* they call 'em, but they will not be socializing with the women, and they will never be taking meals with them. They do not spend time with the opposite sex. Separate living, separate sleeping, separate eating. That's the way it's gonna be here."

I noticed that I was the only one of the drivers writing anything down, and I questioned Sami about this. "No need, *chica*," he said as he tapped his temple. "Gotta keep it all up here. Safer." I put my pencil down then. I didn't want to appear overly studious. It turned out that most of the information was incorrect anyway, or accurate for a short time only, and we were told very little in any case.

Right from the beginning, we weren't told the actual name of the family, just that they were Saudi royals. Nor were we told the full name of any of the members of the entourage, usually only a name that was reduced to something like "Cousin" or "Auntie." The cryptic briefing extended to the details of the family's stay as well, which were doled out sparingly on a need-to-know basis only. Regarding their arrival, we were told simply that they'd be coming soon, maybe the next day, or the next evening, maybe the day after that, and their day of departure might be sometime several weeks hence, or maybe more. Nor were we told how they might spend their days, where they might go, or whom they might visit. It would all be discovered during the course of the job. This was highly unusual in the chauffeur business. Before any of my previous jobs, I always knew the name of the client, where he lived, where he worked, where he was going, where he was going after that, whom he was sleeping with, what medication he was on, whether he was a closet cross-dresser. That's one of the perks of hiring a premier car service: it offers customized handling based on the details known about the client, which have usually been given to guarantee very personal attention. On the Saudi job, we'd be flying blind, and it was apparent that the family preferred it that way. None of the drivers in our group even spoke Arabic. I assumed that the family would have liked to have Arabic speakers who could translate for them, but I was told that they specifically didn't want any drivers understanding what they might talk about in the privacy of the car. They spoke to us in English if they wanted to be understood. All of the royals spoke English well, especially when they wanted to make their wishes known.

In general, chauffeurs hear everything that is said in the car if they care to listen, and even if they don't. The accurate interpretation of even an overheard one-ended telephone conversation is also remarkably easy. Once I picked up a famous music producer and a friend of his after their weekend outing in Vegas. They came in on a private plane to Van Nuys Airport both reeking of marijuana and body odor and carrying several bottles of beer in their jacket pockets. The music producer was a burly bald man with bad skin and a wet mass of chest hair bursting out of the top of his shirt, and he wore a $2,000 suit that needed to be thoroughly dry-cleaned pronto. His frothing friend sitting in the car beside him hung on his every word like a happy sycophant. As the mogul reminisced about the weekend's merriment, he repeatedly said things along the lines of: "Those chicks were hot, smoking hot," and "I'll do that bitch again anytime." I thought he was charming. Then he received a cell phone call from someone he addressed as O.J., and O.J. was undoubtedly in some financial trouble. The producer had hesitated before taking the call and complained that "the guy will not leave me alone; ten times in the last twenty-four hours he's calling me." He then had to stay on the phone a long time to talk O.J. down, saying things like, "Man, I'm sorry, that's rough, real rough, O.J., but I don't have access to that kind of cash. I feel for you, man, but I told you, I just don't have it. Yeah, I know, but you gotta think of somebody else, bro. I can't swing it." When he ended the phone call, the producer then did a play-by-play of the conversation for his buddy, so it was impossible not to know what had transpired. I practically had it memorized. By the time we arrived at the mogul's McMansion in Calabasas, the cohorts had both fallen asleep and were snoring like bears, with the sycophant drooling on his friend's suit jacket lapel. I couldn't wait until they were out of the car.

Stu reminded us to try to keep a low profile—we should be seen and not heard. We were not to ask questions of the royals unless absolutely necessary. It was considered rude and presumptuous to suggest anything to the royals or to try to anticipate their wishes. We were not to contradict them even when we knew there might be a problem with what they were requesting. For example, if they asked me to take them to the Beverly Center mall and I knew that it was already closed, I could not tell them so. I had to drive them to the mall in case, perhaps, they only wanted to do a tour of the parking lot while it was empty. I didn't see the point in this.

We had to be sure that our cell phones were charged up and accessible at all times, day or night. We were under strict orders not to talk on the phone for any reason if the client was in the car. This turned out to be impossible to sustain. The royals and the entourage repeatedly asked their chauffeurs to make phone calls for them on our own phones when they were in the car, and even handed us their phones to take calls while we were driving. Sometimes I had to juggle two or more calls at once, trying to find out information that they were demanding to know immediately, or to communicate with another group they wanted to join on an outing or to give another driver directions to meet up with us. It was round-the-clock royal ground traffic control. At first, I tried to pull the car over whenever they asked me to use the phone, but that was vetoed in short order.

We were instructed always to wait for our clients within a block or two of where we had dropped them off. This also turned out to be problematic because often the person I was assigned to drive would hop in somebody else's car and be driven to another location, without giving me any heads-up at all. Hours later, I might get a call from security demanding to know why I wasn't with my client at Chanel on Rodeo Drive, when the last time I had seen her was when she was scarfing down pasta at the American Girl Café in the Grove mall. Normally clients tell you if they are changing plans; in fact, they actually want you to know where they are so that you can provide good service; it's in their best interest to help you help them. On this job, I learned to

31

tail whoever I was driving by making visual sightings of them at regular intervals throughout the day so that I could be sure to know where they were at all times. I felt ridiculous doing this, but it was the only way I could think of to maintain an accurate assessment of their whereabouts. Even so, I sometimes felt as if they were purposely trying to avoid being tailed or found out. It was kindergarten antics; a peculiar little palace game of hide-and-seek from the chauffeurs. But why?

Stu had told us that the Saudi group would be staying in many different Beverly Hills luxury hotels, including the Regent Beverly Wilshire, the Four Seasons, the Peninsula, L'Ermitage, and the grande dame of them all, the Beverly Hills Hotel—occupying several floors of each. This is one of the few bits of information that turned out to be true. Most of the women stayed in one hotel, most of the men stayed in another, the eldest son of Princess Zaahira stayed with his male friends and staff at another, and several older important-looking men with mustaches (who were all driven in the pricey Bentleys that I saw at the airport pickup) stayed elsewhere. Various other family members were sprinkled over the Beverly Hills environs in private estates and compounds. There was no socializing among the men and women, not even for meals, although Princess Zaahira's children sometimes visited her.

I hardly saw the Saudi men, and they didn't seek me out. Occasionally a tight cluster of them would stride in or out of the hotel at odd hours, talking gruffly and smoking as they walked, but none of them engaged me in conversation or even glanced my way. If we happened to arrive at the lobby elevator together, they'd invariably stand off to the side and I'd ride up alone while they waited for the next elevator car.

4

Where Are the Veils?

*A*t the airport, the Saudis breezed right through customs, just as Sami had said they would, even though I was told they had a chest full of American dollars. One of the guys at the FBO said it was $20 million: $1 million in stacks of hundred-dollar bills weighs about 20 pounds and fits into a 5-inch Halliburton attaché case. Twenty such cases would fit into a chest big enough to carry a large human body. That's a lot of moola.

"Every one of these Saudi groups comes with cases of cash," said the guy from the FBO. "That's the way they roll. They like to have stacks and stacks of cash, and they like to show it off. Some of them even come in on their own 747. Talk about a humongous plane. That's some friendly skies." He told me many of the planes have their insides completely gutted and redecorated to resemble the inside of the *I-Dream-of-Jeannie* bottle with plush velvet-tufted settees, king-size beds, 50-inch flat screen TVs, and Turkish baths with 14-carat-gold fixtures. One Saudi prince even owns a jet that houses a baby grand piano and a cocktail lounge. Playing the piano at 35,000 feet has some serious wow factor.

Fausto hand-signaled to the chauffeurs to stay sharp and keep our eyes peeled as we waited for our passengers near our cars. As the royals started exiting customs, we all livened up. Several clusters of dark-haired, mustached, well-suited, but weary men walked out first. They moved with great focus and force but as if they were dragging boulders behind them, their shoulders prone forward with the weight. They immediately headed toward the Saudi officers gathered with the consul staff and conferred with them in husky whispered voices. They didn't look at or speak to any of the chauffeurs.

The women exited separately, and as they started to trickle out I thought, *Where are the Saudis? Where are the veils?* I was expecting to see women coming out in black robes and head coverings, but the ladies coming out didn't look like Saudis; they looked like a bunch of Brazilian hotties going nightclubbing. Many of the women were scantily clad in Versace, Gucci, and Prada with inch-long flashy fingernails, lustrous jet-black hair flowing down to their waists, and layers of perfect makeup in smoky tones. *Could a flight from Rio have come in at the same time as theirs?* I wondered. More women joined them, older and less audaciously dressed but still chic and modern. Behind them trudged another group of women, most of them dressed in traditional Islamic garb with covered heads and modest clothing. Many were very young and petite, with dark skin and no hint of makeup. They looked exhausted.

As I made my way to them, thinking that they were the Saudi royals, one of the half-dressed, bronzed-up sexy chic ladies turned and spoke brusquely to them in Arabic. As a group, in sharp unison like a flock of draped birds, they flinched in response. I realized that the downtrodden-looking ladies were the servants and that the sexy chic women were the royals and their traveling entourage. The sexy chic women paraded past me without acknowledgment, but almost every servant woman smiled and dipped her head at me as she walked by. A few of them looked at me with puzzled expressions as if to say, *Who is she? What is she doing here?*

I was puzzled too. I hadn't expected the Saudi royal women to look so done up or so Westernized. An oil engineer I met told me that when he flies commercially from Riyadh to Paris, he invariably witnesses a spectacular transformation. "I'll be in first class with a woman from Saudi Arabia seated next to me dressed in a long black cloak, black gloves, and black veil—the whole deal. I can't even tell what she looks like, she's so covered up. Sometimes even their eyes are covered, and they have black booties on, so no skin shows at all. Then the plane takes off, leaving Saudi airspace. She goes to the bathroom and then a minute later a glamour-puss in high heels and a short, short skirt takes her place.

Chanel from head to toe. Same woman. She's wearing the stuff underneath her cloak. This happens every time I fly. Sometimes there are a whole lot of them. They look like a dark cloud getting on the plane, and then they suddenly strip down, half-dressed and sparkly. And then you notice: Saudi women are good looking," he said.

In the Kingdom, it's the law that a woman must be completely covered when out of the house, but once she's out of the country, she can wear whatever she wants, and the Saudi women do. The servants were religious, however, and I soon saw that they dressed in complete cover at all times no matter where they were, indoors or out.

The head of the family was Princess Zaahira, who was traveling with a number of her sisters, friends, and cousins, several of her many prince sons and one princess daughter, of whom I was told by one of the servants, "she squeezed out at the last second with great happiness." She wanted a baby girl and finally had one, last in line. All of her children had friends joining them for the trip—other young princes and princesses—and servants—an astounding number of servants, and secretaries, and nannies, and tutors, and trainers, and cooks, and doctors, even a psychiatrist, a massage therapist, the royal hairdresser, and a bunch of other people hanging around kind of like court jesters—that was the entourage. There were about forty people in all accompanying the family of seven.

Princess Zaahira was in her late thirties and strikingly beautiful, really princess-like, with long, black, perfectly coiffed hair that she wore in elaborate and artful arrangements, and flashing dark eyes that carefully monitored everything happening around her. She had an open smiling face with high, wide cheekbones and luminescent flawless skin, and all her movements were measured and graceful. There was nothing rough or rushed about her. Maysam, one of the palace's teenage servant girls from North Africa, said that Princess Zaahira was worshipped by her husband. I thought it must be because she was so beautiful, but I was told that it really was because she gave him seven sons. Because of this, she was his favorite of his many wives, and she basked in his favor. She was also far more beautiful than any of the other women in the group, even her sisters; it was as if an aura of shimmering light enveloped her, making her life magical and effortless. She had the "money shine," as my driver friend Sami says: wonderfully waxed, perfectly polished, and beautifully buffed. Whenever her bulletproof-armored Mercedes-Benz pulled up to the hotel entrance signaling that she was coming or going, the employees at the hotel—men and women alike, who were accustomed to regular celebrity sightings and were pretty blasé in general—would invariably stop what they were doing to better position themselves to get a glimpse of her. She was that beautiful. It was easy to forget that this was probably partly so because she was surrounded by a highly skilled and accommodating staff tending to her every need.

I was told that I was specifically hired to drive a young princess, a niece of Princess Zaahira. Fausto had given me a sign that said "MICHELE," similar to the ones you see chauffeurs holding in front of baggage claim when you deplane. As the girls and women passed me, I pointed to the sign and asked, "Michele? Michele?" All of them giggled and quickly skirted by. I saw that most of the Saudi teenage girls were also dressed in thousands of dollars worth of fashionable clothing; they were ultra-chic miniversions of the older women. Saudis buy over 75 percent of the world's haute couture, so I guess they start the girls off young.

I continued to seek out Michele until a thin-lipped English woman with tightly curled apricot-colored hair, a chaperone to one of the young Saudi teenagers, reprimanded me for bothering the girls: "You are asking the wrong people. Michel is a man, the princess's hairdresser. He is over there." She pointed to a very tan middle-aged man dressed in a sequined T-shirt and tight, low-cut jeans, smoking a cigarette near the curb. He had a huge potbelly that poured out over his pants, and silver-streaked reddish wiry hair that struck out from his head in all different directions à la Don King. This was Michel. He wasn't a Saudi; he was a Tunisian hairdresser whom the princess had met in Paris and now traveled with—the royal hairdresser. I was so disappointed. *What the hell!* I thought. *Where's my little princess? And he's supposed to be a hairdresser? This guy needs a comb and some serious face time with a mirror. I don't want to drive him, not without inoculations. He looks like he bites.*

The passengers didn't walk out with any suitcases because there were two huge cargo trucks at the back of the limo line with a bunch of guys to grab the luggage. There were hundreds of bags, some as big as a Volkswagen. Many were shrink-wrapped in plastic like gigantic frozen TV dinners. Most of the cases were made by Louis Vuitton, Gucci, or Coach, and some of them cost as much as a year's rent on my apartment. The servants lingered behind to make sure all the bags were accounted for and transported to the correct hotels. They sat on the suitcases, guarding the bags they were responsible for like roosting hens on their eggs.

The Saudis traveled large, like a military operation. I discovered later that all of that shrink-wrapping covered furniture, fine silk rugs, all kinds of tchotchkes, Limoges china, special cookers, chafing dishes, lustrous silver serving trays, ornate gilded and ceramic Persian samovars, extraordinary coffees, teas, dried fruits, rice, beans, grains, spices, candy, and rich chocolate that you can get only in the Middle East. They brought a whole palace with them. Maybe several palaces. They even brought incense.

Not all families travel this way. A friend of mine does staging for luxury homes in Los Angeles, and she was hired to completely redecorate a home for a Saudi princess who would be renting it for a short stay. The princess didn't like the priceless antiques in the house and had it redone in an ultramodern style costing tens of thousands of dollars for a one-week rental. The princess didn't bring anything with her when she arrived, and she left everything she'd purchased at the house.

One of the shrink-wrapped monstrosities turned out to be a tea set that had its very own $500-a-day hotel room to itself: servants would go in and out at all hours preparing tea for Princess Zaahira and her entourage. The tea set had it made. It didn't have a suite, merely a regular room, but even so, its hotel bill must have been close to $25,000 for a seven-week stay, and it had a balcony overlooking Beverly Hills. My rent was two months behind and I was rifling through my jewelry looking to see what I could sell to keep the sheriff at bay. I would have been happy to bunk up with that tea set anytime.

The servant girls then got busy flitting agitatedly around the baggage, making sure that the carriers handled the family's tea set and other treasures properly. Later in their stay, the girls would serve me tea too—once they got to know me and grew fond of me, as I grew fond of them.

I pulled my gaze away from the avalanche of luggage and shadowy figured women to glance briefly at the gathering of glinting royals waiting near the Lincoln Navigators and Porsche Cayennes parked at the start of the vehicle line. I would get to know some of them too, especially the young women. I smiled as I passed by them, but they took no notice of me, and then I made my way over to the royal hairdresser who was smoking angrily on the curb, glaring into space.

He looked like he was going to be trouble.

5

Palace Intrigue

I quickly discovered that there was an elaborate hierarchy and pecking order pervading the royal family's and accompanying entourage's behavior at all times. I noticed that no matter the position in the detail's hierarchy, everybody wanted to have someone beneath them to order around. There was always a pecking order. The security guys liked to lord it over the drivers, the tutors liked to lord it over the nannies, the nannies liked to lord it over the servants, the servants liked to lord it over the hotel maids, and the drivers liked to lord it over the hotel valets. It was insidious and endless. At first, I didn't realize the extent of its pervasiveness and assumed that the ubiquitous vying for power was an aberration perpetuated by a few miscreants, but I soon saw that it was standard operating procedure that clearly came from the top down and also served as a form of entertainment. The royal hairdresser was the worst offender of this. The first day at the airport, after he had been pointed out to me, I approached him politely, "Michel?"

He gave me the once-over, looked away in disdain, and turned away from me. I adjusted to be in his eye line, but then he turned away again. I adjusted again, and again he turned away. It was a weird dance we were doing. It took me a few turns to realize that he was purposely facing away from me to demonstrate that he didn't deem me worthy of occupying space in his field of vision—I was just a chauffeur, a nobody.

"WHAT? WHY?" he screamed at me with a thick French accent after we had danced around a bit more and he saw that I wasn't going away. He was Tunisian but had a lot of French attitude. He told me many, many times that he had spent much time in Paris, that he loved Paris, and that he preferred to be in Paris. And he was a screamer.

"WHO ARE YOU?" he screamed.

"I'm your driver, sir. How do you do? I hope you had a nice flight." He scowled at me. "WHERE IS CAR?"

I pointed to a black Crown Victoria parked a few feet away in the convoy of cars.

"WHERE IS SUV?" he asked. "YOU ME DRIVE MYSELF IN SUV!"

"I'm sorry, sir," I answered. "This is the car that's been assigned to you." He scowled again and moved away from me. I discovered that there was a hierarchy to the selection and distribution of the cars as well. All the princes and princesses had a luxury vehicle or one of the armored Mercedeses; most of the entourage had SUVs or some other high-end automobile that they had requested; those lower on the totem pole had town cars such as the Crown Victoria that was assigned to Michel. He wasn't a member of the family or in the upper echelon of the entourage, and he was unhappy that he wasn't being chauffeured in an Escalade or a Navigator. Maybe he'd gotten one in the past, or perhaps he'd requested one for this trip, but later when I mentioned his dissatisfaction to the security who had arranged the cars, they laughed with derision.

An agitated woman in her thirties, dressed in a colorful mélange of flowing silk scarves that trailed behind her, approached us and demanded a cigarette from Michel. She glanced charily at me as if I were a rude interloper even though I was just standing there quietly, waiting for him to get in the car or tell me what to do. Then she began talking to Michel in a mixture of Arabic and French. She spoke in a loud and impassioned voice and gestured wildly as if she were performing in an old-fashioned melodrama. I waited. Every now and then, she'd spin around and glare at me. There was some kind of problem, but I couldn't understand what it was in spite of all the elaborate histrionics. The drama escalated as she got further along in the story.

Suddenly, she pounced on me and announced, "I will ride with Michel." She had moved very close to my face, inches away, and I could smell the cigarettes on her breath. "First, you must drive us to the Beverly Hills Hotel, and then after we will go to the hotel where the princess is staying. We must change the hotel. *C'est très* important. My driver will follow us. You must tell him now. *Tout de suite. Merci.* That is all."

She hadn't bothered to introduce herself, but I sussed out later that she was Princess Zaahira's secretary, Asra. I looked around for her driver, hoping that he was nearby. I knew only two other drivers, Sami and Charles, and I had no idea yet who was assigned to whom on this job. There were too many of us.

"Who is your driver please, Madam?" I asked her. She didn't answer but instead stepped away from me sharply to make it clear that the discussion was ended. Then she and the hairdresser stood shoulder-to-shoulder, conferring again in their fervent Franco-Arab mix, smoking cigarette after cigarette, lighting them butt-to-butt, so that they sometimes each held two lit smokes at once with a haze of fumes enveloping them. Every now and then they would look at me accusingly as if challenging me to do or say something—I wasn't sure. I could understand only a few words and phrases of what they were saying, and I was starting to get nervous because I could tell that something troubling was going down. I am a very observant person and have relied on this ability my whole life; I am usually able to glean what is going on and how to handle a situation from the bits and pieces of information I can gather if I keep my eyes and ears open. This was my first experience where it was clear to me that I was being purposely excluded from a conversation, but could also sense that I would be held responsible for any information that I missed—which had perhaps been deliberately kept from me—as well as the ultimate outcome. It was a safeguarding strategy that I came to call the *scapegoat factor* and was a consistent technique used within the royal family and the entourage to cast blame on others, spread misinformation as a way to obfuscate, or as a way to disassociate oneself from those potentially at fault. This made for a very tense environment in which no one could be trusted. It became apparent to me that it was systemic to the workings of the royal household.

There was relentless rivalry within the group as well, but I couldn't determine to what end. Were they competing for better salaries, or for an early cushy retirement, or just for the Princess Zaahira's attention and good favor? I had no idea, and within a few days of exposure to this, I didn't really care either. I'm normally curious, but palace intrigue held no interest for me; it was too mean-spirited. I'd rather read a textbook on particle physics—in Russian, which I can neither read, write, nor speak—than try to unravel the machinations of the royal household; it was just too convoluted and unsavory.

I found out later that Asra was unhappy with her room assignment and was angling to get a larger, more comfortable suite. Most likely, she was displacing one of the tutors or nannies and was petitioning the hairdresser to align himself with her. She knew he had Princess Zaahira's ear. Later in the seven weeks, some of her family who lived in the States came to visit, and she needed the extra room for her guests.

As I was quizzing the other chauffeurs on who was assigned to Asra, her driver, Jorge, came charging up. He was a young thick-set Latino in an ill-fitting tight polyester suit, and he was sweating profusely from running around the terminal trying to find the woman. He had left her at the curb to bring the car closer, and she had disappeared. I told him I'd be driving his client and mine to the Beverly Hills Hotel and he should follow.

"I don't know where that is!" he said, wiping the sweat from his brow with his fingers. "I don't want to get lost on my first day!"

"It's on Sunset, north of Santa Monica Boulevard, at the northwest corner of Crescent, near that five-corner funky intersection that meets Beverly." Chauffeurs are used to giving directions to each other and always want street corners and compass points.

He looked alarmed. "Is that in Beverly Hills?" he asked.

"Yes," I said. "It's the *Beverly Hills Hotel*. Just follow me in. Watch out for the hairpin turn into the hotel so you don't miss it. Punch my cell number into your phone, and call me if you get lost." I could tell he was going to have difficulty on this job, especially working for Asra, and I'd known her for only a few minutes.

I learned later why Jorge was so nervous, and it wasn't just that he was an inexperienced driver. He was desperate to keep the job. His brother had recently been deported, and Jorge was supporting his ailing elderly mother as well as his brother's two small children. Jorge was also an undocumented worker constantly looking over his shoulder for the cops to nab him. Because he was an illegal immigrant, he lived with an unrelenting amount of stress and was taking a huge risk by chauffeuring and spending so many hours in a car. He felt like a sitting duck. He'd gotten a California license years ago when you still could do so without proving that you were a citizen, but that had expired. If the police ever pulled him over, he would surely be busted and then undoubtedly be deported, leaving his family in the lurch with no one to provide for them. The children were American citizens since they were born in California, and his elderly mother had a green card but hadn't yet been able to secure her son's papers: the changes enacted by Homeland Security after September 11 now make all immigration processing excruciatingly slow.

Jorge told me that he hadn't been to Mexico since he was a teenager and he didn't even know anybody there anymore except his brother. He had lived in the States illegally for more than twenty years and it was the only life he knew.

Sure enough, Asra fired Jorge after only a few weeks on the job. She said that he'd been rude to her and hadn't done what she asked. More likely, she was probably just impossible to please.

I discovered that the duties of the royal hairdresser were to attend to Princess Zaahira's coiffure when she woke up, always late in the morning, and then again before she went out to dinner. So this meant that the hairdresser had a lot of free time. Very rarely, Michel would also do grooming for one of the princess's sons staying in another hotel. He'd known all the children since they were young and behaved rather like an eccentric uncle with them. They tolerated him while keeping him at arm's length, but he was obviously quite close to their mother. Princess Zaahira and the royal hairdresser giggled and yakked together like two schoolgirl chums.

It was my duty to drive him when he joined the princess shopping or, rather, I drove his empty car in a caravan of eight cars as we crawled up Rodeo Drive following Princess Zaahira and her entourage, who were on foot. The first time we did this, I could hear him scream for me a block away when he was ready to be picked up. I quickly pulled his car up just behind the princess's bulletproof Mercedes and chase car, then ran around to open the door for him. He acted as if he'd been waiting for me for two weeks.

43

"WHERE ARE YOU? WHY I WALK?" he screamed.

I was standing directly in front of the Crown Victoria with the door open, waiting for him to get in. "The car is here, sir. Uh, you called for me to come pick you up?"

"WHERE ARE YOU? WHY I WALK? WHY!!? WHY YOU MAKE ME WALK MYSELF!!?"

"I'm sorry, sir. I'm right here, sir. Uh, did you want to walk?"

"*LA* [no]! *LA! LA!* I SAY, WHY I WALK? WHY YOU MAKE ME WALK MYSELF? MISS, WHY? WHY? WHY? YOU WITH ME, ME ALWAYS WITH PRINCESS. WHY YOU MAKE ME WALK MYSELF?"

I looked around for somebody to interpret for me, but the rest of the entourage near us was busy studying the cracks in the sidewalk. They all knew what he was like and didn't want to get involved. The princess was up ahead in a shop and didn't hear any of this; he never would have gone nuts like this in front of her. Around her, he was especially sweet, deferential and affable, but at all other times he acted like a rabid dog.

I figured out that he was pissed off that he had to walk twenty steps to get into his car. Princess Zaahira's car was always first in the convoy, followed by her chase car with her security so that she could make a quick getaway if necessary, as the security's protocol demanded. His car was pulled up just behind hers. The hairdresser wished to be treated like a royal. He wanted Princess Zaahira's cars moved so that he could get into his car where he had positioned himself—at the head of the car line. It wasn't going to happen. There was a pecking order, and he was nowhere near the top.

Eventually he got into the car sulking and lit a cigarette. I started to open a window.

"*LA! LA!* NO WINDOW! NO WINDOW! DRIVE!" And I drove him the three blocks back to the hotel, choking on his fumes.

6

The Spirit of Partnership

*P*rincess Zaahira's husband was a high-ranking prince in the family and a successful businessman. His reach easily extended to Beverly Hills and its hotels. Saudi royals own or are part owners of many of the premiere hotels in Los Angeles and all over the rest of the world. It was clear to me from the beginning that the family's trip was made with Washington's blessings. The security personnel were in daily contact with the U.S. State Department to coordinate the family's movements, so the atmosphere around the group was always highly charged and sometimes volatile, as if the security were protecting touring national treasures.

It's common knowledge that Washington has a long-standing relationship with the Saudi royal family; we've all seen the pictures of smooching heads of state, and the United States has been a major player in the financial growth of the country. It was American hunch and sloggers, wildcatters scouting for petroleum, who discovered oil in Saudi Arabia in 1936 and made the Kingdom rich, along with lining the pockets of American oilmen and automobile makers who wanted to put the railway out of business. Twenty percent of the world's known oil reserves are beneath the Saudi sand, oil comprises 90 percent of its export revenue, and it is the world's largest exporter. Before oil, Saudi Arabia's greatest export was dates.

Full-on production wasn't underway until after World War II, and it was the U.S.-owned Arabian Standard Oil Company that found oil, brought it out of the ground, refined it, and sent it across the ocean. It later became ARAMCO, a conglomerate of several American companies. In the 1970s the Saudi government reached an agreement with ARAMCO granting the Saudis 67 percent ownership; by the 1980s, Saudi Arabia finally claimed full ownership. The Saudi royal family, the major beneficiary of the petroleum boom, now makes billions of dollars a year on oil.

Petroleum oil has been used for thousands of years, but its first most prevalent use was medicinal. It was applied as a liniment, and it must have stunk something awful. I lived briefly in West Texas, and know firsthand that the air surrounding an oil or gas well is rife with the stench of sulfur and chemicals, filling the sky with such a strong smell of rotten eggs that it used to make me gag. Later it was used as a fuel instead of coal and whale oil to light lamps, furnaces, and then still later, locomotives.

But it was the onslaught of the automobile, which Americans made ubiquitous, that has made oil so valuable. The internal combustion engine needs fuel to drive it and oil seemed relatively cheap and plentiful.

In 1945, Franklin Delano Roosevelt made the historic "oil for security" deal that cemented the United States and Saudi Arabia's future together and shaped the course of events in the Middle East for decades to come. FDR gave King Aziz Al Saud his first plane, a DC-10, which he had outfitted with a special swivel seat so that Aziz could always face Mecca when flying. Saudi Arabian Airlines, the largest airline in the Middle East, was the creation and a subsidiary of TWA, which also staffed and trained its crew for the airline's first years. The Ford Foundation spent over a decade helping the Saudis develop a bureaucratic system to run their new country, and Americans established the farming techniques and built irrigation systems that developed agriculture in a country that is mostly desert. The list just goes on and on. Relations are still so good that in 2011 Washington made a deal to sell the Saudis $60 billion worth of arms that includes F-15 fighter jets and Apache helicopters. It is the largest arms deal ever made, with tens of billions more in the works for the future.

I soon felt the long reach of the Saudi arm, even on the left coast. On the first night (or rather early morning), after we'd finally delivered the family to the hotel, I was on my way home to get some sleep when Fausto ordered me to haul ass down Wilshire Boulevard to deal with the Beverly Hills Police Department. It was an emergency. As I was driving along Wilshire, with no idea of what lay ahead, I heard sirens and saw flashing lights. Wilshire was cordoned off at Comstock Avenue a half-mile in both directions. Fausto had told me I was needed there because of a problem with the two rented cargo trucks that had transported the family's luggage from the airport to the hotels, but I didn't see them anywhere, only a stretch of blazing bubbles. There were several Beverly Hills Police SUVS, several more black and white Los Angeles squad cars, a sturdy-looking bomb squad that was armoring up, and a cacophony of helicopters circling overhead.

I was driving one of the family's loaded brand-new Lincoln Navigators instead of the hairdresser's Crown Vic, and before leaving the hotel, I had taken a business card from the head of security suspecting that it might come in handy sometime on the job. It was an imposing laminated card with several official-looking seals, longer and thinner than an ordinary business card and oblong shaped with beveled corners. "Dignitary & Executive Protection Services" was written in raised letters on one side. It looked more like a membership card to a private club than a business card. I had tucked it into my bra for safekeeping and occasionally felt its edges bite into my underarm flesh as I maneuvered the SUV's steering wheel.

As I slowly drove west on Wilshire toward the lights, the cops blocking the street shouted at me, "Turn around! Drive away! Turn around!" Sitting high up in the Navigator, I felt a sudden surge of invulnerability, as if I were being lifted above it all, and even though my heart was pounding, I ignored the shouts and drove up as close as I could to the flashing lights. Police were charging about in all different directions, and the atmosphere was frenzied. Then I saw the two abandoned cargo trucks in the distance, parked on the corner of a side street in front of a high-rise apartment building on Wilshire, bordered by a wide parameter of police cars. I realized that Fausto had sent me to convince the cops that the trucks were not improvised explosive devices. He probably chose me because he suspected that I could handle the Beverly Hills police force better than anybody else in the detail, but it didn't seem promising.

The sergeant on duty was a forty-year-old All American–looking surfer type, which is typical for Beverly Hills, with sun-streaked blond hair slightly graying at the temples. The Beverly Hills Police Department must have special divisional requirements because they all seem to be tall and blond and buff; the occasional deviation is usually only even better-looking, more exotic looking, or more buff. This sounds like an exaggeration, but I don't think it is. I'm sure there are some women in the department, but I've never seen any, not one, and I've lived in Los Angeles for more than a decade. This guy was particularly beef-cakey, and it was clear he loved his job and his uniform. It was a balmy dawn, and he had a short-sleeve shirt on. He made a point of flexing his muscles every few moments to show off his action. The sergeant looked good, and he knew he looked good.

Time slowed as he ambled up to the SUV, assessed me and examined the car, circling it once and making note of the paper plates—police parlance for no license plates because the brand-new Navigator was from a high-end rental agency. He decided that I was worth some of his attention, probably because I had rolled up in a $65,000 car tricked out with all the bells and whistles. As he approached the driver's side window, he flexed his action a little more, smiled sweetly at me, introduced himself as if we were at a country club dance, and then waited patiently for me to speak. I was still pumped up from getting through the police barricades so it took me a moment to compose myself, and frankly I was a little discombobulated by this excruciatingly handsome cop. For a moment, I thought maybe I was on an episode of *Punk'd* and Ashton Kutcher was going to pop out at any minute. Finally, I said that I worked for a *family* staying in several Beverly Hills hotels. I don't think I said "a Saudi family" but said something inane like "an *oil family*" to indicate vast wealth. I whipped out the fancy card (I noticed that he noticed that it came from my bra) and said that the *family's* security had sent me to speak with the police regarding the cordoned-off cargo trucks. Each time I reiterated the word *family*, I said it slowly and with great gravitas. I explained that the trucks had been used for the *family's* stupendous amount of luggage and were to be returned to the rental house when they opened. The sergeant said that a tenant in one of the corner apartment buildings had watched, from their balcony, as the Latino drivers had parked the trucks and then taken off. They were frightened and had called the police department, which responded in full force.

I had the truck keys on me and offered to open each vehicle for inspection. He watched me closely as I hopped out of the SUV and I could feel his eyes checking out my suit, my tits, and my ass. I pretended not to notice. I was way past making any assumptions about my femininity or physical attributes diffusing a police conflict in La-La Land.

During a recent snowstorm back east, a cheery Boston cop had helped me parallel-park my friend's Ford Trooper in a commercial loading zone, around and between 9-foot snowbanks, and then made sure I wasn't ticketed even though I was parked thoroughly illegally—all because I smiled at him. But my first week in Los Angeles, I was pulled over by a young mirrored-sunglass-wearing superstud motorcycle cop on Santa Monica Boulevard for failing to wear a seat belt. He flirted shamelessly with me the whole time but still slapped me with a $200 ticket even after I showed him that the rental car's seat belt was broken. "Shouldn't be driving it, then, ma'am," he said as he roared off on his motorcycle.

The sergeant helped me roll up the cargo trucks' back gates. "See," I said. "They're totally empty. It's all a crazy misunderstanding. The *family* came in today, and they just have so much luggage, we have to rent trucks. Can you believe that? But they are totally safe, really. We just couldn't return them until Monday. See? Totally safe." Luckily, they were empty. I had been holding my breath, half-expecting the guys who had loaded the luggage to be sleeping inside after their long night's work.

The sergeant was as cool as a cucumber throughout all this. He nodded several times and then stepped away as he spoke into the radio attached to his shoulder. He calmly accepted my assurances that the trucks would be moved first thing the next morning, but I figured there would be a huge fine at the very least, if not a citation of some kind. I didn't know what ordinance had been broken, but there had to be one. In Beverly Hills you hardly see anything that doesn't look like it absolutely belongs in Beverly Hills: there are no rundown ghetto cars cruising the streets, no homeless people (if you don't count the impeccably dressed Baptist minister–looking guy in a black suit, white shirt, and black tie who always begs for money on the corner of Santa Monica Boulevard and Bedford in front of the Church of the Good Shepherd), no after-hours club-hoppers loitering outside restaurants or bars and whatnot. They have it wrapped up tight. There had to be a "Does Not Belong in Beverly Hills" statute.

A moment later, he smiled again at me, even more sweetly than the first time, and then offered me his card. He asked that I keep in touch with him and graciously offered to assist me in any way he could, "anytime, with anything the *family* needs. Just give me a holler. I'd be happy to help." He said that he was familiar with such *families* and wanted to make sure their stay in Beverly Hills was as pleasant as possible. The sergeant introduced me to some of his buddies, and they offered their help as well, and then I went home for the night with what sounded like a promise of assistance from the entire Beverly Hills Police Department. That was nice.

Everything ended up working out fine because I was working for people with a lot of money and influence. I felt supremely well connected. This was new for me, and I have to admit I found it exhilarating. I thought about how easy it had been at LAX when we picked up the group—essentially shutting down the airport to do so—and I also soon noticed that we were never hassled by the police anywhere in Los Angeles, even when racing in a convoy at 50 miles an hour through a residential district, blowing through stop signs and sometimes even red lights. We were impervious.

I couldn't help but wonder if every cop in Los Angeles County was in the Saudi royal family's pocket. After a few days on the job, it was apparent that none of us was ever going to be ticketed by the parking police no matter where or how we parked. The parking enforcement heads must have been told to stand down as well, which is quite a feat in Beverly Hills since they will ticket you for just looking at them the wrong way. The BH Police Department site lists six core values that they hold dear. The last is: "Spirit of Partnership: In partnership with our community and other City Departments, we are dedicated to creating a caring environment which enhances the quality of life for everyone." I'd say that was true.

Even so, I considered my late-night police détente quite a coup and wasn't surprised when the next day Fausto asked me to be in charge of the drivers and act as liaison between security and the chauffeuring staff. I accepted, even though there was no increase in my pay, because I was grateful that he had included me in the detail and I thought that he needed my help. My exact new job description was never made clear to me, but I spent most of the day in a command post in one of the hotels, getting a primer on the workings of the detail. "Getting a primer" is a stretch really. Mostly I ran errands for the security personnel on duty and watched them do their job as they worked the phones or computers. Occasionally they would ask me to go find a particular driver whom they couldn't access by cell phone, or they'd quiz me on the Beverly Hills shops and restaurants whenever someone in the family or entourage asked for something obscure. Still, this meant that I had easy entrée to the upper floors of the hotel for the rest of the seven weeks. Everyone assumed that I was more important than I was.

One of the security personnel named Al, a wiry fireball, regaled me for several hours with his previous Saudi security detail stories. "You know the ranking of importance in the household, right?" he asked without waiting for my answer. "For the Saudi man, first most valuable is the horse; the horse is numero uno. Then comes the camel, then the sheep, then the goat, then way far down in the household comes the woman." He paused for emphasis and sipped on a can of soda that he held in his hand. "She's at the bottom, sometimes even after the chickens and the dogs." He laughed so hard when he told me this that he spat soda out of his nose.

Less than twenty-four hours later, I was relieved of my supervisory duties. Fausto called me on my cell phone in the early morning, roaring, furious. He said he had received reports from the other drivers that I had treated them in an arrogant and condescending manner, and he accused me of "not being humble." He ordered me to stick to driving and instructed me to stop talking down to the other drivers. I was dumbfounded. Where was I when all that happened? I couldn't figure it out. I hadn't changed from one day to the next, or had I? Had I started to lord it over people in less than twenty-four hours? Was it like a virus? Had I contracted a virulent "lording-over" virus without even knowing it? It didn't sound like me. How had I missed that? I'm usually pretty aware of how I'm behaving, even if it's badly. Actors are all about behavior—theirs and others'.

Then I realized what the real problem was: I'm a woman. The other drivers, mostly Latino or Eastern European and relatively new to the States, were accustomed to the social mores of their own countries and were pissed off that a woman was telling them what to do or was even in a position to possibly do so. I knew this because for the one day that I was promoted, they had sneered at me when I walked by them. At the time, this perplexed me because the day before, most of them were friendly or had even tried to flirt with me. The truth is that I did little to antagonize or insult them; they were simply affronted that a woman had been placed in a position superior to them. To make matters worse, they started gossiping about me, making up stories that portrayed me in an unsavory light. Sami pulled me aside and told me that they said I was sleeping with so-and-so, and also so-and-so, and even so-and-so. Apparently, in the space of only a few days, I had managed to sleep with almost everyone I had ever met on the job and at the hotel. I was really getting around.

I've worked in many industries amid groups of men and women together, and there was generally a lot of camaraderie and goodwill. One summer, to help pay for graduate school, I worked long hours in a busy nightclub in New York City where I was one of the few native-born Americans on the job. There were six bars and several dance floors, and throngs of people packed the club each night. The place was jammed five deep at the bar from sunset until four in the morning when the liquor was finally cut off; my hands and wrists ached from pouring thousands of long island ice teas, sex on the beaches, and white russians. I had coworkers from Jamaica, Guatemala, Ireland, Germany, and many other countries—even a young man from Liberia, who was the only person I've ever met from there—but we all worked together as a team regardless of sex or native nationality. We helped each other and we looked out for each other; that was the only way to make the job somewhat bearable—camaraderie in the face of adversity. But that was not the case on the Saudi detail.

Later that night, I was standing in the back alley outside the hotel with Charles and Sami, who had given me the lovely turquoise compact now in the mermaid's possession. They knew that I was generally a nice person, or at least tried to be most of the time. As we were going over the details of my unraveling management career, Stu called my cell phone and said that there had been a terrible mistake, and that the jefes needed me to be in charge and wanted to reinstate me. He said that Fausto shouldn't have dismissed me, and he offered me the job again (still with no additional pay) saying, "You are absolutely vital to the success of this operation." I had the speakerphone on so that my friends could hear; Charles shook his head at me, and Sami glowered. I told Stu I would think about it. Then another head security jefe called and offered me the promise of more money—he couldn't guarantee it—but only if I was onboard right away. I demurred again. Then they tried to strong-arm me into accepting their offer with a barrage of phone calls and a blitz of one-on-one "chats"; they even promised a future management position in an upcoming detail for another Saudi family due to arrive in September. The sudden intense pressure was strange; they seemed to have decided out of the blue that I was indispensable.

Between strikes, Charles advised me not to bend under the relentless attention: "I done be warning you, it can only backfire on you, girl. You gots to look out for *herself*." Part of me wanted to relent; the jefes, after all, had said a lot of flattering things about my intelligence and capability. My automatic reflex was to respond by proving these things to be indubitably true, but in spite of the pressure, I also knew that they said what they said just to get me to do what they wanted. I had to remind myself that chauffeuring wasn't my career, it was an interim and short-term fix. I suspected that they would only demote me again or release me in a day or two anyway. After only twenty-four hours, several chauffeurs had already been fired for no apparent reason: some because they hadn't answered their cell phones quickly enough, another because one of the security guys didn't like his face, and another because the client was pissed off that the driver hadn't instantly known the address of a restaurant even though the client had not actually given the correct name of that restaurant and that is why the driver couldn't place it. There was a terrific attrition rate, and the casualties were staggering. We were totally expendable.

I listened to Charles's counsel, knowing that he had my best interest at heart, and I held firm against the onslaught. I was going to fly under the radar as low and as long I could. "Just takes the money and run, girl," Charles advised me. As appealing as the higher-ranking job sounded in theory, I decided that I had to look out for *herself.*

I thought about that evening later—how I had remained stalwart, in spite of the intense pressure from my superiors, and had taken care of myself *myself*—and I wished that this had been truer of me throughout my life and reflected in more of my life choices. Some people are really good at looking out for themselves, getting what they want, and making sure life works in their favor. This supreme sense of self-preservation and self-assertion comes naturally to them; it's instinctive. But I have repeatedly ended up in situations in which I wasn't properly acknowledged for my efforts and achievements or was passed over for someone less talented or conscientious than I was. It's not that I exactly allowed it to happen, but it was as if I could see it transpiring out of the corner of my eye and was powerless to intervene.

Some people are born with a sense of entitlement that enables them to see and put an immediate stop to anything that undermines or disenfranchises them in any way. I was not. Often people who are extremely good at getting what they want are also incredibly self-serving. But I want to be a good person who also gets what she wants—instead of cutting off my nose to spite my face, which is what I've been known to do in the past. Some people even have the ability to see far ahead and position themselves so that they benefit no matter what obstacles or hindrances are thrown in their way. I do not. I don't think you would assume any of this to be so if we met casually or socially; I'm too good at masking it. I've been told that I have a confident and self-assured manner, but the bigger truth is that I wish I were more of a dick. It would be more fun.

I'm sure this is why I was attracted to the small amount of power that my association with the Saudis afforded me. I walked through the luxury hotel lobbies, acted as if I belonged there, and was treated as if I belonged there by the guests and staff alike. The hotel doormen greeted me by name each day and even gave me chilled Evian, fresh fruit, and the daily international newspapers. They knew I wasn't a guest at the hotel, but I worked for the Saudis and that was almost as good.

One evening, early in the job when I still made some attempt to fix my hair and face nicely and was dressed in one of the beautifully tailored Italian suits that my restauranteur sister had given me, I was standing at the top of the lobby stairs encircled by several of the entourage's hulking security and drivers, to whom I was giving directions, when I felt a gentle tug on my sleeve.

"Excuse me, are you a movie star?"

I looked down to see a pretty little pink-cheeked very self-possessed English girl looking expectantly up at me. "No, sorry, I'm not," I said. Even a small child knew what a cluster of security meant—somebody important was around. I was at the center of the cluster, so that meant to her that I was somebody important.

"I was so hoping to see one. Please, do you know where I can find a movie star?" she asked.

"Well, I guess you could try the restaurant around 1:00 P.M. when they're all having lunch with their agents, or you might get lucky up at the pool at cocktail time," I told her. I smoothed my hair with one hand and straightened my suit with the other, pleased that somebody had noticed me even if it was only an eight-year-old girl.

There were other aspects of my employment that were equally gratifying. I noticed that when I was dressed in a dark suit with my hair pulled back, and especially if I was driving or even standing near the black Crown Vic, I was often mistaken for an FBI agent or some other law enforcement official. I liked this newfound sense of power, and I worked it. Sometimes I would hold my finger to one ear as if listening to an ear-bud radio device like the Secret Service use, and I noticed people would make a beeline away from where I was standing but watch me with great interest from a distance. Once in a while, I would dead-eye somebody as I was getting into line at Starbucks and they would pull back and let me ahead of them, indicating that my time was more valuable than theirs. I'd speed through intersections cutting other cars off, then nod tersely, acknowledging that the other drivers were doing the country's civil servants a good turn. People invariably waved me on politely. It felt as if I was wearing a terrific suit of armor. I didn't *feel* corrupt in the least, but of course I was. I considered buying one of those fake police ID billfolds from a Hollywood prop house and placing it in the windshield of my car, but then my sister, a dynamo trial attorney who has a lot of experience with law enforcement, told me this was unwise because I could get arrested for impersonating a police officer.

7

How Many Hermès
Are Too Many?

*S*hopping trips with Princess Zaahira were brutal—first, because she went almost every day, sometimes all day, and second because she bought so much shit. It was endless. If it was indeed true that the family flew in with $20 million, as the kid at the FBO had said, then they must have spent every pretty penny. I know they paid the hotel bill in cash—at least fifty rooms for seven weeks, including the presidential suite that cost $10,000 a night. Room service and whatnot had to be several hundred thousand dollars a day. That's $5 million minimum for a seven-week stay.

On the shopping trips, one of the head servants was in charge of the cash; they paid for everything in hundred-dollar bills. None of the royals ever touched the money. Except for one young princess, I never saw them handle any money ever. They strolled and shopped only, and the servants took care of the mundane details of the transactions.

If you were assigned to drive someone who had decided to join the princess on a shopping expedition, you had to follow in your empty car as they strolled with the princess up and down Rodeo Drive from boutique to boutique. Usually no one ever actually rode in the car, but we had to be there just in case anyone wanted to be driven back to the hotel, which was two blocks away, if they had a call of nature or decided that they'd had enough of the relentless California sunshine. Evidently shopping with millions of dollars can be exhausting, and a two-minute walk after such strenuous activity could be life threatening.

So we'd be seven, eight, or nine cars in a row crawling up the street, all empty, following a princess and her entourage as they strolled along, stopping in each store along the way even if they had cleaned it out the day before. The shopkeepers were ready, though. They were on it. They must have spent each night restocking, because there were always more purses to purchase.

Every once in a while, one of the servant girls would hurry over to the line of cars with bags and bags of Jimmy Choo shoes, or armloads of Christian Dior dresses, or Hermès Birkin crocodile handbags in any and all the colors available (those can cost as much as $150,000 apiece). A stylish woman in my yoga class has a black one; she told me with glee that she was on a waiting list for three years to secure it and said it was well worth it. "It's magnificent," she said, "and it has all the hardware I wanted!"

The servants never left the shops carrying any boxes because they were too hard to pack to send home. They even eschewed the magnificent orange Hermès boxes, which can double as installation art. My designer friend, Theodore, has a collection that he uses to decorate a house when he's staging it for selling. He arranges them artfully in the wardrobe closets as if they were priceless sculptures and keeps an eye on the count as people tour the home because they're frequently pilfered.

All the booty would be thrown into the back of a waiting van that would make periodic runs back to the hotel to dump the goods. I watched as every week, hundreds of huge moving crates were filled and then shipped out to Saudi Arabia to be opened and sorted by the servants back at the palaces in the Kingdom. There was absolutely no regard for what something cost, no inquiry whatsoever. If they wanted it, they bought it, then bought more, then bought more, then bought more. It was like a really expensive fairy tale. *Lordy!* I thought. *I wish I could sneak into the store with one of the Saudi ladies for only a nanosecond, just so I could toss one of those Hervé Léger bandage dresses on the pile. Size medium in amethyst or peacock blue, please, and I wouldn't even register the dress's serial number (they all have one). I'd just wear it around my apartment and keep it safe.*

After several long afternoons spent watching this impressive display of immense wealth, I started to think that perhaps the Saudi women shopped not just because they liked to have beautiful new things, but also because it made them feel better. If I'm feeling down and go out and buy a special something to give myself a little lift, it often works, especially if I've gotten it at a bargain. Ask anybody who has spent hours on eBay or QVC, and he'll tell you that this happens to him too. But there are a lot of other options for me if I want to brighten my spirits: I might go to the SLAMMO! batting cage in Culver City, or see some friends perform naked in an avant-garde dance piece in a downtown loft, or go to Gold's Gym to watch the bodybuilders pump iron in their purple leopard-skin tights—that can be immensely entertaining and uplifting, especially when they start grunting.

But there were very few other things that the Saudi women were allowed to do, and most, if not all, of my pick-me-ups were off-limits to them.

In Saudi Arabia, many women send a male relative or servant into shops to do the sizing and purchasing of, say, their panties and bras. Traditionally, retail shops are staffed by men. There are very few woman-owned and -operated shops, since it is considered by conservatives to be forbidden by Islam for a woman to work outside the home, where she could be viewed by any passing man. Female sales personnel in a store that sells undergarments and cosmetics and caters to a female clientele are only now becoming more prevalent because of royal decree. In America, where there are so many female-staffed businesses of all kinds, the Saudi women can shop more freely everywhere. So shopping in the United States was perhaps empowering for them as well as comforting. I wondered if perhaps this gave them a thrilling measure of control: they can look at and purchase whatever they like, wherever they like, and buy it from whomever they like. They can choose.

The Saudis were also making money as they were spending money. Each member of the family and the traveling entourage had an assigned vehicle. All of those sedans and SUVs, which were kept idling throughout the day, needed gasoline, and all of those cars lined up behind us, trying to get around the convoy—because naturally we blocked the street for hours every afternoon—also needed gasoline. The Saudis were tying up Beverly Hills, wasting gas, which likely had been imported by the United States from Saudi Arabia, setting the price of as well as driving up the cost of gas because of demand, and then making money on that gas all the way down the line. The economic through line didn't seem to be calculated, though. It just was brilliant.

One of the first royal women I was assigned to drive was Fahima, a cousin of Princess Zaahira. She was a well-preserved woman in her fifties, with a strong jaw line, deep-set penetrating eyes, and shoulder-length, perfectly blown-out hair that looked as if it was a helmet. Fahima was always impeccably dressed in chic but conservative clothing with acres of expensive jewelry. Chauffeurs aren't supposed to ask questions, in fact can be fired for doing so, but she usually tolerated my inquisitiveness with measured graciousness. She was multilingual, worldly, and well traveled, and surprisingly patient with my questions as I chauffeured her around the city, usually to get the British cigarettes she smoked, which are available only in specialty tobacconist shops. She was a heavy smoker, as were many of the other Saudis in this group—even some of the young women chain-smoked—and carried her own Fabergé portable ashtray in her purse. The Saudis regularly depleted much of the supply in Beverly Hills, so we often had to travel to Westwood or Santa Monica for her preferred choice of nicotine fix.

Fahima didn't hide the fact that she felt vastly superior to me but also that her sense of noblesse oblige compelled her to be generous with her knowledge. It wasn't that she ever overtly insulted me; her condescension was subtler and more sophisticated than that, but it was clear that she thought me to be less worthy than herself. She seemed amused by my ignorance and naiveté, as she saw it, and therefore treated me like a child who needed her help. It was in her company that I first felt the pang of being an infidel, a heathen, a nonbeliever. I tried to ignore it.

"I am sure it is difficult for you to understand the uniqueness of our society, but I am happy to help you to know more about my country and our customs, Janni Amelia, if you insist," she said. "Please, what is it you would like to ask?"

"Why do you have to wear the *abaya* [black cloak]?" I asked. I really wanted to ask why the Saudi women spent so much money on designer clothes and jewelry and then let themselves be wrapped up in a black blanket, but that didn't seem politic.

"Please understand, Janni Amelia, in the Kingdom, a woman must be fully covered, in *abaya* and *hijab* [headscarf], and sometimes the *niqab* [veil], when in the company of any male who is not a son, brother, husband, or father. Of course. Not to do so is tantamount to prostitution. When we are inside our home, with our children and family, we do not have to cover. But we do not walk on the street without the *abaya*, we do not talk with a man who is not a relative, we do not sit in a Starbucks café with a man who is not a son, brother, husband, or father. Nor do we care to do this! There is always a very comfortable family room in the back for the women and the children, where we are more at ease," she told me.

"But why is it up to the woman to cover herself? Why can't the men just not look? Why is it her problem?"

"You see, Janni Amelia, women tempt men. We are temptresses. It is our nature; we cannot help it. And if men respond to the temptation—a glimpse of a cheek, or a wrist, or an ankle—then chaos will ensue. So we women cover. It is our duty, or we will provoke chaos, and then society and all mankind will suffer."

"Then why don't you have to cover when you're not in Saudi Arabia? Doesn't Allah see you always?" I asked her.

"Yes, of course, but most Saudi women do not cover when visiting your country because we do not like to capture attention or discrimination, especially since the unfortunate tragedy of September 11. But in the Kingdom, we must cover, or we may be arrested for indecency. This is the law, of course. For the Saudi woman, this is shameful behavior not to do so, but the American woman has no conception of this," she said. I got a little irked then because it sounded as if she was calling me a floozy.

In much the same offhand patronizing manner with which Fahima treated me, it didn't seem to register with the other royals that their drivers were actual people, with personal lives and families waiting for them at home. In spite of the many hours they spent with their employees, it didn't appear that the royals ever considered for a minute that their servants and chauffeurs were working impossibly long hours, were likely desperate for money, and might not actually enjoy dedicating their entire existence to the whim and fancy of the uber-rich. The Saudis just didn't seem to think about it. Why would they?

If you've always had money, say hundreds of millions of dollars, it must be almost impossible to negotiate a path of empathy toward understanding what it's like to have nothing, or to work night and day for a few hundred dollars, or to save for years to buy a coveted item. It's just so foreign. And even if you come from nothing and then you have money, usually you try to forget what it's like not to have any. You put it out of your head, very far away. As far, far, far away as possible because it makes us feel inferior, and we define ourselves by our superiority to others: We want to forget that we were ever inferior.

Aristotle called this philotimia—the love of honor, the need to feel morally superior. But if you take the moral aspect out of the equation, I think we just need to feel superior because feeling inferior makes us feel shame. I see that this shows up in how we live, where we live, and what we have. It's not just things we own; it's other stuff too: the influential friends we know, the talented children we have, my two Ivy League degrees, for instance, that I consciously and sometimes even unconsciously mention when I want to advance my standing or support an argument that I'm making—so people think better of me. These elements document our superiority, and that superiority validates us. Having people think that I was an FBI agent, armed with important information, survival skills, and perhaps even a handgun, when in actuality I was just an overworked and mistreated lowly chauffeur, made me feel better about myself. The same must go for princesses who cannot vote or drive but who have a different Birkin bag for every day of the month. These things make us feel more worthy. I don't know why we need it, but we do. I need it, the Saudis need it, we all need it—except maybe the Dalai Lama. I'm really hoping he doesn't need it, and I doubt he does much shopping anyway. He looks so darn dashing in those saffron robes that they're probably custom-made for him.

8

I Will Survive!

*A*fter the day's shopping and evening's coiffure were wrapped up, the royal hairdresser insisted I drive him to the casinos near Palm Springs, where he drank, smoked, and gambled all night. Every night. Michel liked to play slots. The only slots near Beverly Hills are 120 miles away, just outside Palm Springs on the American Indian reservations such as Pechanga or Morongo.

Gambling is a big business out on the reservations. They've worked out a deal with the state of California that only certain games can be played in certain locales. So even though you can play cards at Hollywood Park Casino in Los Angeles, where I'd try to persuade the hairdresser to go to avoid the Palm Springs schlep, the only slots permitted in California are on the reservations.

Morongo is particularly surreal. When you come upon it at sunset, silhouetted against the glowing orange desert sky, it looks like a mirage. It's as if a Disney-inspired high-rise space station were plopped down in the middle of the sand as a kind of freakish Sixties-style oasis, pulsating in garish neon light to attract the masses. It even features an oasis pool and waterslide.

It takes two hours to get to Morongo from Los Angeles, and that's if you're driving 90 miles per hour in the middle of the night with no traffic. But at 5:00 p.m. in bumper-to-bumper traffic, the trip could take three and a half hours or more, and that's always when the hairdresser was ready to go.

"NOW WE GO CASINO! NOW! NOW WE GO!" he screamed.

"Sir, this is not a good time," I said. "Everyone's trying to get home from work." I don't know why I bothered to call him *sir*, he was acting like a three-year-old.

"WE GO DIFFERENT WAY NOW!"

"Sir, there is no different way, at least not one that's any faster. There's only one road to Palm Springs, and everybody's on it," I said.

"TELL THEM OFF THE ROAD! WE GO CASINO NOW. LATER THEY GO HOME!"

"Uh, that's not the way it works in this country, sir. They have a right to be on the road just like us."

"TELL THEM OFF THE ROAD!"

He must have been joking when he said that because obviously there was no way I could tell all of the thousands of drivers to make way for us, but it didn't appear so because he was practically spitting with rage. He had a terrific sense of entitlement that at the time I found loathsome but in retrospect I quite admire. Maybe I'd have nailed more movie roles and more credits on films if I'd had a greater sense of privilege and demanded what I wanted even half as often as the hairdresser. *NOW! NOW! I am star of picture! I am producer! I have single title card! NOW!*

He chain-smoked in the car the whole way there without letting me open the windows (*"LA! LA,* NO WINDOW, *LA!"*) and sang along to the music he liked on the radio, loudly and badly. He sounded like a wounded dog with damaged vocal chords, crying for his master to come home. His favorite was Gloria Gaynor's "I Will Survive," which he wailed between drags on his cigarette. He didn't know most of the lyrics, but that didn't stop him from yelping along at the top of his lungs with complete and enviable abandon. My ears rang with pain.

Casinos are an odd environment—almost like an enormous man cave but where women are allowed and even encouraged to visit, preferably wearing miniskirts, sporting high hair, and carrying trays of free beer or rum and Cokes. There are no windows anywhere. The lights are kept at a consistent level so you don't know whether it's day or night, your circadian clock goes awry, and you never know when to be tired, so you just keep on gambling. A hotelier friend from undergraduate school told me oxygen is pumped in to keep you awake to help you stay at the tables longer. The casino owners ply you with free booze so your judgment is severely impaired, and you're likely to gamble away your house or baby daughter after you've been awake for seventy-two hours and eaten nothing except pretzels for forty-six of them.

A few years ago, I did a voice-over campaign for a major casino chain, and the read they wanted for the narration was "a cross between Cate Blanchett's fairy queen in *Lord of the Rings* and a sexy dominatrix who's totally intimidating but still totally hot." Okay. The ad copy was equally challenging; it went something like this: "You are KING of the world! MASTER of all! Everything can be at YOUR disposal! BUT you must EARN it! You must LEARN how to be a king. At our SUPREME resort you will LAVISH yourself with sumptuous SPA SERVICES that cater to your every need, the finest culinary DELIGHTS in the world, and five thousand GAMING tables, all at YOUR command! It is your time to REIGN!" In other words, come to our casino so you can spend most of your money on massages and hookers and learn how to act kingly, lose whatever you have left at the blackjack tables where the house always wins, then end your suffering by jumping out a window when you finally realize the havoc you've wrought. Thankfully, most casino hotel windows specifically don't open in order to prevent such a demise.

Michel took to the casinos like hairspray on a beehive hairdo and loved spending hours on a stool surrounded by dirty ashtrays and half-chewed plastic cups filled with gaming tokens. After a few double whisky sours, he often became quite chatty. He told me that even though there is no gambling in the Kingdom, he had frequented casinos all over the world while traveling with Princess Zaahira, who spent a large part of the year away from Saudi Arabia visiting family and friends in London, Paris, and Marbella. Now that her children were all nearly grown, she went home only when her husband summoned her or when duty called, for example, if she had to attend the funeral of a relative. Michel said the husband gave her a long leash because he was so fond of her.

The hairdresser claimed that Le Grande Casino in Monte Carlo was his favorite gambling spot because he loved the beautiful people there, but I don't see how he ever would have been allowed entrance to such a posh place. His hair looked like a science experiment, and I never saw him outfitted in anything but distressed dirty jeans and smelly T-shirts.

Then again, maybe he owned a tuxedo that he whipped out if Princess Zaahira had a hankering to go to Monaco. She must have bankrolled him too, because he seemed to have an endless amount of cash.

He also loved Morongo because it has over two thousand slot machines, including *Rich Little Piggies, Dean Martin's Wild Party,* and IGT's video slot *Marilyn Monroe,* which features a lifelike voice-over of Marilyn cooing as she's being played. I thought that was a nice touch.

The first night I took him there, he won $40,000. I know this because the casino demanded an address for his tax information; they wouldn't accept the hotel as a valid address, so they asked for mine as well after I confirmed that I knew him and verified that he was staying in Beverly Hills. Then they flooded my mailbox for months with promotional material: fanny packs, foam beer koozies, and dozens of coupons for free weekends, which I distributed to my casino-loving friends.

After the happy blush of those first huge winnings, the hairdresser lost thousands of dollars night after night and became surly and abusive. He would gamble until 4:00 or 5:00 A.M. while I waited in the parking lot drinking $9 espressos. Casino parking lots are lonely; there isn't much activity. The gamblers park their cars and then disappear for days. The casinos suck them in like a neon black hole. Periodically throughout the night, I'd wander inside to go to the bathroom or check on the hairdresser, to get him cigarettes or save his place at his machines while he went to the loo, and I'd watch the action at the tables or the slots. No one seemed happy.

On the way home, the hairdresser would sleep in the back stretched out on the leather seat—grunting, snorting, and farting—while I drove 90 miles per hour back to the hotel. The California Highway Patrol never bothered the Crown Vic. It's a cop car, so they probably thought I was an undercover cop cruising by on official police business. This one was black, so that made it particularly undercover police–like, although I've also seen them in army green and dark blue depending on which governmental organization is using them. The Federal Building on Wilshire Boulevard has a parking lot filled with white and gray ones, usually with several long curved antennas coming out of the back hood and windshield. When you see one of those pass you on the 405 freeway, especially if it has four fierce-looking men in it sporting aviator sunglasses and flat-tops, you can be sure it's the Feds. The cop version is called the Crown Victoria Police Interceptor (CVPI) and is not available new to the general public, but it is widely sold or auctioned off as used, which is how they end up at rental agencies.

Racing back to the hotel, I thought about how the hairdresser had dissed the Crown Vic that first day by insisting that he was meant to be in something more substantial. He was sadly mistaken. I learned quickly that the Crown Vic has a 250 horsepower V8 engine that picks up powerful speed in seconds and also has a hard-as-hell chassis, which is useful for tactical ramming and maneuvers in car chases, so it's the sedan of choice for law enforcement agencies. I know it sounds like I'm a car chick, but actually I am not. It's just that after months of being stuck behind a wheel for hours on end, I couldn't help but develop a profound respect and appreciation for a vehicle that was so smooth and so fast. I nicknamed my car "The Rocket." One morning, The Rocket and I made it back to Beverly Hills from Palm Springs in 85 minutes instead of the usual 2 hours; we were flying. That car was my friend. Usually Rocky would get me home at 7:00 A.M. to catch a few hours sleep.

Each afternoon back at the hotel, Princess Zaahira wanted to hear about the previous evening's escapades since she did not go to the casinos. I presumed she was forbidden to do so by her husband, but perhaps it was her own sense of propriety that prevented her. I knew the Saudi Army officers on constant duty carefully monitored her activities, so she had little wiggle room in any case.

The hairdresser had noticed that I was a pretty good mimic and started to enlist me to help re-create his activities from the previous night. "COME, Janni!" he yelled as he waved for me to join him next to the princess's Mercedes parked in front of the hotel. He wanted me to act out the goings-on at the poker tables and slot machines that I saw when I went in to check on him.

"NOW! Tell the princess how you see at the blackjack! NOW! Tell the princess!" He pushed me toward the open door of the car, and I could see the princess sitting in the backseat looking relaxed and regal. She smiled benevolently at me and waited expectantly.

"NOW!" he said again. My participation was not a request; it was a demand.

Michel set up the blackjack table scene for her in Arabic, and then I cursorily portrayed all the different characters one after another: the disinterested croupier, the drunken loser, the tentative newcomer, working up to the main action featuring the hairdresser. As him, I looked around as if I were at a poker table, mimed looking at imaginary cards on a table in front of me, lifting the edge of my cards covertly, and checked out the other imaginary players and the imaginary croupier. Then I looked at my cards again. I sighed. Then I mimed sipping a drink from a glass and grimaced to make it clear that it was a strong alcoholic beverage. I glanced around worriedly. I counted imaginary chips. I checked my cards again. I wiped imaginary sweat from my brow. I checked my cards again. I scratched my head as I mumbled to myself: "Card? No card? Card? No card?" I pretended to ask a player next to me: "Card? No card? Card? No card?" I paused, checked my cards again, and then said reluctantly, "Hit me." I watched the cards, cringing with dread as they were dealt. I paused dramatically, then cried "Noooooooo!," throwing my face into my hands and fake sobbing with despair. The princess and the hairdresser howled with delight.

Princess Zaahira asked me to act out various scenes for her again and again; this regular ritual was my only contact with her other than when I delivered things to her hotel room, the Presidential Suite. I could sense that she envied our nights out on the town. I also thought that in spite of her lavish lifestyle and limitless access to everything that money can buy, there were many things the princess probably wished she could see and do and yet could not. She seemed to accept her fate with grace and equanimity, but with a little sadness too.

I could see that Michel had his own buried sadness. It seemed clear to me that he was gay but had sublimated his own desires and needs in service to the princess, as if he were a court eunuch, and that the repression was making him mean. I had tried several times to take him to the West Hollywood clubs (anywhere instead of Palm Springs) so he could at least dance off a little of his bad temper, but he always adamantly refused to go. Sometimes I even went out of the way to drive him home along Santa Monica Boulevard or past the Abbey on Robertson so he could see the early morning boy-on-boy action that he was missing in Boystown. He never acknowledged what he saw as we drove by and never asked me to stop. Homosexuality is forbidden in Saudi Arabia and punishable by death, so perhaps he had just shut that part of himself down forever, even though he spent much of the year in Paris and elsewhere traveling with Princess Zaahira.

We had developed a curious semblance of camaraderie, and I knew that he liked me, in his screaming way, but three weeks on the job was about all I could stomach of the nightly driving jaunts to Palm Springs with the hairdresser. Michel was extremely difficult to be around. He was overbearing, demanding, and insulting, and my lungs took a beating every night because of his incessant chain-smoking on the long drives. I could see that he was lonely and unhappy, but it didn't make the abuse any more forgivable.

One morning, I stumbled into the command post and told security that I was going to quit if they didn't reassign me. I was still considered a lowly member of the hierarchy, but I knew that it reflected badly on the whole group if someone resigned in spite of how quick they were to fire. The royal family didn't want defectors. Also, by this time, they didn't want to lose me. I had started to become somewhat valuable, and I knew this—there are some things they could or would ask only a woman to do. Security agreed but said that I must clear the change with the hairdresser.

I told Michel that I couldn't drive him at night anymore because my "husband" was unhappy that I was coming home so late. Within the first few days, I had already started wearing my grandmother's wedding band to support my "husband" story, as well as to deflect advances from the chauffeurs and security, so this worked out quite well. Pretending to be married was a trick from my bartending days that came in very handy as a chauffeur, and then especially with the Saudis. In Arab culture, it is understood that a husband has every right to forbid or approve his wife's activities. Even so, the hairdresser was clearly hurt that I left him, and from then on, he would look away like a jilted boyfriend whenever I tried to say hello. I didn't miss him.

9

Who Are These People?

I had never met any Saudis before I started the job, so whenever I had a free moment, I would steal away to surf on my laptop as I waited in my car for the next call from security. I didn't have an Internet card so I would drive slowly along the Beverly Hills city streets near the hotels, trolling for a signal on which I could piggyback.

Saudi Arabia is mostly desert, or semidesert, and only 2 percent of the landmass is suitable for cultivation. There are no permanent year-round lakes or rivers. There is very little tourism except for religious reasons. Saudi Arabia is considered the birthplace of Islam and is home to the two holiest Muslim shrines: Medina, the burial site of the Prophet Muhammad, and Mecca. To be a good Muslim, you are obligated to visit Mecca at least once in your lifetime; the *hajj* is one of the five pillars of Islam.

During the yearly pilgrimage to Mecca, there are as many as 1 million people circling the Kaaba at one time and several million more in the surrounding area. The Kaaba is the sacred black stone that is the most sacred place in Islam, the place where Allah revealed his will to the Prophet Muhammad, and Muslims worldwide face in its direction five times a day to offer prayer.

If you are not a Muslim, you are not allowed in the city. The ancient city has no airport, railway, or water system within its limits. A Muslim friend told me, "If you want in, you gotta walk in, you gotta be Muslim, and you're gonna be thirsty." It's all about prayer and sacrifice, not comfort. But he also told me that just outside the city is a plethora of Burger King, McDonald's, and Kentucky Fried Chicken joints.

In the old days, Mecca was hard to get to, and a pilgrim might endure great hardship and sacrifice to make the journey. It took my friend's grandfather six months to travel there by camel from Morocco and six months more to get home. He spent a year riding through the desert and died shortly after. Nowadays you can just catch a flight to be one with Allah, and millions of people a year make the pilgrimage. It's a popular place. In 2006, a stampede in nearby Mina, during the *Ramy al-Jamarāt* ritual ("the stoning of the Devil," wherein pilgrims throw stones at three different pillars), killed more than 340 people, and over 300 were injured. In 1990 more than 1,400 people were killed in a tunnel crush underneath the Kaaba. Since then, the Saudis have improved traffic flow.

As a single woman, I would not be granted a visa to enter the country unless I were sponsored by a government agency or operating in some official capacity (think State Department or the *New York Times*) or if I were stationed there for business (think Boeing or Coca-Cola), but such visas are extremely hard to come by. An average woman like me couldn't go there alone as a tourist to check out the holy sites, do a little water skiing in Jeddah, or try my hand at some camel racing. On a rare sanctioned visit, a man would have to meet me at the airport and escort me wherever I traveled at all times.

Modern-day Saudi Arabia is named after one family —*Saud,* which means *fortunate.*

The Saudi royal family comprises the family members of *Al Saud,* the House of Saud, and are descendants of Muhammad bin Saud, who lived in the eighteenth century. The most powerful are the descendants of his great-great-grandson, the legendary warrior Abdul Aziz Ibn Abdur Rahman Al-Faisal Al Saud, who unified the region in 1932 and formed the Kingdom of Saudi Arabia. It was under his watch that oil started flowing. The king of Saudi Arabia is head of the state and head of the government. The law of the land is Islamic law, or Sharia. There is no written penal code, and Sharia is interpreted by sitting judges, assigned for life, who have studied the Quran and the Prophet Muhammad's teachings.

King Abdul Aziz had forty-two known sons by his twenty-two wives, although some reports have the number of wives as high as one hundred. There are no public birth records for the girls. It's not that the girls were less loved, but perhaps they were just less valuable, so didn't need to be documented. There are now thousands of princes and tens of thousands with prince-wielding influence.

It is estimated that King Fahd, Abdul Aziz's son who died in 2005, had more than 100 wives. Abdullah, his younger brother who succeeded him, has reportedly wed more than 30 wives so far, which means he's behind. According to Saudi custom, a man can have as many wives as he wants during the course of his lifetime, but he can keep only 4 at a time, and he must treat them all equally in terms of lifestyle maintenance, nights spent in each bed, gifts bestowed, beatings, and so on. As recommended by the Prophet Muhammad, it must be truly equal, or he must not keep them, and 4 is deemed the limit of a man's ability to spread the wealth.

If he is a bedouin in the middle of the desert, then he just has to have four tents that are all the same—one for each wife. But if he is a prince with millions of dollars, then it has to be four palaces—all the same.

Originally this custom was the result of tribal warfare after which many widows and children were left without protection and sustenance. It was a man's duty to marry and provide for the wives of his fallen brothers. Nowadays Saudi middle-class men have trouble managing this system. They usually can't afford more than one or two wives. I'm sure that's a letdown for them.

King Fahd was a benevolent and beloved ruler, renowned for his generosity, but I've seen pictures of him and he wasn't exactly what you'd call a stunner. Good looks was definitely not how he persuaded so many women (100!) to marry him. Fahima, Princess Zaahira's cousin, explained to me that many were probably given to him by their families as bonds to foster carefully chosen strategic tribal alliances. The Saudi royal family uses marriage to align interests just as the monarchies of France, England, and Spain did for many centuries. King Abdul Aziz was a master of the tribal bedding that strengthened his sovereignty, and he made sure that his sons were equally adept.

Fahima told me many modern Saudi women like this arrangement because it gets the men out of their hair when the husband spends time with his other wives. I couldn't help but wonder if it doesn't make for a certain amount of competition among the wives, especially if one or more of them happened to be in love with the husband and didn't want to share him. I wondered if there are wives who fight over a husband, or his attention, even if they had married not for love but to advance their family's standing.

"Can a woman marry who she wants?" I asked Fahima on one of our drives.

"Please understand, Janni Amelia, the customs of my country are different than yours. In Islam, the woman has every right to agree to the choice of the husband, of course, but a Saudi woman's groom is often chosen by and must be approved by her *mahram,* her male guardian, who would be her father or her brother until she is married. Then the husband is her *mahram.* This is done in her best interest for a happy and peaceful marriage and for the benefit of all involved. To secure her future, a Saudi woman understands that it is important to cultivate her husband's good favor to protect the longevity of the union. In this way, it is an exquisite . . . dance that she enjoys to do to maintain a happy household and the interest of her husband. A Saudi woman knows this."

It is estimated that the 42 known sons of King Aziz married more than 1,400 women, an average of more than 33 wives for each son. Now that's a party, or a nightmare. Many of my married male friends are fascinated by polygamy and are disappointed when I tell them that I haven't been able to speak to any Saudi men regarding this custom. They just won't talk to me. I've tried. But I do know that many Saudi men have only one wife their whole lives, probably because even one can be a helluva lot to handle, much less four.

As an outsider, it was difficult for me to know who was who in the group or even in the family, especially since I was never told anyone's proper name. I figured out who some of them were by ferreting out clues as I eavesdropped on the security personnel. But I could tell that the Saudis in this group were definitely higher-ups in the royal line because there was a lot of security from Washington, many ex-military guys with big egos and bad attitudes, and there were also security personnel hired from local Los Angeles–based private protection firms. Most of them were American, but there were several from other countries as well; almost all were ex-military or had worked in law enforcement, and most of them were armed. The upper-echelon male members of the family, who were known collectively as the sheikhs and whom I rarely saw, traveled with an elite security detail from the United Kingdom, but Princess Zaahira had locally hired boys. Most of the security were exceptionally well mannered and accustomed to working in high-stress situations with little fanfare, just as Stu was, but a few of them were scary rough around the edges. One guy in particular, Jaco, gave me the heebie-jeebies since he appeared to be synapses away from being a sociopath. Jaco had a constant need to demonstrate his virility and dominance over everyone in his near vicinity—women, men, even an idling Cadillac Escalade—and was tedious to be around. He would regularly come up alongside my parked SUV outside the hotel to make a point of proving that he could rock the truck forcefully enough, with me in it, to knock it on its side if he had the desire.

A Saudi Army colonel, two majors, and a captain were also escorting the family. None of these guys ever looked me in the eye even when they were speaking to me. They always addressed the men near me, as if I were invisible. I'm not sure they would have acknowledged me even if I had spoken to them directly by asking a question that required a response. A female air traffic controller I met told me that there had been a big brouhaha with the FAA and the air traffic controllers union when a Saudi pilot refused to be guided in by a woman—Saudi men do not want women giving them orders. The pilot adamantly demanded to communicate with a man only, and it was reported that the FAA complied with the request. The union was called in after the female controllers complained. There are records of this happening several times, most notably when King Abdullah visited former President Bush on his ranch in Texas.

The Saudi colonel was particularly menacing looking, with a stern gaze and bulging black pouches under his eyes as if he hadn't slept in months, and his voice was a low cigarette-ravaged growl. He had an imposing stocky build, but it was clear he'd eaten a few too many cupcakes so he was big and soft around the middle, as if that part of him forgot to be intimidating and was just hanging out and having a good time. At the beginning of the detail, he spoke to all of us about what to expect on the job.

"We are traveling with the family as protection and advisers. Please know that we are here at the behest of His Royal Highness. Please know that we are always on duty. We are always here. *We are always here.* You are also on call twenty-four hours, seven days a week. You must be ready and available at all times. This is understood. You have been informed of the protocol that must be followed. If you are driving a principal, always maintain less than a car's length between the principal vehicle and the chase vehicle. Be vigilant. Your assigned security must control all door locks and windows. Please do not interfere with this. If you do not have security in the car with you, please keep all doors and windows locked. *This is essential.* It is paramount for the protection of the royal family as well as for yours."

Sometimes, though, I would catch the colonel looking at me when he thought I couldn't see, and he would quickly avert his eyes. I passed him many times each day going in and out of the hotels, and I didn't understand why he always turned away. Later, an Arab friend explained to me that in polite Saudi society, a man doesn't look a lady in the eyes because she belongs to another man—a father, husband, or brother. And he must have noticed my grandmother's wedding band that I was wearing; the colonel was just being polite to me and my man.

In the Kingdom, the sexes do not mix at all when they are out of the home, and in many homes the family compound is separated into areas: one for women and small children only and another area for the men. Cafés and restaurants and even malls are segregated. Women do attend university in Saudi Arabia, but they can be taught only by men via video transmission, never in person. King Abdullah recently celebrated the opening of King Abdullah University of Science and Technology, where men and women do join in classes together, but it is the only school of its kind in the country, and it is hidden away on a remote compound in the middle of the desert far from prying eyes and the zealous religious police. The Committee for the Propagation of Virtue and the Prevention of Vice, the *mataawa,* is a volunteer group that must be some scary dudes; wielding whips, they patrol the city streets looking for infractions of indiscretion. Abdullah wanted to attract major teaching talent from American universities, and in order to do so, he had to guarantee a certain measure of personal and academic freedom.

A woman cannot travel out of the country without written permission from her *mahram,* her legal guardian from her immediate family, even if he's her ten-year-old son because all her grown male relatives are dead. She also needs his permission to work, study, or receive major medical care. As of 2012, women still cannot vote, but there is the promise of election reform in the year 2014, and rumor has it that a woman will not need her *mahram's* permission to do so.

Asking permission from a man, particularly a brother or a nephew, to do what I want whenever I want, and especially to wear what I want, would be hard for me to stomach. One of my first boyfriends used to try to dress me in long Laura Ashley shifts that were popular at the time and to arrange my hair in an upswept Victorian fashion that he said was most flattering to me. Finally, I just flat-out refused in protest at the constant styling. The truth is, part of me wanted to dress in whatever he liked just to please him, but a bigger part of me hated that he relentlessly tried to conform me to his will by telling me what to do and what was best for me. "If you want a doll you can dress up," I told him, "then go buy one."

I did take care of *herself* sometimes.

But I can also imagine that there must be a sense of great comfort in knowing that as a Saudi woman, I would be forever looked after—that my well-being would always be considered, even if carefully monitored. I think I would feel very safe. It might be a comfortable conundrum to be in, but one that still rankles. My first apartment in Los Angeles afforded me the opportunity of living in a condition that I called "condo-bondage." It was in the heart of Hollywood, and the contiguous traffic was abominable; helicopters roared overhead all night long followed by blaring sirens, and the building was a dreary Seventies modular style with hideous wall-to-wall dirty white shag carpeting. But it had a tennis court and a huge heated pool, which my roommate and I blissfully swam in every night after we barbecued on the outdoor grill, lolling around in the warm water from dusk until midnight. It was hard to give up when the time came to move to a sweet little craftsman cottage with a yard and a lemon tree, because it had the soft, sweet stranglehold of condo-bondage.

10

Shoot the Go-To Girl

When I started the job, I brought my computer with me every day. I was one of the few chauffeurs with a laptop, and many of the other drivers didn't even know how to use a computer, or didn't have one that they could carry with them because their families shared one. I had quickly become the go-to Internet girl. They all demanded that I do research for them or their clients: Where is the best late-night chocolate soufflé in Los Angeles? When is the last showing of *Alvin and the Chipmunks* at the Century City AMC? Does the Beverly Center mall have a Gucci shop, or is there only Dolce and Gabbana? I was now becoming the all-around go-to girl as well. I was sent on problematical errands because I usually came up with the goods when no one else could. In a short time, my job had become increasingly more difficult because I had made it more difficult—I made myself the problem solver and troubleshooter—and I paid the price for it by being constantly in demand.

One afternoon, it was brutally hot upstairs on the hotel pool roof deck in the midday sun, especially with my black wool suit on. Security had sent me up there to do an errand for Princess Zaahira's daughter, Princess Anisa, but she and her companions were floating around in the pool and nobody was bothering to issue a directive to me or to release me. No one was even looking at me to acknowledge that I was waiting there in the sun for forty minutes, steaming from collar to cuff. I could

77

feel the sweat trickling down my spine and pooling at the top of my panties. Even though it was not required, I had continued to wear suits because I thought it made me look more professional, but all of my suits were expensive hand-me-downs from my stylish sister in the Northeast who didn't dress for the Beverly Hills summer. All of her clothing was gabardine wool, worsted wool, or just plain wool. I was sorry that I hadn't invested in a light linen number, but I hadn't wanted to spend the extra money, and now I was suffering. While I waited, I vowed to ransack my closet for any long pants and thin cotton blouses that I could wear from that day on.

The hotel had a tranquil swimming pool bordered by private cabanas with billowing white curtains lining the perimeter, and a secluded garden area at the back that had a cool eucalyptus mist spray shower. I wondered if I could somehow stage slipping into the pool or tripping into the shower so it would look like an accident (I was good at pratfalls), but I didn't want to ruin my sister's beautiful suit.

There was an opulent spa next to the pool, but the Saudis never used its services. They preferred massages and pedicures in their rooms administered by their personal staff. Sometimes they hired outside massage therapists, always incessantly cheery and intensely pert young women, who came and went from the hotel rooms at all hours lugging their portable tables behind them. One of Princess Zaahira's cousins had a massage every day to help her relax. *Why the hell does she have to relax?* I wondered. *She doesn't do anything all day except shop and eat.*

The first thing I noticed about Princess Anisa was that she had inherited neither her mother's beauty nor her mother's good nature. She was plump and pouty, with a constant sour expression on her face as if she had just inhaled something foul or as if life was not kind to her. She was sixteen, she was a princess, and she had three maids. How bad could it be? I'm sure there was more to the story (there always is), but even so, it was hard to feel sorry for her. She traveled with several companions who acted like ladies in waiting. They didn't clean up anything or pack anything or carry anything. They just trailed around after Princess Anisa and giggled a lot, making her look good. You could easily tell who was the princess in the group, and she didn't let anybody forget it either.

With Stu's directive ricocheting in my hot, heavy head—"Do not speak unless you are spoken to"—I swayed at the edge of the pool, melting away, waiting for instruction. Finally one of the companions, Yasmina (perhaps?), skipped over to me. I wasn't yet sure of all of their names, and they spoke little English. They could, however, recite most of the lyrics of every hit pop tune: "Baby drop another slow jam . . . And all us lovers need hold hands."

"The princess, she says to Mac drive?" said Yasmina.

I thought about that for a minute. "Oh, she wants to go to the Apple store?" I asked. "Okay, I'll pull the car up and wait downstairs until she's ready." Anisa had her own car and driver, so I had no idea why I was now being asked to chauffeur her or why I had to stand in the scorching sun for almost an hour to find this out, but I didn't argue. She must have heard that I was the go-to girl, and that's why she had requested my services.

Yasmina reached into her robe pocket and handed me a few hundred-dollar bills. "The princess, you must to bring her iPhone."

"She wants me to go to the Apple store on my own and get her an iPhone? Does she know she has to sign up for service if she wants it to work as a phone?"

Yasmina looked at me blankly and I demonstrated with my phone. "AT&T," I said. "She has to sign up for AT&T. I can't do that for her. She has to have a phone service contract for it to work here. It's a two-year commitment."

Yasmina called out something in Arabic to the other ladies in waiting, and their heads spun in my direction. Then one of them snapped her fingers at the servant girls sitting by the side of the pool. One of the girls who spoke the most English hustled over to me.

"Janni! Please, the princess, she must to have the iPhone!" she said.

"I'm sorry, your name is Zuhur, right?" She nodded yes. I had started to be embarrassed that I had to keep asking them their names over and over again, and I was trying hard to learn them, but I had almost no conversational reinforcement. And no one seemed to care about my correct name so I don't know why I was worried about getting theirs right. Every member of the family and entourage called me by a different name: Janni, Jennie, Joanie, Junie, Yianni, Yanie, Yoanie. And I had learned to respond to them all.

"Yes, Zuhur, I know that she wants me to get her an iPhone, but she needs to sign up for cellular service for it to work as a phone; otherwise it'll just be an expensive iPod." Perspiration dripped from my upper lip, and I dabbed at it with my fingertips as I looked around for a tissue. There was nothing but green-and-white-striped pool towels stacked up near each cabana.

I could see that Princess Anisa was watching from the corner of the pool while she floated around on a green foam lounge chair. An iced drink was in the cup holder near her right hand, and she was slapping the water with her left. She was slowly spinning on the foam lounge with a tight frown on her face, and it was obvious that she was following the action. She hissed something in Arabic in our general direction, and Zuhur jumped at her words.

"Yes, here is cash." Zuhur handed me another wad of hundreds, about a thousand dollars. "The princess she says three iPhone. You must bring now. Three iPhone. Okay? *Yalla!* [Hurry.] *Yalla!*"

"But they won't work if she doesn't sign up for service." I said this very clearly and loudly to be certain that Anisa could also hear. "She has to give them a credit card, they run a credit check, and then she signs up for two years of service. That's just the way they do it. It's not my rule; it's how Apple sells them."

The roar of a jet plane overhead interrupted us. That was unusual because I didn't think the FAA flight plans permitted flyovers in Beverly Hills; I'd never heard one there before so it must have been a military plane. We both tilted our heads up and watched the plane's long white contrails for a few moments.

When we faced each other again, I saw that Zuhur was now hopping back and forth from one foot to the other as if the soles of her feet were burning on the concrete, but I knew that the ground wasn't hot; it was a specially treated surface resorts used so that their guests were comfortable walking to and from the pool. She repeatedly looked back at the princess, then at me, then at the princess. Something else definitely was making her uncomfortable. Anisa hissed again, and Zuhur grimaced. Two of the other servant girls joined us, flanking Zuhur on either side. They all looked at me with worried eyes.

"Please, it must to phone. It must to phone or the princess, she is unhappy," Zuhur said. It dawned on me that she, or perhaps even all the girls, would be held responsible if Anisa didn't receive her working iPhones. It wouldn't be their fault if the iPhones weren't activated, but they were obviously frightened that it might not be done. Perhaps they were worried only that the princess would be unhappy, but it seemed more ominous than just that. They wouldn't have been so agitated if they didn't fear some kind of repercussion if Anisa's wishes weren't fulfilled.

My instinct was to speak to the princess myself and explain the problem. But I wasn't allowed to speak to her unless she addressed me, and that clearly wasn't going to happen. She was acting as if I wasn't even there.

I dropped my voice. "Okay, Zuhur, let me go talk to security and ask them to speak with Princess Zaahira's secretary. Maybe they can help, and I can figure out a way to get the phones signed up. Okay?" I had a few friends who worked at the Apple stores around town and hoped that maybe they'd work something out for me.

"*Yalla,* Janni. Please, please to do this, and I will tell the princess," she said.

I was afraid that Zuhur would tell the princess that it was a done deal and then we'd both go under. By this time, several more drivers had been fired for lesser infractions than disappointing a princess. The day before, a driver had been fired because his client didn't think he was paying attention to her, but it was more likely that he was just trying not to be rude by paying too close attention. It was a fine line to navigate.

"Please tell her that I will try my best, but also that this has nothing to do with you," I said. "Tell her what I said about it being Apple store policy. It has absolutely nothing to do with you or me."

I wish there was a way for me to make it clear to Anisa that I'm not doing this to make her happy, I thought. *I'm only doing it so that these girls don't catch hell for it.* Just weeks before, I would have been eager to do whatever I could to please a princess, no matter what she asked of me, but that was starting to sharply erode.

"*Yalla,* Janni!" she said. "Please, please to make the iPhone to phone," she said.

As I turned toward the elevator, Zuhur squeezed my arm softly. "*Shukran* [thank you], thanks you, Janni, thanks you. *Yalla!*" All the servant girls scurried back to the far end of the pool to attend to the princess's and her companions' needs.

I was able to buy the iPhones for Princess Anisa, but I left it up to security to arrange for them to be unlocked and activated, and I tried to avoid any further dealings with her. Eventually I learned to leave my laptop at home or in the trunk of my car and use it only out of sight of others. I also learned to take less initiative, make fewer offers of assistance, and often to say no outright even when I was sure something was possible. This was a hard lesson for me.

When I was a little girl, I thought that the world was a meritocracy—that if you have some modicum of talent and nurtured it with hard work and perseverance, then you would succeed and be rewarded. It was at this time in my life, more than any other in spite of the many disappointments I have had, that I began to see that this is simply not true. Your future can be determined by an accident of birth or a stroke of good luck. Sometimes you are just *fortunate*.

11

Like a *Hijab* in the Wind

I was finally assigned to be the regular driver of another young teenage niece of Princess Zaahira, the little Princess Rajiya, who had arrived after most of the rest of the family. A group of us drove several family members in a convoy of six cars to greet her at the airport. I was told that at home in the Kingdom and also when traveling, a large group would always convene to pick up a friend or relative at the airport even if the journey was several hours long and they'd seen them only a few days before. If no one ever has to work, then several trips to the airport each week was common and possibly a nice diversion.

When the young girl exited customs, I saw that she had traveled with three servants accompanying her; each servant came out of customs wielding two luggage carts weighed down with at least eight enormous bags and boxes. This was how a thirteen-year-old girl traveled. All the family members drove back in one Navigator together, and the rest of the SUVs were used to transport her baggage.

Each client had his or her own car, and Rajiya had requested to be driven in a convertible as her regular personal vehicle. There was some pushback from security about whether one would be procured for her because convertibles are much harder to protect—they're too vulnerable. But Rajiya was adamant and had persuaded the family that she absolutely had to have one; Fausto scrambled to find an available high-end black convertible midsummer in Los Angeles.

I picked up the car at a Beverly Hills car rental agency early in the morning and then had it meticulously detailed and prepped as usual with goodies, tissues, and bottled water. The cars had to be immaculate inside and out at all times, no matter the time of day or how many hours it had been driven, and loaded with anything the royals might request. Santiago's bookish prince preferred lukewarm Evian and Doritos. He usually took only one sip of water and ate one or two chips at a time, but Santiago had to make sure that new bottles and fresh bags were always available. For Princess Rajiya, I stocked my car with snacks that didn't melt—no chocolate or candy, and luckily she didn't ask for any, which would end up in a gooey clump after a day of driving. I had learned that the messy hard way when I had to spend a whole morning scraping chocolate from the cup holders and carpet after a client had opened a bag of M&Ms, eaten a few, and then dumped the rest, thoughtfully leaving them to bake in the California sun the remainder of the day.

The family was exiting the hotel en masse when I finally pulled up, and I hustled to jump out and open the car door for Rajiya. I still didn't know what she actually looked like—she had moved so quickly at the airport before leaping into the SUV to join her cousins that I didn't get a good look at her then. I only knew that she was petite and dark-haired. So I just stood there with the door open, smiling politely, hoping somebody would get in the car.

A striking woman with an air of great authority, wearing a *hijab,* long pants, and a matching long tunic, introduced herself to me in excellent English. "So! You are to be Rajiya's driver!" she announced. It was hard to guess her age without seeing more of her, but she had dark pencil-thin eyebrows and dark kind eyes, and a smooth handsome face with few lines. She wore no makeup, but her skin looked soft and shiny.

"Yes, ma'am," I said.

"My name is Malikah." She held my proffered hand firmly in both of hers for a long moment, looked at me appraisingly, and then patted my hand as she said, "I am very pleased to meet you. Rajiya is my angel. You and I will guard her with great care."

"Of course, ma'am," I said.

I assumed this formidable woman was little Princess Rajiya's mother, but it was her nanny, Malikah. She was a devout Muslim and dressed with arms, ankles, and head covered at all times. Most of her outfits were made for her in Lebanon, where she was from, in styles that she saw in Paris when traveling with the family and then modified and had made more cheaply in Beirut when she visited for Ramadan. I'd never seen anybody dressed like this up close. It was exquisite. Malikah wore lace-edged gauntlets to make sure her wrists were covered, and even at the beach she wore finely woven cotton leggings and ballet slippers on the sand. Many of her clothes were made of finely embroidered silk, and her headscarves were matching and often colorful, so her wardrobe was always a collection of elegant but strangely modest ensembles.

"This is good. I can tell by looking at your face that things will work out well between us," she said as she winked at me. Then she walked away and was quickly besieged by the other nannies and servants. This would be true throughout the family's stay. Malikah was clearly the thought leader of the household help, though she was too modest to have ever called herself that. All the staff looked to her for innovation, information, and counsel.

Everyone was talking at once and most of it was in Arabic so I couldn't tell what was going on, but there was some kind of hullabaloo afoot. It was impossible to know what was expected of me or what I was supposed to do next. I glanced around worriedly to see what my next move might be, but then one of the security personnel came over to the convertible and introduced himself to me.

George was one of the few black Englishmen on the job. He was from the West Midlands, with a short-voweled, lilting musical accent, and had been a decorated soldier in the English military. He had broad, square shoulders and a highly developed muscular upper body with burly, hairless arms. A long, angry-looking pink scar traveled down one arm; it looked like it had been made with a sword. He was handsome, soft-spoken, and courteous, almost chivalrous, and all the women loved him—royals and servants as well as the entire female hotel staff. He seemed to have a warm relationship with everyone he encountered. When George gave an order, he'd cleverly turn it around to sound as if he were asking me to do him a favor to make his job easier instead of issuing a command, which was what he was actually doing. He'd touch me on the elbow lightly and lean in close as he spoke—it was respectful but still carefully manipulative. And he always said, "Thanks, love, you're a dear," after I agreed to do what he asked. I felt that he meant it when he called me a dear.

George informed me quietly that I would be driving Rajiya and her cousin, Princess Ava, to a restaurant in Beverly Hills to join other members of the family for lunch. The family had decided that Ava would be allowed to join Rajiya in the convertible even though the security had made it clear that they preferred that she didn't. George was Ava's family's regular security and traveled around the world with them so he, or Ava's full-time female security, accompanied her wherever she went, along with Ava's nanny, a Frenchwoman. Ava was fourteen and had a lanky tomboyish build, with long curly hair that she always wore pulled back behind her ears. She was interested in music and art, and had a thoughtful and studious manner (her brother was the young prince taking classes at USC), but she was a loner and it turned out that she rarely cavorted with any of her teenage princess cousins.

Rajiya was thirteen years old, sensitive, spirited, very fashion conscious, and willful as hell, with a sweet moon-shaped face framed by black soft ringlets. She and Ava had very little in common besides blood. The girls got in the backseat of the convertible, and George sat in the front. He reminded me that he would be in charge of controlling all door locks and windows; then he powered the convertible top down on the car, and the girls squealed with glee—so they had that in common. I got the idea that this was truly a rare occurrence for them, especially for Ava, whose family had very tight security. Just before we drove off, Malikah came up to the car, smiled at the girls in the backseat, laid her hand again firmly on my arm, and said to me, "I will see you in a moment." It almost sounded like a threat, but a nice one.

Ava's nanny was already in one of the family's SUVs ahead of us on the way to the restaurant, but Malikah watched us drive away, then quickly jumped in an SUV following close behind. She was like a hawk. Wherever little Princess Rajiya went, Malikah followed. Rajiya called Malikah "my flag" because she knew that as long as she could always see Malikah's *hijab* in her eye line then she would never be lost, never in danger, no matter where they were, even if hundreds of strangers surrounded them. Rajiya knew that Malikah would always guard and protect her.

Malikah was more than just a chaperone. She was a compassionate teacher as well and monitored Rajiya carefully as she helped her to negotiate any new situation that the young woman might encounter. Rajiya relied on her for guidance as well as advice, even when they argued about what she was allowed to do. Malikah would never forbid her to do anything—it wasn't her place to do so—but she would firmly remind Rajiya of her obligations and commitments. There was a constant tug of war between them, but ultimately Rajiya could do whatever she wanted as long as she got clearance from her mother, whom she lobbied regularly and often successfully, but Malikah was such a worthy opponent that her sound counsel often superseded Rajiya's pleas.

When I started the job, I wondered why the family needed so much supervision and security. Most of the Saudi families I met were heavily guarded. Were they afraid of kidnapping and ransom demands? Were they concerned about Islamic extremists who objected to the royal family's Westernized way of life and conspicuous consumption? Had something happened that made them feel threatened?

One of the top American security personnel, Rick, offered his opinion on this: "I've been working with them for years, and the way I see it is like this: they're used to the protection and they like the attention, makes them feel special. Do they need it here? I doubt it. Back home in Riyadh, no one messes with them for sure. They speed around 70 miles an hour in a convoy of SUVs just to meet up at the Häagen-Dazs in Kingdom Tower for an ice cream cone, and the regular folks jump out of the way because they know it's the royal family coming through. Now, the most worry we have here is keeping the young girls in line because they're so happy to be in the States. But there's nobody coming after them, per se; we just have to make sure they aren't approached by any young men who want to get to know them, who want to talk to them. That would be a problem. Their fathers would be plenty upset about that."

It was hard to believe that so much money and effort was going into protective measures that were seemingly more for appearance than actual necessity. But the legion of support staff around the members of the royal family was perhaps a way to keep them insulated as much as it was to keep them safe. The family liked to have a bolster around them; it made them feel special. It made them feel superior.

Rajiya was at a vulnerable age, and the family preferred to surround her with women. I could understand this. I went to an all-girls middle school, and it was a huge shock for me when it merged with a school for boys partway through my high school years. Suddenly I was painfully conscious of my hair, my face, and my figure. One of my brothers repeated to me that his friend called me "Orca" after seeing me at a swim meet wearing a white bathing suit. I was crushed, and I know my education suffered.

The pressures that all teenagers face as they begin to interact with the world independent of the cocoon of their families can be disconcerting, but the pressures a young Saudi girl faces are much greater than just having her feelings hurt by an unkind remark. Her life can be ruined if she dishonors her family (or, rather, dishonors her father and the men of the family, because that's the way it is perceived) by committing an act, either intentional or not, that compromises her reputation in any way. Even an innocent conversation with a boy who is not a blood relative could be considered a grievous infraction depending on her age and the temperament of the family. She can be punished severely for any breach of misconduct, and it is her father's right to punish her however he sees fit, even put her to death, for a major contravention.

I have a handful of protective brothers (even the one who repeated his friend's remark probably did it to curb any possible interaction between me and his friend) and a father who was old-fashioned and rather proper, but none of them would ever have felt compelled to punish me to release them from shame. My father wouldn't have hurt me if he'd found out that I kissed a boy in seventh grade during a game of spin the bottle, much less beat me to death because I had a conversation with a stranger on Facebook—as an aggrieved Saudi Arabian father who felt he had been disgraced by his daughter's online communications did recently. As I grew to understand more about the culture of the young princesses in my charge, I became protective of them as well. I couldn't help but be so; I felt it was my duty as a person and as a woman because their future well-being was at stake.

After lunch, Ava, George, and her nanny drove with the family back to the hotel, and Rajiya jumped in the front seat of the convertible with me while Malikah got in the back. "Please, driver, I would like to see Los Angeles!" Rajiya said to me without looking at me. "Can we go see everything? Is it far to Hollywood? Are there any stars that we can see? Can we see them now? Where is the beach? Where are the best shops? Is there a Jamba Juice nearby? My friends say it is the best. Is it very far? Where is Melrose Avenue? I want to see all the shops. Can we go there now? I want to go to a studio so I can see the making of a movie. I want to go to the Universal City, I have heard it is the best. Is it very far to Disneyland? Can we go there too?" Rajiya spoke into the windshield as if I wasn't there and she didn't wait for my answers to her questions; she constantly looked to Malikah for confirmation and approval.

"Yes, yes, Rajiya," said Malikah. "We will now go on a tour." Malikah leaned in to speak to me from the backseat and spoke quietly as if confiding in me. Rajiya had cranked up the music at this point, but Malikah was right on my ear so I could hear every word she said as clear as a bell. "Please, Janni, will you take us to see some wonderful things? This will make Rajiya very happy. This is the first time for Rajiya in Los Angeles so she is in high spirits and wants to see everything. This may seem strange to you, but she is a teenager so this is natural."

"Uh, sure," I said. "I guess we could go to Hollywood if you like, and then we'll work our way back from there." I just wanted to go home and get underneath the covers and never come out, and it was only early afternoon. A daunting, oppressive feeling came over me as if I were being locked up in a dark room—the same feeling I used to have when I had to begin a 3:00 P.M. shift at a nightclub that I knew would last until five the next morning. The end seemed so far away. But it was only a few weeks into the job, and I had to keep going. Even though the start of it had already been unfathomably grueling, I had to believe that maybe it would get better. It had to; it couldn't get worse. *Buck up,* I said to myself. *Just buck up and do it.*

"Perhaps you do not have children?" Malikah asked. This was not the first time this question had come up on the job, and I was gearing up to invent an unfortunate malady that sadly prevented my "husband" and me from conceiving, but there was something about Malikah and the way she asked me that prevented me from doing so.

"No, no, I don't have any children of my own," I said. "But I have lots of nieces and nephews, so I think I know how to make sure Princess Rajiya has a good time."

"And are you sure you do not mind to do this?" she asked.

"No, of course not, it's my pleasure," I said.

"Let us go, and I promise you that we will all have a good time. I will be sure to make this so," Malikah said as she patted me softly on my shoulder.

Malikah was on the ball. She'd obviously noticed that I was uncomfortable even though I was trying to hide it. It was distracting to have Rajiya sitting up front, where she constantly fiddled with the radio that she liked to play at top volume. She peppered me with questions but still ignored me completely, she kept on changing her mind about where she wanted to go and what she wanted to see, and she insisted on having the top down even in the midday sun. I had forgotten to put on sunscreen and was getting terribly burned. I also hadn't thought to put my hair back, so after a few hours in the convertible it was a big tangled catastrophe circling my head. I wanted to tell Rajiya that only tourists drove with the top down before sunset, but that seemed mean, so I held my tongue.

I drove Rajiya and Malikah around Beverly Hills and Hollywood for several hours, showing them all the important landmarks. This turned out to be fortuitous for Rajiya because she was one of the youngest in the group and had never before been to Southern California. Prior to 2001, many Saudi families came to visit regularly, but that slowed after September 11 and Rajiya's family had visited America only a few times to go skiing in Aspen. Many of her cousins' families owned homes in Bel Air and Beverly Hills, which they kept year round, and many stayed in rented estates in the summer months when the Saudis like to visit. The other girls her age knew where to go and what to do and who was who and what was what, but Rajiya did not. She was smarter than they were, though, and a quick study. But she wasn't sure how to treat me because my position in the hierarchy was ambiguous. At first she completely ignored me, but then she saw that maybe that wasn't to her advantage. I was a good resource, so perhaps I should be consulted more. After one fast and furious tour with me as her guide and Rajiya paying close attention, she was all over it like cheese on chili fries, as if the little Saudi princess had SoCal in her blood.

I drove Rajiya along the Sunset Strip and showed her the music clubs: the Whisky, the Roxy, the Viper Room, and then the Sky Bar at the Mondrian (that really wowed her), and of course the Chateau Marmont Hotel. There was a modeling shoot going on there, and she was in heaven. We checked out Grauman's Chinese Theater, where I pointed out the costumed superheroes in front of the theater posing for pictures with sunburned potbellied people in shorts and T-shirts that said "Made in Hollywood." I offered to double-park so she could get out to walk closer, but also intimated that she probably wouldn't want to get too close to the polyester-caped aged Spiderman. She looked at him and frowned, then nodded her head in affirmation. We went to the Roosevelt Hotel, where the *Jimmy Kimmel Show* is filmed, and I told her I could get her tickets from a friend if she wanted to go see it or to any other show that sparked her interest. We went to the original Fred Segal on Melrose Avenue, where we had ice cream in the café and saw a slew of stars; then I took her down Melrose to the funky hip stores, to the Pacific Design Center, and to the trendy shops in the Robertson area where the celebutantes shop: Kitson, Lisa Kline, and Curve. We didn't do any shopping then, just made quick hits only so that Rajiya could get a sense of where she was and what was going on in La-La Land.

Rajiya would speak to Malikah in Arabic whenever she didn't want me to understand what she was saying or when she didn't know the correct words in English. On the way back from our tour, they talked softly in Arabic for several minutes, and then I heard Malikah say in English, "Perhaps you should ask her then?"

Rajiya finally looked at me and asked, "Why are you my driver?" By this time, she knew that I had gone to Cornell as an undergrad (we had passed the Tesla studio on Santa Monica Boulevard and I'd pointed out that he had done much of his most important work at Cornell) and then to graduate school at Harvard (she heard me talking to George about the razing of the Tasty, a classic greasy spoon that's no longer in the Square). I was so markedly different from most of the other chauffeurs she had ever met that she couldn't put it together. "Well, I'm between jobs, as we say. I'm in the entertainment business, so sometimes there are lulls in employment and I have to do other things to make ends meet. That's not unusual," I said. I didn't want to elaborate any further. The truth is I felt that I had sunk pretty low. And Rajiya was only a teenager who was too young to understand how debilitating money troubles can be, and she was certainly never going to have that problem anyway. She'd have her fair share of difficulties, I'm sure, different from what I would ever know, but probably money would never be one of them.

A short while after this conversation, Rajiya saw me in a late-night rerun of a television show. "If you are a TV star, why are you here as my driver? Why are you not with the show every time?" she asked me.

"I'm not a TV star, and I was just a guest star on that show, not a series regular, which means you're on the show every week. Unfortunately, I was on it only a few times," I answered.

"So they did not want you to be the series regular in every show?" she asked.

That hurt because I knew it was true. "No, I guess they didn't."

"But why did they not want you?" she continued.

"I don't know," I said. "I just really don't know." That was the truth. It's an absolute mystery to me why some people make it in the entertainment business and some people don't. But there I was explaining to a girl one-third my age why NBC didn't want me acting on their show so I was acting as a chauffeur instead. I cringed inside.

Rajiya began to watch my every move and constantly quizzed me on my opinions about everything from David Beckham to limited-edition collector sneakers so she could get a better read on me. She went on the same mega-thousand-dollar shopping sprees that the older ladies loved and then modeled the clothes for me to get my take on her purchases. She never openly agreed with me and barely acknowledged that she was even taking in my views. In fact, sometimes she was even coldly dismissive, but I noticed that she still clocked everything that I said to the extent that I began to be careful about sharing my views.

More than once, I heard her repeat a paraphrased version of something I'd said the day before: "I must drink fresh grapefruit juice every night so that I can lose weight! That is what all the stars do!" I heard her say to one of her friends. She was referring to my "Hollywood Royal Flush" cleanse, which contains whole fruit only, *not juice,* which is basically just a glass of sugar, and she forgot a crucial step: massive amounts of caffeine. I would have been more careful about my choice of words if I'd known I was going to be quoted as a diet expert. Also, it saddened me that she felt she had to lose weight anyway because she had a perfect little figure; but like most teenage girls, she was starting to worry about her curves.

I decided to be more judicious in my speech and figured she didn't need to know that I thought all celebrity idolatry was bullshit and that stars are just like real people—many are deeply flawed—or that the only reason I'd ever wear someone else's name emblazoned across my chest or ass is because they are paying me to advertise them, not the other way around. She was enamored of American pop culture, and I decided to let her enjoy it; she was, after all, only thirteen.

In many ways, Rajiya was oddly inexperienced and naive, even for a thirteen-year-old. She noticed that I kept a supply of energy bars in the car for myself since there were often huge gaps between stolen mealtimes, and she asked me to take her to Whole Foods so that she could buy some for herself. At the store she chose box after box of different varieties, costing over $300, filling up the shopping cart. I pointed out that she could buy just one bar of each, taste them and see which flavors she liked, and then come back to buy more. She scoffed at me when I suggested this; it was unseemly. It was un-princess-like. Buying just one bar would appear as if the whole box couldn't be hers if she so desired.

Malikah used the opportunity at Whole Foods to educate Rajiya about the use of physical currency, which she would need to know if she attended university in the United States. Malikah knew that Rajiya had her heart set on this and was thinking ahead for ways to help prepare the teenager. At the register, the princess gleefully counted out and then placed several hundred-dollar bills on the counter. Then she walked away, satisfied with herself for a job well done. The surprised cashier laughed and called out to Rajiya, "Hey, you forgot your change!" Malikah stopped her and explained that there was change due, and that

Rajiya had to wait for the cashier to give her the difference in what she had paid and what was owed. Rajiya was mortified, and stood before the cashier red-faced and shaking. She was pained with shame. It was a surreal moment. My heart went out to her even though a moment before I had silently been disparaging the prodigious supply of energy bars and her wastefulness.

Recently I watched my four-year-old niece buy her first ice cream cone with the three dollars her mother had given her, but my niece had negotiated her first purchase better because she had seen her parents do it many times. Rajiya had probably never had that everyday experience. She was thirteen years old and had never paid for anything in her life nor had she watched her parents do so because the servants always took care of such mundane tasks.

Rajiya had a nanny and her own maid, and several other household servants also waited on her. When she'd come home at night, she'd strip off her clothes as she walked and leave everything on the floor to be gathered by the servants. She didn't do anything for herself.

When I was just a year or two older than Rajiya, I had a summer job at a chain restaurant near my home. My parents were generous and provided everything we needed, no small feat in such a large family, but it was the children's responsibility to earn any extra spending money for things we wanted but weren't necessary. I had started to play golf, and I wanted a new set of Ping golf clubs. I really, really wanted them, and I was sure that new clubs that were sized just right for me, instead of the lousy rentals or my brother's old clubs that I'd been using, would make me a much better player, maybe even shave twenty strokes off my score. I was optimistic about that. My dad suggested that I get a summer job and promised to match whatever I saved as a contribution to my golf club fund. I already had some part-time work experience doing filing and working the phones at his office during previous summers and holidays, but this restaurant job was my first foray outside a protected family environment.

The café was jammed from sunup until midnight; there was never any downtime when I could actually learn my duties and figure out how to do them well with any semblance of expertise. To top it off, I had to wear a uniform from hell—a truly hideous gray polyester dress with orange trim that was tight in all the wrong places and made my skin itch as if I were wearing a hair shirt.

One morning, I was assigned to make the iced tea that would be served for the busy lunch crowd. I made several pitchers successfully, but then a glass pitcher shattered when I was filling it with boiling water; it exploded all over me, silencing the entire restaurant in a shush of shock. I can still practically feel the thing vibrating and then bursting in my hands. The front of my gray and orange hair shirt was soaked with black tea (it looked like I had peed on myself), and I felt completely humiliated. I was so shaken that I couldn't finish the rest of the shift, and the manager sent me home. Of course, I didn't want to go back to work the next day, but I had to; I was hired for the summer and obligated to stick it out. The next morning, a kindly older waitress showed me how to put a silver spoon in the pitcher before filling it slowly to prevent the glass from cracking. Other messy mishaps followed, but somehow I kept the job and even made enough money to buy myself the new set of Pings, a new golf bag, and even snazzy new white leather golf shoes. My dad didn't contribute at all; I paid for everything myself. It was truly a rite of passage, and I remember a flooding surge of pride when I showed off my new gear to my family. As I watched Rajiya at the market, I saw that it was unlikely that she would ever have that same rush of accomplishment if everything was always given to her—as if anything and everything was hers to possess, in a way, but not to truly enjoy because she hadn't earned it.

Rajiya hid her face from me the rest of the day and did not speak to me again until the next afternoon. I understood that in her eyes, her first attempt to operate as a normal American teenager had transpired badly. She appeared particularly upset that I had witnessed the incident. I know that she was confused and conflicted about who I was and my role in the palace hierarchy, and this must have deepened her embarrassment.

In spite of her privilege, Rajiya was never mean-spirited or unkind in any way, at least not purposely. When we arrived back at the hotel late at night, Rajiya would always turn down the music as we neared the hotel entrance. At first, I thought this was because she had finally grown bored with the repetitious station selections, but then I realized that she was doing it out of consideration for others who were sleeping. Many of the hotel balconies and windows faced the circular driveway entrance, and the thumping music from the car radio could easily have woken guests up if their windows were open. I credit Malikah for that because she took great care in showing the young girl the importance of being a thoughtful and polite person, and she always set a tremendous example for her as well. Just being around Malikah could make anyone a better person, and I loved spending time with her.

She and I had frequent long conversations as we waited together outside a prestigious learning center in Beverly Hills where Rajiya took tutoring classes. The teenager had made a deal with her mother, Princess Aamina, Princess Zaahira's sister-in-law, that if Rajiya took classes three mornings a week, then she'd be free to pal around with her girlfriends the whole rest of the day. Rajiya's mother knew her daughter wanted to be admitted to college in the States, so she was making sure that Rajiya was receiving the extra schooling that would make that easier. Rajiya was the only one of her friends who was taking classes, so my chauffeur hat's off to Princess Aamina; she had the vision to help prepare her daughter for globalization and a rapidly changing world.

Malikah and I sat with each other in the café next door to the learning center, with Malikah's eagle eye fixed firmly on its door, guarding her charge. She had been the little princess's nanny since Rajiya was an infant, and was a sibling's nanny before that; she loved them all dearly and had a vested interest in Rajiya's success and future happiness.

She was from Lebanon and had been a nanny for the family for most of her adult life. When Malikah was a young woman, civil war devastated her homeland, and her parents were killed. Thereafter, she supported her family and had even put her three younger brothers and sisters through college. Perhaps because of this she had never married. My biggest worry was whether I could pay my cell phone bill and still have any money left over to buy organic grass-fed New Zealand beef at Whole Foods for eighteen bucks a pound, and she'd put a whole family through school on a nanny's salary. She also gave away a substantial amount of what she made as alms to the poor and would never have considered not doing so. One of the five pillars of Islam is *zakat*, alms-giving, and Malikah took this very seriously. She had a sunny nature too in spite of all that sacrifice. She was eternally good-spirited, tolerant, and charitable and acted as a sort of den mother to all the household staff. It was through her, and her serene teaching, that I was able to understand much of what I saw happening around me. She became a heroic figure to me.

Malikah patiently answered many of my questions, just as Fahima had done, by explaining the Islamic custom compelling women to cover. But I wanted to know more about why it was so important to the women to do so, especially Malikah. She often told stories to illustrate a point.

"Okay, okay, Janni. So, you love salad, *nam* [yes]? Yes, I love salad too. I could eat it every day. I love a beautiful salad with many different delicate lettuces and vegetables. A very good salad has everything you want and expect, and then something else that completes it in a way that you cannot expect. For me this is the lemon. The final addition to a delicious creation that makes it more complete. Yes, it is very, very good with just the oil and salt, but it is the lemon, at the last moment, that makes it more complete.

"For me, the *hijab* is like this, Janni, the final ingredient. I do honor to Allah with all my deeds, but it is the final act of wearing the *hijab* every day that makes all my other actions more complete. This is why I cover."

"But why is it up to the woman?" I asked. Fahima had already explained that women are temptresses, but I wasn't buying that. There had to be more to it.

"Janni, in Islam *both* men and women are asked to behave with modesty and decorum; that is the word, *nam* [yes]? But the woman is considered more desirable in every society; look at the beautiful paintings all over the world and you see that this is true. So she wears the *hijab* when out of the home to protect her but also, more important to me, she wears this so the attention must be drawn to her personal qualities rather than her physical qualities. So that her actions are considered, not just her physical beauty.

"Everywhere in Los Angeles, you see the vulgar exploitation of women, and men and children as well, and the human body for marketing purposes and pornography. This can only end badly, Janni. Sexuality is a natural human expression, but it is a private concern, meant to support a happy home life. It is not meant to sell toothpaste, it is not meant to sell sneakers, it is not meant to sell at all. *Nam, nam.*"

As many women do, I struggle with objectification and the desire to be heard and respected regardless of my beauty (or lack of), but in spite of that, I also spend a lot of time and attention on the care of my physical self to try to make myself as beautiful as possible. Granted, I am often rather lax in my beautifying efforts, but it's a constant conundrum. I think this is so ingrained in the feminine psyche that it was true even for Malikah, in spite of what she said.

One day when I arrived a few minutes early before my scheduled morning pickup of Rajiya and Malikah, I heard a soft whistle and looked up to see Malikah smiling down at me from one of the upper hotel balconies with her hair uncovered. "Do you see me, Janni?" she called out, and then ducked back inside the room. This was the only time I had ever seen her head bare, and I just stood there for a moment gawking. She had beautiful bright red hair hanging down to her waist, freshly hennaed. She colored it even though it was always hidden underneath her *hijab,* and no one ever saw it but herself.

A similar paradox occurs in the wearing and the attributes of the full cover itself. The black covering that women are required to wear in the Kingdom consists of many complicated interdependent pieces, and there is a vast selection in terms of choice of material, variations, and adornments. Some women wear covering that has sparkles, embroidery, or beading, and some even have diamonds or pearls sewn into the material. The most important articles are the *abaya,* the long black cloak that is the outer layer, and the *niqab,* the long black veil, which is usually triple layered with fine netting over the eyes that allows for a diffused but sharply limited peripheral view. The *hijab* and hair covers are often three or four pieces together and are almost always worn, even inside the house, to completely cover the hair and neck. Pins are used to secure the pieces, and these are sometimes valuable pieces of jewelry. There are also gloves, ankle covers, and even gauntlets for the forearms, that a woman may choose to wear.

The veil and *hijab* can be used as tools that a woman manipulates to subtly communicate or generate interest—the constant adjusting required to keep them secure and well placed, the seemingly accidental slippage or displacement—these actions force attention on the hair and face, as well as on the woman's eyes and expression. What is meant to deter a focus on appearances can actually create the opposite result by thrusting continuous attention on the covering itself, as well as constant speculation about what is underneath, real or imagined. Even an escaped lock of hair takes on great significance. The cover has become part of a woman's allure, because it draws men in as they try to see what treasures may be buried beneath.

I admire the women for being able to just walk in the *abaya* and *hijab* at all, and they did much more than just that. I tried on an *abaya* and *hijab,* and I couldn't even walk across my bathroom in the get-up, and I couldn't make it down the hallway without crashing into the walls. Malikah was an avid skier, and accompanied the family to Gstaad and Aspen where she hit the slopes in full *hijab* with a full-length tunic, which reached down to her ski boots, under her parka.

"Since I was a little girl, I enjoy all the sports," she said. "Luckily I can practice these activities I love when I am traveling with the family, since it is usually not possible to do so in the Kingdom. It is no more difficult for me with the cover than it is for anyone else. It was I who taught Rajiya how to ski, not the father or the mother. I have even learned how to jet-ski on the water in Jeddah, and I swam in the sea there too, but only in the middle of the night, when everyone else was asleep and no one can see me."

The door of the tutoring center flew open, and Rajiya ran out cheering, elated that her daily lesson was finally over, and then we all climbed back into the car and took off to join her cousins. I saw that Malikah was struggling in the backseat: the convertible was whipping her *hijab* around, and she was in a battle to keep it on. I started to power up the four windows to block off at least part of the wind to protect her but Rajiya stopped me. "No, Janni. We like to feel the California breeze. We love it," she said as she cranked the radio. Malikah smiled at me in the rearview mirror and held on tight to her *hijab* flying in the wind.

12

The Real Housewives
of Riyadh

*W*e need twenty-seven bottles of Hair Off®! *Yalla* [hurry], Janni! *Yalla!*"

Princess Zaahira's secretary, Asra, had just ordered me to get twenty-seven bottles of Hair Off (for "Anti-Irritation and Ultra-Moisturizing Hair Removal"). She didn't want Nair and she didn't want Veet; she wanted twenty-seven bottles of Hair Off, and she insisted they were all needed right away. "*Yalla!*"

Were they having a Hair Off party? I wondered.

On my way out of the hotel, Maysam, one of the princess's nubile teenage servant girls from North Africa, pinched my arm and begged me again to hurry as if her life depended on it. "*Yalla,* Janni, *yalla!* The princesses, they need tonight, Janni, tonight, tonight, tonight! *Yalla!*"

I went to every Rite-Aid, Sav-On, and Walgreen's within a 20-mile radius. I went to over 20 stores; most stocked only two or three bottles at once, so I had to drive all over LA County.

Couldn't they just go for a little laser action? I thought. *That's how we do it in Southern California. Two or three visits, and you've got a Brazilian forever whether you like it or not.*

I had started work at ten o'clock in the morning, and twelve hours later I was driving around trying to score twenty-seven bottles of cream depilatory. I thought I had become valuable because of my resource-fulness, intelligence, and conscientiousness. Now I was beginning to suspect that it was probably because they didn't want to send a man on this kind of errand. I was only midway through the time the family was expected to stay, and even though I'd known it was going to be demand-ing, I wasn't prepared for this. I had already driven 4,000 miles, some-times 400 miles a day, pulling 16-hour days, and I was getting 4 hours of sleep a night. I was a wreck. I was afraid there was no way I was going to last seven weeks. But I knew that the Saudis tipped only at the end of the job, so I couldn't quit. I had to hold out for the tip. I had to keep my eye on the prize. I had to get the Hair Off, but really I just wanted to tell Asra to get on the horn, make some appointments, and get those women under some laser light.

The Saudi women had come to Los Angeles for plastic surgery; it was clearly one of their main reasons to visit Beverly Hills, the mecca of surgical enhancement. Most of them already had liposuction, tummy tucks, rhinoplasty, mammaplasty, blepharoplasty (eyelid lifting/stretch-ing/cutting), and even vaginal rejuvenation, which I had never heard of before but now know is a startlingly popular procedure.

There is a glistening 14-foot-tall silver sculpture entitled *Torso*, by artist Robert Graham, which stands on a high bronze pedestal at the intersection of Rodeo Drive and Dayton Way in Beverly Hills. It has no head; it is a female torso with perfectly proportioned breasts and but-tocks. In spite of its beauty, there is a distressing anonymity to the piece, and since it is carefully composed of polished aluminum segmented blocks, it gives the feeling of being built piece by piece, as if the best possible parts were chosen to comprise the most perfect torso. Somehow the combination of the headlessness and the idealized body parts is an enigmatic summation of the power and allure of cosmetic surgery. I find the sculpture cold and disconcerting; it even looks chilly, and I've often thought about wrapping it in a pashmina when I drove by it late at night. But the Saudi women would invariably oooh and aaaah with admiration when they saw it, as most people do.

An older member of Princess Zaahira's entourage, a prune of a woman whom everyone called Auntie, had full-on bodywork: she had a facelift, chinlift, liposuction, and breast augmentation, all in a few weeks' time. In the beginning, it was mind-boggling to me, but after several weeks on the job, I saw that for many of the women this was routine. I had wondered at first, as most people do, why the Saudi women, who spend much of their time in the Kingdom covered up in black garments, would spend so much money and time on their appearance that almost no one sees. But of course, they do it for the same reasons American women do: they do it for themselves, they do it to hang onto their youth or to create a body they've always dreamed of, and they do it for the rush. One surgery often leads to another, and then another and then another.

One afternoon I had to pick up Princess Zaahira's friend, Amsah, after an office procedure at one of the Beverly Hills surgical clinics on Spaulding Drive. Amsah was at least fifty-five years old and was a substantially endowed woman, with dyed mahogany-colored hair, heavily tattooed eyebrows, and coarse piebald skin. She wasn't exactly a beauty queen, but she was friendlier and more easygoing than most of the other Saudi women I had met so far, and I liked her. I had no idea how many days or hours she'd been at the clinic but was told that she'd be ready for a noon pickup. I waited. In the early evening she was finally escorted downstairs in a wheelchair, drifting in and out of consciousness. The nurse accompanying her gave me instructions on Amsah's care for the ride back to the hotel and then scurried off. They were hopping upstairs, and she had to attend to other patients. As soon as the nurse walked away, Amsah nodded off.

"Amsah! Amsah! Wake up. C'mon, Amsah, wake up!" I clapped my hands in front of her face but she didn't stir. *Shit, shit, shit, she won't wake up.* I thought. *There's no way I can get her into the car like this.*

I looked around and saw several Saudi women exiting the garage elevators, including Amsah's cousin, Sajidah, who had been upstairs for a checkup with the same doctor. She was walking stiffly and with great difficulty because she'd had a bunion removed the previous week and wore a special shoe to protect her foot as it healed; she was also sporting a thick white chinstrap, so I guess she was getting work done top to bottom. Sajidah and her cousin looked so much alike they could have been mistaken for sisters, but Sajidah spoke better English. She had family in the States and visited both coasts regularly.

"Sajidah? Could you speak to Amsah in Arabic, please? To help me wake her up? Tell her I can't get her into the car unless she wakes up," I said as I walked over to her.

"Do not interrupt. I am talking to my son in Washington," she said, holding a cell phone to her ear as she moved away from me. She had already told me that her son was a hugely influential businessman and that she was very proud of him. As I've already mentioned, sons are important in the Saudi family—so much so that when a Saudi woman gives birth to a son, she is thereafter often known by the name of her son, as in *Umm Amad*, or Mother of Amad.

"Amad is doing business in Washington. Washington, D.C.," she said as if I hadn't known she meant the nation's capital.

"I'm sorry. I didn't realize you were on the phone. It's just that Amsah . . ." I knew that she'd been on the phone; I was just hoping that maybe Umm Amad would interrupt her important call for a moment to help her unconscious relative. No such luck.

"You must wait; my son needs my attention," she said and walked away. She didn't seem at all put out by the fact that her cousin was out cold. I considered going upstairs to get backup assistance, but I didn't want to leave Amsah.

I called the hotel on my cell phone. "May I have room 1205, please?"

"What is the name of the guest, please?" said the hotel operator.

"I . . . I don't know the name. Room 1205," I said.

"I'm sorry, but I am unable to connect you with room 1205 without a hotel guest name."

"There is no name!" I said.

"I'm sorry, but I am unable to connect you without . . ."

"I mean there are a lot of names. It's the security room for the family staying on the twelfth floor. The *whole* twelfth floor, and the eleventh floor, and the . . . Are you new? I work for them. Please connect me right away, thank you."

Boyd picked up. My heart pitched. He was a pompous ass, a real thug, and probably a failed Green Beret who now considered himself hugely important because he ran high-security details for visiting luminaries needing protection while buying 300 purses on Rodeo Drive. He demanded to know why I hadn't yet returned with Amsah when I had other things they were waiting for me to do, implying that I was purposely hanging out at the medical clinic for jollies. He'd obviously heard about my penchant for post-op antics and comatose patients.

"We're downstairs in the parking lot and Amsah's out cold. The nurse brought her down in a wheelchair, and then she just took off. I can't get her into the car myself, Boyd. She's at least 180 pounds, and I think she had butt implants! They told me not to touch her butt. How am I supposed to lift her up into the SUV if I can't touch her butt? You have to send someone to help me."

Amsah started to whimper.

"Oh, I think she's waking up. I'll call you back." I hung up the phone.

Then Amsah started to cry. "Oh, oh, okay, Amsah, it's okay," I said to her. "I'm sure it hurts to sit down, but you'll feel better soon."

Then she murmured something that took me a moment to decipher. It sounded like ". . . the lovely bottom, yours such the lovely bottom."

"Oh," I said when I finally understood. It was thoughtful of her to compliment my bottom when she was clearly in agony, but I knew then that she must have been delusional because it is definitely not one of my best features, in spite of years of doing squats. I wanted to be gracious but didn't know how to reply to that kind of remark, especially from an older woman who'd just had balloons stuck in her ass cheeks.

"*Shukran* [thank you], Amsah. *Insha'Allah* [if it is God's will], hopefully your bottom will be as beautiful as mine soon too. *Insha'Allah.*"

"*Insha'Allah,*" she moaned.

I saw my window of opportunity and I jumped through it: "*Insha'Allah,* Amsah. But right now, *Allah* wants you to get in the car. That's right. *Allah* wants you to get into the car. Then you can go home to the hotel and lie down in your nice soft bed, I mean lie down on your side, in your nice soft bed. Okay, Amsah? Okay. I'm just going to ask the valet guys to help us." I ran over to the valet parking attendants nearby.

"*Hey, guapos, pueden ayudarme por favor? Um, um, yo quiero levantarla a ella para arriba en dentro el SUV? Por favor?*" I said. I don't know why I was trying to practice my lousy Spanish at that moment.

One of the guys finally said in perfect English, "Relax, miss, we'll help you." They must have been accustomed to dealing with post-op patients all day because they immediately understood the problem. They quickly encircled her and started to lift her up, but it all went way wrong right away. Amsah screamed in pain. I guess they'd never dealt with butt implants. "*Cuidado!*" I yelled. "*No toca el culo!* Don't touch the butt!" Amsah screamed again and passed out.

It was truly awful. We finally got her into the SUV after a lot of struggling and crying. Sajidah rode back with us to the hotel and suddenly took an interest in her ailing cousin. She prayed to Allah the whole way, wailing and keening, begging for him to save Amsah, acting like Amsah was near death from a sudden and unavoidable accident. It was hard to drive with the racket she was making. Amsah drifted in and out of consciousness, moaning, groaning, and whimpering as her cousin yowled. It was like an episode of *The Real Housewives of Riyadh*. I didn't think that this was Amsah's first time around the surgery block, and she'd probably known what she was in for. In spite of the fact that Amsah was in such pain, I was embarrassed for both of them and wished they'd show a little self-restraint. I doubted it was Allah's idea for her to have ass surgery, and it seemed inappropriate to be begging for his ministry once the deed had been done.

As we neared the hotel, security phoned and said they had notified the family doctor to meet us, and instructed me to deliver Amsah near the private elevator that is accessed via the underground parking garage. I was met at the hotel's driveway by two security personnel who ran ahead of the SUV clearing traffic as I wound my way down—the wrong way down—the garage's circular ramps so that we wouldn't be hit by oncoming valets bringing cars upstairs. Down and down we went to the very bottom, the two stalwart men flanking the vehicle as if they were escorting the president of the United States. It was ridiculous, but I was thankful to have them there. By then, Amsah was out cold and had been so for some time. I was worried that maybe she was in trouble and that, as usual, I'd be held responsible. When we arrived at the elevator, the doctor was there waiting and men expertly swooped her up and out of the SUV and into a pillowed wheelchair waiting at the elevator entrance, and they then whisked her away without saying a word to me. Sajidah ignored me as well.

I just sat in the SUV for a little while enjoying the quiet of the car. I felt as if I had just been through a terrific battle but, miraculously, had walked away unscathed.

When I had picked up Amsah, I couldn't help but notice that the waiting room in that medical clinic on Spaulding Drive was packed with women—not just Saudi women but Beverly Hills women, with big rocks on their fingers and platinum hair piled high. The Saudi women were no different from the Los Angeles women I saw walking down Melrose Avenue with huge balloon-shaped breasts and stiff silicone-enhanced monkey lips. They were all doing the same exquisite dance to maintain their value and a happy household, and hopefully their husband's good favor.

Later the next night, I was leaving Princess Zaahira's hotel when one of the family's Porsche Cayennes pulled up. Several thin effete-looking young men got out, all giggly and excited. Then a tall figure with long black hair and narrow shoulders sidled out of the backseat. All of the other drivers and doormen standing in the hotel breezeway whistled under their breath because this chick had a magnificent ass. Huge, high, and supple, and perfectly round, like a gigantic ripe peach—beautifully displayed in tight, stretchy jeans. And then the figure turned around and we all gasped: she had a moustache. It was a guy, one of the princes in the group. The best ass in the family, the best ass in the whole group, belonged to a young prince. I do not know if his was surgically enhanced, but it was truly awe inspiring.

Anyway, I don't recommend ass surgery, not unless you're a real glutton for punishment.

13

Un-Avoidable

One day, I was asked to drive Princess Zaahira's cousin, Princess Soraya, who was seventeen years old. She looked nothing like the other young Saudi girls, who emulated the older women's fashion look with layers of haute couture, heavy makeup, and lavish jewelry. She was slender with short black hair and dressed simply in a striped T shirt, pressed jeans, and clean white sneakers. Soraya reminded me of Audrey Hepburn in the movie *Roman Holiday*, the one in which she plays a European princess who falls in love with an American. The young Saudi girl looked pleasingly fresh, almost impish, but with a serene, composed countenance as if she were older than her years.

"Thank you, you are very kind," Soraya said to the hotel doorman as he opened the car door for her. She got in the back of the black Crown Victoria town car and smiled broadly at me.

"Hello, driver," she said. She spoke English with a refined, slightly British accent. "My name is Soraya. It is a pleasure to meet you. I would like to visit the Krispy Kreme, please? And I would like to visit the UCLA, please? And I would like to visit the beach, please. Thank you." As I drove out of the hotel driveway, I could see that she tried to power down the window. It didn't budge. She frowned and she tried again.

After a few moments she said, "Excuse me, please, driver? Will you unlock the window, please?"

I remembered what the colonel had told us about keeping all the doors and windows locked. "I'm sorry, Soraya, but I was told . . . ," I said as I glanced into the rearview mirror and saw her looking hopefully at me with a beseeching expression as if to say: *please, no one will know.* I unlocked the controls.

She beamed at me. "Thank you!" she said. Then she stuck her head half out the window and smelled the air like a big puppy, smiling as we drove down Wilshire Boulevard toward Westwood. I watched her in my side mirrors as she pushed up the drink holder console in the center of the back seat and slid from one side of the car to the other, looking out the windows the whole time. After a long while, Soraya brought her head back inside the car and beamed some more.

"You are so lucky. Do you like to drive? I would like to learn. I am sure I could learn." She pointed to a car we passed. "Oh, there is a little car with the sign that says 'Westwood Driver Education' on top." She looked hard at the car. "The instructor is a man?" she asked.

"Yes, most of them are. Not because they're better drivers, though."

Soraya looked down at her hands for a minute. "It is not possible for me to learn how to drive," she said. "I must return home to my family soon. It is un-avoidable." She said *unavoidable* as if it were two separate words. Un-avoidable.

"I would like to stay here very much. I would like to study here. I am studying philosophy. I like philosophy. I have just come from a summer program at Berkeley, and now I am enjoying a short visit with my favorite cousins."

"That's a great school," I said. "I've a lot of friends who went there and I would've liked to as well, but somehow I got stuck on the East Coast hiking through 10-foot snowdrifts with 20 pounds of books strapped to my back. If you fell in that kind of snow, you might not be found 'til spring."

She cocked her head at me then. I supposed she hadn't heard yet about the overeducated female chauffeur. "Oh," she said. "Berkeley is very warm. I do not think one can fall into a snowdrift there."

"Did you like it?" I asked her.

"I loved it. I learned a great deal," she said. "It was a course on the writings of Ralph Waldo Emerson. Do you know him?"

"Yes, I do," I said. " 'The infinitude of the private man.' "

"Yes!" she said. "Yes! Exactly! 'The infinitude of the private man.' I am so happy you know this. I have been thinking about his belief that it is one soul that animates all men—that we are all part of God. Do you believe this?"

"I'm not sure exactly, but I suspect that it might be true, or rather I should say, I hope it's true. That's pretty heady stuff that you've been reading."

"Heady? Yes, I suppose it is," she said quietly and smiled as if we were sharing a secret. "It has been a wonderful summer. I have been so happy in San Francisco because it is a great walking city, and this was new for me, and I had a very pleasant time enjoying the activities on the Embarcadero. It was immensely pleasurable."

"Your English is exceptional," I said.

"I am a good student," she said in the same tone that I recently heard my five-year-old nephew say: "I like myself. I am so proud of myself." It was declarative and definitive, but not boastful in anyway. Just unquestionably true.

"I enjoy school very much. It does not seem like work to me," she said.

"I felt that way too," I said.

"I wish that my father would permit me to stay for this year, but that is not possible. I have asked him many times, but he always says no."

This was perhaps the longest conversation I'd had with any of the Saudi royals so far, and for a moment I forgot that I was a lowly chauffeur. I practically gurgled with glee as I drove us north up Westwood Boulevard.

"Is this the UCLA?" she asked me as she stuck her head out the window again. "Oh, I like it! So many trees and flowers. So many people. This is lovely. I am sure I would like to stay here to continue my studies, but I cannot."

"It's a pity you can't stay longer," I said.

Soraya was quiet for a minute and then said, "I must return home. It is un-avoidable." As she spoke, she slowly powered the window up and down.

Up and down.

Up and down.

"All my family will celebrate. It is time. It is un-avoidable. I will make my family proud. For this I am happy. I am very happy." Then I heard her begin to cry softly.

I watched her in the rearview mirror, her head bowed. I wasn't sure what to do, and I didn't want to intrude on her. Eventually I thought to hand her a handful of tissues, which she accepted without comment. I continued driving us west on Sunset for a long time toward the beach, and all the while I could hear her sob; it was the weeping sound of resignation, not indignation.

When we could go no farther west, I stopped the car along the Pacific Coast Highway overlooking the ocean.

"Here we are at the beach, Soraya."

She wiped away the tears from her face with the back of her hand and looked out the window. "It is so clean," she said. Then we were both quiet for a while and watched the waves and the surfers checking out the incoming wave sets. Armored in black wetsuits and silhouetted against the setting sun, they seemed like warriors at sea guarding the coastline against attack.

"They look cool, don't they?"

"Yes, they look cool," she said. "Very cool."

I continued to watch her in the mirror, trying not to stare so I wouldn't disturb her. She was pale with red-rimmed eyes and blotchy tear-stained crimson cheeks. She continued to look out the window as she wiped her eyes again with the back of her hand, pressing the tissues in her other fist as if she were afraid to let them go.

"Are you okay?" I asked her.

Soraya didn't answer right away, but after a while she turned to catch my eyes in the rearview mirror. She knew that I'd been watching her. "I am to be married. My husband is waiting. He is a colleague of my father's. I am to be his third wife. I was told he is very kind."

"I see," I said.

"So I am happy, I am very happy. I will make my family proud."

Time passed, and we said nothing.

"Don't you want to get out?" I finally asked her.

She seemed surprised by my question. "Oh, no, I will just look. Thank you."

"Are you sure, Soraya? Don't you want to get out and walk on the sand or put your toes in the water?"

She continued to look out the window. "No, thank you. I will just look. Thank you. I will just look."

I drove Princess Soraya around all afternoon. We stopped at the Krispy Kreme on Wilshire Boulevard, where she asked me run in to buy her several dozen assorted doughnuts to take to Princess Zaahira and her family back at the hotel. I got extra of the dulce de leche doughnuts because she said they particularly liked those, and she insisted that I keep a box for myself to take home. In Santa Monica, Soraya asked me if I would like a Wetzel Dog, and I told her that I'd never had one. "You will love it," she said, then gave me money to buy us a take-out soft-pretzel hotdog lunch at Wetzel's Pretzels on the Promenade. I double-parked at the end of the alley, and we ate quietly in the car as we watched and listened to crowds of chattering shoppers pass us by. I noticed again that the cops never bothered any Saudi car and especially not a Crown Vic. Soraya nibbled at her lunch as if she were a little bird pecking at seeds. Later I found her half-eaten hardened pretzel sans hotdog in the backseat pocket.

We spent six hours together, and she never got out of the car. Not once. She just looked out the window as if memorizing everything within her view with a solemnity that suggested she was saying hello and good-bye to it all at the same time.

I didn't see Soraya again after that day, even though I repeatedly looked for her. Because I couldn't speak to Princess Zaahira or any of the royals about her, I asked security and the servants if she had gone home, but no one could or would tell me anything. I even asked the doormen if they remembered the lovely slender girl who now seemed like an apparition, but they did not recall her. I presume that Soraya did return to her family and to the future that awaited there in her homeland, and I hope that she is happy.

14

Kill Me but Make Me Beautiful!

$\mathcal{L}$ate one night, I had a run-in with Princess Zaahira's secretary, Asra, who I'd noticed had watched me with hooded eyes when I performed my little casino pantomimes for the princess. She was an Arab but looked startlingly European, with porcelain skin, perfectly dyed blond hair, pale eyes, diminutive fine features, and a tiny hourglass figure. She looked like a doll, except a doll that furiously chain-smoked. Her English was excellent, and she spoke several other languages as well, including French. Asra was Princess Zaahira's right-hand woman and was shown great respect by the servants and the rest of the entourage. She was beautiful, but word on the street was that she was treacherous. I knew she had already dismissed several drivers assigned to her, including Jorge, and the rest of the drivers had warned each other to stay on her good side if at all possible. She was not to be trusted.

Asra was the one who had sent me out for the 27 bottles of Hair Off; later she called me to her room to pay me after my mission. Her hotel suite was near Princess Zaahira's room, and although it was large and luxurious, it was in complete disarray. There was only one lamp turned on and the room was disconcertingly dark. The television flickered in the corner, muted. Clothes were strewn everywhere, and it stank of stale cigarettes and dead flowers. I wanted to leave immediately. I knew that she was working very long hours tending to Princess Zaahira's needs, and it seemed apparent that she didn't want the hotel cleaning staff to disturb her few hours of rest, so the room was much neglected. She reclined on the bed as she spoke to me but did not ask me to sit.

"*Merci, merci,* Janni. *Je suis fatigué.* Please forgive my state of *déshabillé.* You understand me? *Je suis fatigué.* I am so very tired," she said as she covered her bare shoulders in a shawl. I wondered if she had ever called any of the male drivers up to her room.

"You are so very helpful. I will tell the princess that you are very helpful, and she will be sure to reward you. She is very generous. I am from Paris, of course; that is how I know the princess. I was in fashion. She bought much beautiful haute couture from me, and then she asked me to come work for her. Only me! No one else! I am very happy with the princess, but I am very tired."

She sighed deeply, lit a cigarette, and then picked up a tray of Belgian candies from the coffee table. "Would you like some chocolate?" she asked as she offered them to me but then quickly pulled them away before I could even make a move to take one.

"These are *très* delicious," she said as she bit into one herself between puffs of the cigarette. Bits of chocolate stuck to her lip, and then to the edge of the cigarette. "Now, please do not tell the princess that you delivered these bottles. I will tell her. I appreciate so much that you are so helpful in this way. Now! I need you to do this for me. Let me think how to explain, I need this something to shampoo the hair without the water. Do you know this?"

"You mean like dry shampoo? The spray stuff?"

"No, this is not what I want," she said. "The hair has to be shampooed with the water; this is necessary. But the neck and shoulders cannot approach the water. One does not bathe the body, but still the hair is to be shampooed because of this device."

"You mean kind of like a shampoo bedpan? They use that in hospitals when people have surgery?"

"Yes, yes, that is what I want. I need this tonight, Janni! Tonight! *Yalla!*"

"Tonight? Oh, no, I'm sorry. I can't get it tonight; it's much too late.

There's nothing open, and besides I'll probably have to go to a hospital supply store to get one, and they definitely aren't open at night."

"Hmmm, I see," she said. She looked around the room, her eyes darting from the drapes to the carpet to the door. "That is fine. Please do this and bring to me in the morning, *tout de suite. Merci*. You are very helpful. *Merci*, Janni. The princess is sure to reward you." Then she waved me out of the room.

The first thing in the morning I went shopping to find the contraption to wash the princess's hair—a small horseshoe-shaped sink with a short hose to attach to a faucet. As soon as I had it in hand, after scouring five hospital supply stores and finally finding one beneath a dusty pile of home care aid devices, I rushed back to the hotel to give it to the secretary. When I encountered her in the hotel lobby, I thrust it at her, proud of my expediency and resourcefulness. She looked at it disinterestedly. "Yes, Miss. What is this?"

"It's the thing you asked for last night, to wash the princess's hair?" I said.

"No! It is too late," she said as she turned from me and walked toward the elevator. "The princess, she does not need now. She said you were to bring her last night. She has left." Then she disappeared behind the elevator doors.

I knew Princess Zaahira needed the hair-washing apparatus because I saw her getting dropped off from a doctor's visit the previous day all bundled up, so she probably had a procedure of some kind. I also knew she was still at the hotel because her armored Mercedes was parked outside. You always knew where the royals were by where their cars were, and of course I'd just passed their security guys and drivers standing around checking out chicks in the hotel breezeway, which seemed to be their primary activity. I was the only chauffeur always working. I'd become the go-to girl, the go-to Internet girl, and now the go-to-get-shampoo-bedpan girl, while they napped in their cars or stood around getting a tan as they practiced their pickup lines. One time one of them said to me, "Yeah, I'd fuck your mother." I think he meant it as a compliment to me and my mother even though she wasn't there. I understood the underlying message to mean something like: "You're kind of old, but still okay-looking so your mom's probably still okay-looking too. Congratulations! You're both still fuckable."

Later that day, the head security guy pulled me aside and asked me why I hadn't done Princess Zaahira's bidding. There had been a complaint.

"Stu," I said. "That's not fair. I told Asra that I couldn't get it last night; it was way too late by the time she asked me. I got up this morning at 8:00 A.M. to try and find the stupid thing. I had to drive all over Los Angeles; it's not exactly a regular item. I'm lucky I even found one."

"She said you were supposed to deliver it last night," he said. "Listen, missy, all I know is that the princess is unhappy. You got that? Stay out of the way, and quit doing favors for everybody. It only gets you in trouble. You show off too much. You got that? Remember your place!" he said.

My place? I thought. *I have an education, and now I'm driving around trying to score a shampoo bedpan, so don't tell me about place. I got that!*

I found out that the secretary was supposed to get the hair-washing contraption thing herself during the day but couldn't find it, so she pushed the whole problem off onto me—the scapegoat factor and the pecking order, all in one go. I couldn't help but wonder why she needed to make me look bad; I was already so low on the totem pole that I was no threat to her.

All my life I had been the kind of person to say: "Yes, I can help. Yes, I can do that. Yes, that is possible." But I now began to consider that maybe I should join the masses to make my life easier. I realized that many people do not live as I did because it is easier to do nothing, or to pretend to not know something just to get out of further work, responsibility, or potential culpability.

I tried to steer clear of Asra after that, and even let calls go to voice mail when I thought it might be her trying to reach me, knowing that I might possibly be fired for doing so.

I figured out later, after the family had left, why I was asked to get the bottles of Hair Off. When a Saudi girl is married—sometimes soon after she becomes a woman, when she is required to begin wearing the *abaya, hijab,* and veil in public—part of the traditional matrimonial preparation is to wax off all body hair, except from the head and eyebrows but including all the private parts and even those little tiny hairs around the backside. Everything goes.

This ancient custom, *halawa,* is in part for the comfort of the man, and I understand and appreciate this. In fact, I've spent hours preening and prepping for the pleasure and comfort of men, and often it pays off. The word *halawa* actually means sweet, and it is also the name of the boiled sugar paste that is used for hair removal. The complete body waxing is also to ensure that the woman is made *sweet*—that she is clean and pure, and ready for a man. For many Muslim people, removing pubic hair is one of the parts of the *fitrah* (natural disposition or customs of nature) as enjoined by the Prophet Muhammad.

A young girl, maybe thirteen, fourteen, or seventeen years old, about to be married to perhaps a sixty-year-old man as his third or fourth wife, has all her pubic hair waxed off so that she looks more like a ten-year-old instead of a thirteen-year-old. I couldn't help but think of Soraya. Perhaps the Hair Off was for her and her wedding? Princess Zaahira had a son who was in his midtwenties, and she was thirty-eight or maybe forty years old—so she may have had him when she was only a teenager. Her husband was over eighty, so he was at least fifty-five when they had a child. And as for Soraya, as the third wife of the man her family had chosen for her, perhaps she had returned home to be married to a man old enough to be her grandfather.

Then it is the preference for many women to continue to wax in this way every forty days. I don't know why they do not choose to have the hair removed permanently, but I suspect it has something to do with enjoying and maintaining the ritualistic aspect of an ancient custom—the custom of preparing oneself for a man, just as American women do but in different ways. I started performing similar rituals in high school, way before I'd ever even been with a man, and I like doing them now too and even step it up or change it up depending on who I'm with, or the season or even the circumstances. A week in Key West calls for different ablutions than a week skiing in Vermont. I've seen by looking around me in the changing room at my yoga studio that I'm not alone in this and that there is an astounding variation in the color, shape, and style of the private parts landscape. I've even seen a pink Mohawked vajayjay, and one that was bejeweled. After a few excruciating experiments and mishaps of my own, I know that pain goes with the territory.

My Persian friend, Giti, taught me the Farsi expression "Kill me but make me beautiful!" which women say in different languages all over the world. I don't know of an equivalent expression for men.

In their travels these modern women must have figured out that Hair Off is a lot less painful than waxing. Now that I know what they need it for, I want to send them cases of the stuff.

15

Alhamdulillah

*J*anni like Saudi tea?" Maysam asked as she gently tugged at my
sleeve one day when I passed her in the hotel hallway.

"Uhh, sure, Maysam. I've had Turkish tea, is it like that?"

"*La* [no], *la, la,* Janni. This is special tea from Arabia. Here, come
to the tearoom, sit, sit. I make for Janni." She brought me into the tea
set's hotel room and I sat down on one of the comfy Parisian chaises
that the Saudis had brought with them on the plane. The hotel rooms
were already beautifully appointed with Italian silk damask upholstered
furniture and walnut tables, but the additional accoutrements that the
Saudis had brought made them even more opulent. The Saudis also
burned a lot of incense, so their rooms were also filled with exotic and
seductive smells that reminded them of home. My clothes often carried
the lingering odors of ambergris and orange blossom *bakhoor* (incense)
long after I had visited them.

I watched Maysam prepare and then infuse the tea. She was not more
than sixteen years old but had already worked for the family for many
years. Her English was halting, but her intelligence and common sense
pervaded everything she did, and I enjoyed her company very much
without us ever speaking many words to each other. She was round all
over—even her wrists were round—and she wore a constant smile as
if she was just happy to be alive. She always hummed to herself as she

worked. She moved swiftly but with great grace, as if all her movements were so well practiced that they were now effortless. As she poured the tea into a china cup, she draped a funky-looking root over the spout of the teapot, so that the liquid passed over the root as it entered the cup. It looked like a fat bug with long hairy tendrils and a rank smell even from five feet away; like something from *Fear Factor*. I hoped she didn't think I was going to eat it.

"Whoa, whoa, Maysam, what is that?" I said.

"This is special spice from Arabia. Special for you, Janni. Here taste, taste, taste. You like?" Maysam forced the teacup into my hand, and I had no choice but to take it. I was relieved that the root bug stayed on the teapot.

I took a little sip and immediately felt woozy. I coughed several times, then was suddenly and sharply clear-headed, as if I had just sniffed smelling salts. The tea was strong, really strong—but good. "Wow, Maysam, this is actually delicious. And it's what my mom would call Sergeant Major tea—gives you a little buzz too. No wonder you ladies drink it all day long."

"What is this buttz, Janni?" she asked.

"No, Maysam, buzz, not buttz. Buzz. Well, a buzz makes you happy in the head," I answered and drank a little more.

"*Aiwa* [yes], Janni, *aiwa!* Take, take. More for your beautiful buttz."

Sometimes I was assigned to drive Maysam and the other servant girls if they had a few hours free in the evening while the Princess Zaahira and the entourage were at dinner. Most of them were teenagers from North Africa or the Philippines who worked night and day for the family, with no days off ever that I could see. The North African girls (many from Somalia, Ethiopia, and Sudan) were Muslim and always wore colorful *hijabs* that covered their hair and neck, and modest clothing of many layers comprising long skirts, shawls, and tunics over long pants. These were usually geometric or floral patterned matching ensembles that covered their legs and arms completely. Some of them were stunning, with exotic good looks and nubile full figures that were alluringly silhouetted by their garments. Many times I saw the doormen and valets at the hotel gape at them with open-mouthed appreciation. Even covered from head to toe, the girls knew how to captivate an audience, and they were adept at casting their eyes this way and that to receive and acknowledge the attention.

When attending to Princess Zaahira or one of her sisters or cousins, the girls always maintained a demure and quiet demeanor. They made soft clicking and clucking sounds that punctuated any brief communication signifying understanding, agreement, or dissatisfaction. At first they were this way with me as well, but I worked hard to win their favor and open communication. Eventually when we were out on our own, in the safety of the car, they were lively and full of energy, and chattered away cackling with good cheer. I played my favorite Senegalese and West African artists for them, and they were impressed that I had such music. The vehicle bounced and swayed with the accompanying rhythms that they made with their bodies and voices; it was like having a twelve-piece band, percussion and all, traveling with me. I snuck my computer and blank CDs into the car so I could make copies of their music, which were always live versions of famous Arabic performers— when we played those, it really felt like there was a live concert in the car—and copies of mine for them.

They were delighted by their new free musical acquisitions, and I was too by mine. Their music was wonderful. I had some of the Arab music lyrics translated for me by a friend. All of the songs were achingly romantic: *"I am always with you. You're always on my mind and in my heart. I never forget you. I always miss you. Even if I am with you."* My friend who did the translations said, "Of course, the man always sings about love to the woman, and she sings of love to him. There is nothing else." The girls would weep with happiness as they sang along.

When they saw that I was computer savvy, they asked for help with the hand-me-down laptops that the family had given them. I showed them how to use Google in Arabic and other languages so that they could read and understand what was going on in their own countries; I mapped out and printed short, safe walks that they could take in the neighborhood when they had a half-hour free and set up Skype accounts for them so they could see and talk with their families back home. One of the youngest girls waited anxiously for me to download a version of Skype that would interface with her laptop's dated operating system, and then cried all evening after she had talked with her sister for the first time since she'd left home, probably several years before.

The girls told me that they loved me.

They liked to go shopping too, just like the rich Saudi ladies whom they served. When I saw that they were buying things to send back to their own countries, things to make their families' lives better and gifts for their little brothers and sisters, I got the idea to take them to the 99¢ Only store, which is famous in Los Angeles as a discount megashop that's amazingly jam-packed with a myriad of low-end goods, all for ninety-nine cents. It's commemorated in a renowned Andreas Gursky photo taken in 1999 at the 99¢ Only store in Hollywood, which sold for $999,999.99. I performed in the legendary Los Angeles yearly holiday spectacle, Orphean Circus's "The 99¢ Only Show," a brilliant and bizarre musical pageant in which all of the colorful costumes, scenery, sets, and props are from the store. My gown was crafted from shower curtains, paper tablecloths, balloons, baby swim floaties (as cap sleeves), crystal garland, and tinsel. My headdress was a tower of picnic plates, knives and forks, plastic flowers, and plastic fruit almost three feet high. I had to cover my body in baby powder every night to keep my costume from sticking to me permanently.

The girls loved the store. They went nuts. They bought dozens of pairs of baby flip-flops, yards and yards of hair ribbon and handfuls of hair bows, piles of tiny socks and baby panties, Sweetee girl dolls, giant magic bubble wands, sippy cups, battery-operated plastic swords that lit up and made swooshing noises, toy cell phones and machine guns, mechanical pencils, Hershey bars, Tootsie Rolls, nail polish, toenail clippers, and bags of Cheetos that they'd eat on the way back to the hotel in the car, licking their sticky orange fingers with satisfaction.

I noticed that they were careful not to waste their money. They would vigilantly look at one item after another, weighing each one in their hands as if calculating a hidden value, going back and forth comparing the attributes of each, passing the item from one girl to another for inspection, before making a cautious decision to determine which had the most bang for the buck. Even so, I often had to supervise their selections.

"Oh, no, Zuhur. That's Spam!!!" I said as I stopped her from putting a dozen cans on the conveyor belt to be rung up by the cashier. "It's made with pork. You don't eat that. It's pork!"

Zuhur was tall and willowy with freckled cocoa-colored skin and moved languorously but always with surprising efficiency. She demonstrated her command of the English language with pride and often acted as the translator for the group even though she knew perhaps less than a few hundred words of English. She was inventive and imaginative, however, and those few words were put to terrific use in refreshingly ingenious combinations. But she didn't know what pork was, so finally I made a snorting noise, imitating a pig, and this stopped them all dead.

"Oh, *la* [no], *la!*" cried Zuhur. "*Shukran* [thank you], Janni! *Shukran.* Thank you for this beautiful rescue, Janni! We do not want the pork! This is *haram* [forbidden]! We must not to enjoy the Spam!"

They were sweet and unfailingly generous to me. Once, when they thought that I had admired a risqué panty in the lingerie aisle of the store—I was actually inspecting the panty from a distance with some trepidation—they later presented me with a gift of three of the same crotchless polyester thongs edged with black fringe in fuchsia, orange, and lime green.

"Wow, *shukran*, thank you. I don't know what to say. These are really quite something. Really unusual. I think you should keep them, though, and take them back to the Kingdom so you'll always remember all the amazing stuff in the 99¢ Only store," I said as I tried to push the panties back at them.

"You must to take, Janni. You must to accept. You must. Is gift!" By this time they were all giggling and hiding their laughter behind their hands. They were teasing me, but I saw that they also delighted in purchasing and handling for a moment something that was clearly illicit to them and then passing it off for me to enjoy. I was touched that even though they had so little money, they wanted to buy something for me that they thought I would like. This happened more than once, and I learned not to pick up or even look at any item when they were shopping, or it would invariably end up as a gift to me.

Once I spotted them all together in a huddle hovering over a display right next to the feminine hygiene section. No one moved. They just stood quietly, frozen, with their heads slightly cocked to the side as if

listening rather than watching. I went over to investigate and saw that
they were standing directly in front of an abundant selection of condoms. There were rows and rows of colorful boxes, but there was also
a huge pile of loose single condoms placed in a big bin as if they were
five-cent condom candy that you could grab by the handful. Out of
modesty, the girls were averting their gazes, but it was apparent that they
were spellbound. They couldn't help but stand inert before the display
just so they could take it all in—a staggering assortment of colors, sizes,
and attributes. They glanced wordlessly at me as I approached. Then one
of them pointed to the exhibit as if it wasn't clear what had transfixed
them. I had to stop myself from laughing out loud.

I knew they couldn't read the print on the boxes and also very likely
didn't want to touch them either to do their usual hand-over-hand
investigation. I picked up a few of the boxes and a fistful of loose condoms from the bin and clumsily conveyed to them that some were fla-
vored (banana, chocolate, strawberry), others had ridges, some glowed
in the dark, were textured, or lubricated, had extra headroom, offered a
snugger fit. The more complicated condom styles were more difficult to
depict, but I made a determined effort to be clear. They just looked at
me, unblinking, following my every word.

I paused for a moment and considered what I was doing: *I am standing in the middle of the 99¢ Only store in Hollywood giving a lecture on
condoms to a bunch of teenage virgin girls from North Africa. Okay!*

I spoke carefully with good diction so that I wouldn't have to repeat
myself. After the tutorial, everyone was quiet. There were no questions.
I walked away so that they would be free to buy what they wanted
without feeling as if they were being watched. I'm pretty sure they didn't
buy any.

One of the girls spent a lot of time looking at lingerie and was particularly interested in low-cut push-up bras. Mouna was petite and round,
and had a smooth, broad face and dark charcoal skin that shone as if
polished. "Why do you want that bra, Mouna?" I asked. "Is it something you would actually wear?"

"Is wedding," she replied, smiling slyly.

"Oh, a wedding. Yes, but are you sure this is what you want? It's
really designed to wear when you want to push your boobs up high, like

this, when you want to show them off, really high." I demonstrated by cupping my breasts and lifting them up high close to my neck.

All the girls tittered. Mouna widened her eyes at me and said, "*La, la, la,* Janni." She looked to Zuhur to better explain.

"No, she does not want such like this. But she must to have the special brassiere for the wedding dress," Zuhur said.

"To wear with your wedding dress?" I said to Mouna. "So you wear a dress with a low neckline? That's allowed? You don't have to be covered up? Won't all the men see you like that?"

"For the men, there is a party only with the husband and the men," said Zuhur. "We do not see them; they do not see us. We are with the women only, so we do not wear the clothing to cover."

"I must to have the special dress such like this," Mouna said.

"When are you getting married?" I asked her.

"I first to meet the husband."

"Ah, so you're planning ahead," I said.

"Yes," she said. "So I must to have the special brassiere." Then she showed me a collection of papers that she carried in a satchel. They were pages ripped from current bridal magazines, some Western but others clearly meant to appeal to Muslim brides with bridal party headdresses, veils, and hair covers. The Saudi wedding party, at least for the royals, usually begins at midnight, and the women's parties can become raucous with singing, dancing, and feasting well into the morning of the next day, sometimes several days, and these headpieces would be removed once the party really got rocking.

I don't know what kind of celebration could be in store for Mouna, a palace servant girl, but she was fifteen years old and imagining her wedding day, just as teenage American girls do. She was taking advantage of a remarkable worldliness at her age, a result of traveling with the family, by stockpiling the things she thought she might want for that day, even though there was no husband on the horizon yet. I admired her initiative.

The other girls too seemed beset with the usual teenage dreams and troubles. Maysam, the tea girl, had bad acne; irritated and oozing dark, swollen pustules mottled her cheeks, and she was painfully self-conscious about it. Individually, each of the servant girls came to me and asked if there were something I could do to help her. I knew she needed to see a doctor. A prescription for Accutane or tetracycline was probably the only way her skin could clear up, and in spite of the multitude of doctor appointments the family booked, a visit to the dermatologist didn't seem to be in the cards for Maysam. Instead, I got her an over-the-counter benzoyl peroxide scrub and a bottle of tea tree oil and showed her how to use them both.

"Okay, Maysam," I said. "You have to use the tea tree oil diluted, or it will burn you. You must be careful, or it will hurt you and hurt your skin." I poured a tiny bit of the oil in a little cup and added cool water to it, then dabbed a cotton ball in the mixture. "It kind of stinks, but it works too. Just be gentle, like this." I lightly ran the cotton ball over her cheeks several times.

"*Shukran* [thank you], Janni," she said. "I use this many times in the day, then will be no more."

"No! No, Maysam. Not many times each day! That's too much. Start with just once in the morning and then maybe after a few weeks, you can apply it at night too. Just be careful. Let your skin acclimate. I mean, let your skin get to know it." Sometimes I sounded like a preschooler trying to put together new thoughts, but I was compelled to be more careful about my choice of words so that the girls could better understand me. "Acclimate " was not in their vocabulary.

The first week of treatment, I kept the bottle and brought it to Maysam's room each day and supervised her because I was concerned that she'd become overly zealous in the application. Her skin cleared up a little but not nearly as well as if she had access to a good dose of oral antibiotics. I started dropping hammer-pounding hints when I was around the Saudi ladies: "Maysam is such a pretty girl; it's really a pity that her skin is so bad, so inflamed. I think it's painful for her too. I'm sure a doctor's prescription would nip that in the bud in a heartbeat," hoping one of them would take her to the doctor. None of them acknowledged that they even heard what I said.

I wondered what it must be like to be a young girl so far from home and her own family, without a mother to take her to the dermatologist or even offer her guidance, as my mother would have done. These girls must have missed their own families terribly. I wanted to ask them about this, but I couldn't find a way to do so without having it sound as if I felt sorry for them, and I didn't feel sorry for them. I respected and admired them—one and all.

Even though I was hired help just as they were, the girls took great pains to look after me the same way they looked after the royal family. They'd noticed that I had lost quite a bit of weight while I was driving because of the long hours I was working; they'd hiss and cluck and pinch my cheeks to signify their disapproval. On the days I drove them, they often ordered room service for me and had it delivered to my car— nice stuff too—steaks, asparagus, and crème brûlée. Or they asked me upstairs and then insisted that I sit and eat while they watched. I was worried that they'd get in trouble for charging meals to their room for me, but they didn't seem concerned. I couldn't help but think: *Hey, Princess Zaahira, let's save a little money on the room service and put it to a dermo visit for Maysam.*

"How is your husband, Janni?" Maysam asked me one day as she served me a medium-rare New York strip steak from the room service tray. She and the other girls were eating chicken paillard, sautéed spinach, and couscous. The couscous came from the hotel's kitchen on the twelfth floor, which the princess's cooks used on a regular basis to prepare special meals for the family. Four of us were gathered snugly around a little table that the hotel staff had wheeled in and set up. The room service table is an ingenious serving apparatus: it has a warmer below for the heated food, and there are two leaves that extend from each side to make the table round once it gets through the door.

It always struck me as incongruous that there we were: a down-and-out chauffeur working around the clock for a bunch of teenagers who also worked around the clock (and were practically indentured servants) for a family of rich Saudis, feasting together on overpriced five-star hotel room service cuisine served on linens and fine china, waited on by accommodating hotel staff who took all the mess away when we had enjoyed our fill. The only thing that could have made it stranger would be if we were sipping Veuve Clicquot champagne too.

"Oh, I don't have a husband, Maysam," I replied truthfully. As soon as I said it, I was sorry. In this moment of happy satiation, I was caught unawares and remembered too late that I already started pretending that I was married.

Alhamdulillah

"I so sorry, Janni. Your husband is died, Janni?"

"No, no," I said. "Nobody is died, I mean nobody is dead. I'm just not married yet."

"*La* [no], *laaaa*, you must husband, Janni. You must husband to protect and take care about you. What must yours Mama and Baba think on this, Janni?"

I've had boyfriends from all over the world, so I smiled and said, "Well, they call me the United Nations of Dating." Maysam somehow understood my sly joke and did not like it.

"*La! La! La,* Janni!"

"It's really okay, Maysam. My parents just want me to be happy." I didn't want to say that my parents were way past the point of worrying about me marrying or not marrying. I am at the bottom end of a big family, and I think my parents are just relieved that they haven't had to pick up the pieces, again, after another child's disastrous divorce. There have been six already and we're still counting.

Maysam began to pray. "*Alhamdulillah.* What will happen to Janni? You must husband to protect and take care about you. I pray for Janni. I pray to Allah for the husband for Janni. *Alhamdulillah. Alhamdulillah. Alhamdulillah.*"

The very idea that I was unmarried upset Maysam and the other girls so much that I began making more regular references to the fake husband I had invented to evade driving the hairdresser, and they accepted this new development without comment. They seemed to forget that I wasn't married. It was easier that way.

I started to make up stories about my "husband." I named him Michael, and I've never dated a Michael, so that seemed fitting for a potential imaginary husband. He was athletic (I like a man who can swing me around a room) and good-natured, with an uplifting playful sense of humor—all of which would be paramount in a "husband" of mine. He was a writer, and we helped to support each other's artistic endeavors by both working when necessary. I even pretended that he had been sick and that I had to work extra hard to pay for mounting medical bills. I was vague about this. I didn't want him to be infirm or require long-term care, and I didn't want them to feel sorry for my imaginary husband. I hinted at knee surgery from an old athletic injury.

Something appealed to me about pretending that I was a doting wife doing whatever it took to make ends meet, but I was a little surprised at how easily the girls, and the family as well, forgot that I had started out unmarried, but of course this made sense. I could see that how I live, how I choose to live, was just unthinkable to them.

In my real love life, I had just started to become close to a man I ended up eventually dating. He was a musician, a painter, a superb athlete, really bright, and the only man I've ever known who'd watch football with me all day Sunday (and patiently explained plays or rulings that I couldn't follow, which weren't many because I'm a fan), and then happily sit through and enjoy several Fellini movies in a row. He was terrific company, funny as hell, and easy on the eyes too. He was tall, with wild hair and a sharply defined massively muscular physique, and he had a deeply pleasing baritone voice that was easy on the ears. I have messages on my voice mail that I've kept and still listen to when I need a fix. In one, he imitates a rough-talking Texan truck driver making his way cross-country in the middle of the night looking for a rest stop (me). In another, he sounds like a lost little girl wondering where her best friend (me) has disappeared to. In another, he is just stupidly sweet.

I'd met him a few months before I started the Saudi job, and our romance was slow to get started—partly because I was working around the clock, but also because he was at the tail end of a relationship that was unraveling and I didn't want to get involved with a man who was still living with another woman. But he was resolute. He used to come to the hotel, wait for me until I had a free moment, and then surprise me with boxes of petit fours and chocolate truffles (which I shared with the girls, saying they were from my husband, Michael), love notes with quotes by Rumi, and sometimes, when I asked for them, a handful of energy bars to get me through the night. He even dropped off and picked up my dry cleaning for me when I had nothing to wear day in and day out because the shops were always closed by the time I was off duty. Sometimes, he'd follow me in his car just to make sure I got home safely after hours and hours on the job. He wooed me fully, thoroughly, and successfully. I felt comforted by his affection and devotion, and his generosity made me feel as if I was wrapped in a constant warm embrace.

Alhamdulillah

I'd usually meet Mr. Rumi around the corner from the hotel so that no one would see us. He was a strapping guy, so I was careful to keep him hidden; one good look at him by any of the family or entourage, and my whole sick husband ruse would have been out the window. Or worse, they might think that I was cheating on my sick husband. Sometimes I'd meet him in one of the alleys off a side street in the flats of Beverly Hills. I'd roll up in a loaded black SUV, dressed tastefully and conservatively, and jump into the backseat of his parked car. We'd neck for five minutes and then I'd emerge from his car with my hair and clothes all akimbo, my face flushed, damp and whisker-burned, with my dry cleaning in hand so I could rush back to the job with a change of clothing for the next morning.

With the girls, I felt like a dutiful wife doing whatever was needed to help my husband through rough times, but Mr. Rumi made me feel like a suburban soccer mom having an extramarital affair with her son's football coach, and I'm sure that's what it looked like to the passersby who saw me exiting his car, with all the windows fogged up, after our assignations.

16

Beach Prayer

O ne day, a beach outing was arranged for all the family and entourage, so most of us headed out to Zuma Beach in Malibu where a huge party had been set up on the sand at the north end of the park. There were balloons and games, and the family hired an In-N-Out cookout truck to serve burgers to everyone at lunchtime. In-N-Out is a popular West Coast family-owned burger chain that serves a super-fresh homemade and seemingly limited menu of burgers, fries, and shakes only. But they also have a secret menu that insiders know about and from which you can make requests for weird and inventive combinations. You can basically order anything—such as a quadruple-patty cheeseburger with extra pickles and tomatoes wrapped in a lettuce leaf stuffed with cheese fries smothered in grilled onions. It will be messy, but it will be utterly delicious. There are also discreet Bible references written on the cups and burger wrappers, which insiders know to look for after they've imbibed.

I was at an In-N-Out the other day with my friend Harlow to load up on some calories and inspiration at the same time. As always, the line was around the block. Her 3 × 3 Cheeseburger (three patties with three cheese slices) quoted Revelations 3:20: "Behold, I stand at the door and knock: if any man hear My voice, and open the door, I will come in to him, and will sup with him, and he with Me," so Jesus was supping with

130

her. That was comforting because that 3 x 3 was a heart attack waiting
to happen. My Double Double (two burgers) Protein (no bun) Animal
Style (with grilled onions and mustard-cooked patties) quoted Nahum
1:7: "The Lord is good, a strong hold in the day of trouble; and he
knoweth them that trust in him." I appreciated that. The Saudis loved
the In-N-Out—we'd sometimes made two trips a day to the Westwood
location—but I don't think they knew they were eating Jesus food.

On the beach outing, I didn't get a chance to partake in any of the
ecumenical fare with the main group because I was driving Rajiya. She
was partying with her Saudi princess girlfriends at the other end of
Zuma Beach a good mile away from the rest of the family and entourage. At first, I thought this was because the girls wanted to distance
themselves from the family, but then I realized it was probably because
their families wanted to protect them from prying eyes. Barricades of
umbrellas had been placed in the sand in a wide arc away from other
beachcombers, and an elaborate spread was set up for the twenty or so
teenage princesses to enjoy. The servers were solicitous men—a small
army of bronzed and buffed eunuchs with short blond hair and glistening muscles—who worked year-round for one of the other families, and
none of them appeared to be in the least bit tempted by the bevy of
teenage Arabian beauties.

Within a few moments, standing in the burning sun at the edge of
the sand, I felt that I was going to roast to death. I wasn't told that we
would be going to the beach beforehand, so I was dressed as usual in a
long-sleeved, high-necked blouse, long black pants, and stacked heels.
Even if I'd known, though, I don't know what else I would have worn.
It wasn't like I was there to swim and sunbathe. The other drivers (all
male) were dressed in shorts, T-shirts, and sandals. It was 95 degrees out,
and there was no shade anywhere unless I sat in the car, which was as
hot as hell in the midday sun. Malikah and all the nannies were dressed
in their regular clothing, covered from head to toe, and didn't seem at
all uncomfortable. I would have given my eyeteeth to be in a bikini and
jump in the ocean for half a minute just to chill down, or even to be
wearing a pair of flip-flops. It felt bizarre to be at the beach fully clothed.
Within a mile of the shoreline, I'm usually already stripped down and

oiled up, ready to get horizontal with a good book the moment I hit the sand. The combination of the long hours, very little sleep, and inadequate sustenance was starting to get to me.

Ten minutes in the sun and I thought I was going to faint, and I knew that it was more than just the heat that was bothering me. I didn't want to be there, and there was no place to which I could escape. I couldn't drive away and tell someone to call me when I was needed. I was expected to stay within earshot in case my services were required. I felt trapped, but in a surreal way as if I were in a Buñuel movie. I wasn't locked in a closet or strapped to a chair; I was enveloped by a huge expanse of sand, an enormous body of water, and a pack of giggling bikini-clad teenagers chaperoned by shrouded, pious women. I started to feel a shortness of breath and a terrible tightness in my chest. This was the worst day of the job for me so far, even worse than the long, lonely hours in the casino parking lot. The minor allure of the employment had totally burned off in the California sun.

Malikah noticed that I was on the precipice of a panic attack and firmly instructed me to sit down under one of the umbrellas that had been put up for the princesses. She wrapped ice cubes in a cloth and draped it across the back of my neck. "Sit and relax here for a moment, Janni. You must relax," she murmured in my ear. Immediately I felt better.

Malikah was devout, and always prayed at the carefully prescribed five times each day. Another of the five pillars of Islam is *salah,* the compulsory daily prayers that are offered to Allah at specific times of the day measured according to the movement of the sun. She told me that Islam is the newest of the big three religions; ironically it was meant to unify the troubled region of the Middle East and to make peace between the Christians and the Jews. It draws many of its stories and precepts from Judaism and Christianity, as well as the principles of what it means to be a godly person. I saw that the servant girls and Malikah were good Christians as well as good Muslims. They demonstrated this over and over again in their kindness and goodwill toward me and others. Malikah taught me that *Islam* literally means submission—submission to God, but also in the sense of submission to peace—peace with God, peace with oneself, and peace with all the creations of God in whatever form they take.

Recently a taxi driver in New York City reminded me that *Assalamu alaykum* means peace to you. This is the greeting that is used for hello and good-bye. And Malikah always meant it when she said it. She wasn't at all judgmental, as I undoubtedly was, about the fact that her employers were as bad as any Westerners in their preoccupations with appearance and possessions; even more so, in spite of the doctrines of the Quran dictating modesty, decorum, and charity to which they purportedly subscribed. She accepted that each person must come to God in her own way and that this must be done in her own time, and Malikah was content to practice her faith as it suited her without casting aspersions on those around her who were less pious.

On the ride out to Malibu, she had alerted me that she needed my help to find a little privacy at the beach for her afternoon prayer, so when I had cooled down, I scouted out an enclave that I thought might work. At the appropriate time, we drove to the far end of one of the Zuma parking lots, and I backed the car up close to a high dune to create a secluded private prayer area for her. She determined in which direction she should face toward Mecca by working an ornate antique compass that she always carried with her, and then she laid out a special prayer rug in the sand. The rug was made of daintily woven silk, thin and delicate, so I insisted on putting a towel underneath it as protection before she set it down. While Malikah rinsed her hands and face with water in preparation for prayer, I brushed away twigs and bits of shell so she wouldn't feel them under the rug. There was nothing precious about what Malikah was doing. She was just efficient and matter of fact. I was the one who was making a fuss.

She then positioned herself on the rug while I stood guard to make sure that no one interrupted or bothered her. During prayer, Muslims must pray as though they are in the presence of God, and therefore must be in a state of quiet concentration and devotion. It is forbidden to fidget or look around. Intention must be pure and one must pray as if it is the last prayer that one can ever offer.

I listened to her pray softly for ten minutes or so. I didn't watch;

I just listened. I thought watching would have been rude, but I was entranced by the sounds of her worship. I could feel and hear her movement even though I didn't see it. She stood first, then went to her knees, and moved up and down several times in succession, prostrating herself at intervals. The ritual prayer is rather like a dance, with prescribed gestures and postures that are specifically executed and repeated along with a recitation. Her pants and tunic rustled with her movements, and it sounded as if she was singing softly.

When I was a young actress in New York, I auditioned for and was accepted into the St. Patrick's Cathedral choir. I wasn't a practicing Catholic and wasn't particularly religious, but I knew it would be a good way to keep my instrument tuned up, and I wanted to be part of the communal cathedral choir experience. And I also thought it would be neat to sing in St. Patrick's—such an imposing and majestic church—and in front of a congregation of thousands. The audition was dauntingly rigorous; I had to do a lot of sight-reading of Handel and Bach, which wasn't my forte, but somehow I squeaked by. And I do mean squeak. At the first Sunday Mass, I was nervous and excited to be there and had hardly slept the night before. The choir had to be at rehearsal early in the morning in order to be warmed up for the singing Mass, the first service of the morning. We wore beautiful plum-colored robes and assembled in a processional to walk down the center church aisle before the congregation, and then climbed up the winding narrow stairs to the choir loft at the back of the church. We sang several hymns, and then the cardinal began his sermon. I was riveted right away—not just because he was a powerful orator with a stentorian voice, but also because he was speaking about the sanctity of life and the immorality of abortion. I was living with a boyfriend at the time, and birth control was a constant preoccupation, problem, and hindrance, so I perched on the edge of the pew paying close attention. After a few minutes, I noticed that the choir had decreased in size, people had wandered to the back rows of the loft, and a short time later, I heard snoring all around me. Most of the singers were taking a catnap while the cardinal spoke and then roused themselves when it was time to sing again. This dismayed me, and it was the same at every Mass. Six months later, I quit the choir.

I thought of this while Malikah was praying at the beach. Her relationship with God was so personal and powerful and seemed to give her an immense amount of comfort and peace. She wouldn't have been put off by a snoring choir, just as she wasn't put off by the hundreds of children shrieking at the waves breaking on the shoreline, or the half-naked people swimming, necking on blankets, and partying on the beach all around her while she prayed to Allah. I was jealous but happy for her at the same time.

After *salah*, Malikah was markedly calm and content, and thanked me profusely for my help. She told me that she had prayed for me, my husband's health, and my complete happiness.

When it was time to leave the beach, Rajiya wanted to get the sand off her and change her clothes before she drove back to Beverly Hills with her friends, piled on top of one another in the SUV in which most of them had arrived. Some of the other girls had already taken off to nearby hotel rooms—even though the families owned homes only twenty minutes away—which one of their fathers had rented so that they could change in private, but Rajiya hadn't been invited to join them and didn't want to visit the public facilities on Zuma. I didn't blame her; they were usually filthy at the end of the day after visits from carloads of families. I powered up the convertible's top; then Malikah and I improvised a makeshift dressing room for Rajiya in the back of the car, and she changed while we kept guard.

One of the few Arab employees who worked for another family chose this moment to try to chat me up. I tried to fend him off, but he was obnoxiously persistent, pestering me with questions and inane remarks ("The beach she is not so soft and beautiful like you"), when I realized that he was hitting on me so that he could steal a look at Rajiya in the backseat of the car while she was disrobing. I shouted at him to go away and to stop bothering us. He laughed and scoffed at me, and moved even closer, as if I had taunted him to be bolder. I became incensed and was readying myself to launch a string of ugly invectives when Malikah quickly stepped between us, put her hand on his arm, and spoke to him in Arabic in a soft voice. Within a moment he slunk away. I'm not sure what she said to him, but I'm sure it had something to do with God, and I admired how she handled the situation with complete graciousness. He had made a valiant effort to check out the beautiful naked teenager, as I'm guessing he felt it was his duty as a man to do, and she had probably reminded him that it was improper and he backed off. No harm, no foul. Watching Malikah handle herself with such ease was a tremendous learning experience for me. She had no need to shame him, and she had effortlessly put a stop to his offensive behavior while still preserving the dignity of both of them. I just stood there watching, still frothing at the mouth.

Malikah turned to me, smiled, and extended her palms as if to say, *See how easy it is.* She took my hand in hers, just as she had done on the first day. "We have a saying in my country, Janni. You must save a little bit of your upset. Do not use it all at once, so that you have some for later."

I couldn't help but smile. She already knew me so well, and it had been only a few weeks since we'd met.

"Are you feeling better now?" she asked me. "Do you feel strong enough to continue?"

"Yes, thank you," I said. "I am much better now. I am strong enough to continue."

17

Shame Is a
Very Personal Thing

*B*y now, I had concocted a more detailed picture of my imaginary husband, Michael, and had also become adept at offhandedly imparting information about him. He was rapidly recuperating from his illness, and I said that I hoped that I would be able to bring him to meet everyone soon because he wanted to thank them for their prayers for a speedy and complete recovery. All the servant girls were especially curious about him and wanted to see what he looked like; they wanted to see who I was smooching when I went home at night. Every now and then I'd wear a different piece of jewelry, and if someone admired it, I would say that Michael gave it to me for my last birthday or Christmas three years ago. The girls would cluck appreciatively. Sometimes they'd ply me with little gifts to take back home to him—usually sweets of some kind.

The man I was semidating at the time, Mr. Rumi, was just as curious about the people for whom I was working. He'd heard many stories about the detail from me (usually during late-night cell phone calls when I waited alone in a dark and dreary place), and he was also especially curious about the girls, wanting to know what they looked like and to see how we interacted. A part of me wanted someone else to bear witness to the phantasmagorical world in which I was enmeshed, but I knew that I couldn't introduce him to the girls as my husband even if he pretended to hobble from recent surgery—I just knew that would be going too far in the deceit. One day, Mr. Rumi followed the servant girls and me to the 99¢ Only store and watched us in the parking lot and while we shopped. He kept a distance, and even though I knew he was there, I didn't acknowledge him. I met up with him afterward, and he said he was so moved by what he saw that it made him want to cry. He said that they were astonishingly beautiful, which they truly were, but also that he was struck by how affectionate we all were together: giggling, touching one another, and leaning in close when we laughed as if we were all young playmates.

The experience also made him see me in a whole new light. Often the 99¢ Only store parking lots are rough terrain populated with homeless people begging for handouts, and the girls always gave their change away when they exited the store. Once a man made a move as if to grab Zuhur's wrist, and I rushed between them and prevented any contact by pushing the man away and wheeling Zuhur off toward the car. I was protective of them with a ferocity that surprised me as well as Mr. Rumi. He said that I looked like a beatific matriarch when I was with them— and that is how I felt when I was in their company, like their guardian angel. I don't have any little sisters, and I really did enjoy my new role; it was one of the most pleasurable perks of the job.

I had told very few people that I was chauffeuring—some of my family and perhaps a few friends only. I definitely did not want to tell my father, and didn't do so until way after the fact. He would have been disappointed that all the money he'd spent on my education was wasted on gassing and washing a Crown Vic. I'm not sure why I didn't tell more people about this career development. It's not that I was embarrassed about the work; I don't think any kind of labor is humiliating as long as you do it well and with attention. But I think part of me hoped that not speaking about it would make it less real and therefore more temporary.

During the Saudi job, every now and then someone who did know that I was chauffeuring would call me to see if I was free to see a movie or have dinner. The ensuing conversations usually went something like this:

"I'm sorry. I'm just too busy to meet," I'd say.

"Okay," they'd say. "Then let's get together on your day off."

"I don't have any days off. We'll have to get together in a month."

"No days off at all? Who are you driving?"

"Members of the Saudi royal family."

"No way?!"

"Yes, way."

"Why'd they hire you? I thought they didn't let women drive."

"I only drive the women, and it seems that's fine here. In fact, I think they like it."

"Well, can we get a drink after work then? Just so we can catch up. I'll come to you."

"No, I'm sorry. The days are really long. Usually I just pass out with a piece of toast in my hand when I get home."

"You must be making a shitload of money. You're getting overtime, right?"

"No, it's a flat fee no matter how many hours, but I'm counting on a big tip at the end. The Saudis are supposed to tip really well if they like you."

"I want to hear all about this. Let's meet for coffee one morning then. How about tomorrow? Or I can do Thursday too. You must have time for coffee."

It was hard to explain the all-consuming aspect of the job. I could hardly meet anybody ever, and then only if they came around near the hotel and also had my dry cleaning in one hand and a bag of almonds in the other. None of my friends could comprehend what it was like to be at the beck and call of an employer day and night, not even the ones who worked in film and were accustomed to great personal sacrifices demanded of them on a long film shoot. We're used to some measure of autonomy and freedom, and we expect it. Working for the Saudi family dictated the opposite of this. Any moment of respite had to be snatched on the fly, catch as catch can. I started to get inventive about how to carve out a little time for myself.

Often I'd be driving someone who accompanied the princess in the evening when she dined at a tony Beverly Hills restaurant. The routine was always the same. Security would call ahead and get several separate tables for a party of twenty or more. Princess Zaahira would sit at a

VIP table with her sisters and friends, the security personnel would sit at another table near the door, the chauffeurs would sit at another near the kitchen, and then if the servant girls were along, they'd sit at another somewhere in between. At first, it was expected that I would join the group for dinner. The Saudis were very inclusive in that regard; if one person is eating, then everybody is eating, whether they want to or not. They insisted that no one should be left out of a meal if you happened to be with them when they were eating. If you weren't with them because you'd been sent on an urgent errand to buy twenty phone cards or six cartons of Carlton cigarettes, no one paid attention as to whether you'd eaten in the last twenty-four hours.

In spite of the promise of a tasty meal, I loathed going into a beautiful upscale restaurant after hours at the wheel and dressed the way I was in wrinkled work clothes and matted hair. I hated having to sit with the other chauffeurs when the servant girls were not along. They were a rude and crude bunch who made no effort to welcome me. I had dined in many of the restaurants before under different circumstances, and I didn't like the idea of running into somebody I knew, or hoped to know, when I was down on my luck. The food didn't taste as good under the influence of humiliation. I didn't realize it at the time, but I know now that I was ashamed to be seen at the restaurant under those conditions.

Shame is an insidious but major player in all of our lives, and for each person it shows up differently, and almost nobody ever talks about it. The silence shrouding it makes it even more potent. Rajiya was ashamed she didn't know how to handle money like any normal teenager, the hairdresser was ashamed to be driven in a Crown Vic because he thought it diminished his stature, and I was ashamed to be seen as a bedraggled chauffeur instead of a successful actor and producer. I suppose a part of me also resented the fact that I was in such a dire situation at all. If I wasn't sitting with the group, then I could continue to pretend that I wasn't really in the group. I didn't want to be associated with them in any case. I wanted to be free. I wanted to be at my own table, with my own friends, and paying for my own meal. It was also difficult to relax and enjoy a full three-course meal when I knew I would probably have to continue working for several more hours, if not long into the night. It was easier to down a few espressos and an energy bar to fuel me through the evening.

I finally relayed to the family that my husband, Michael (I was starting to really like saying his name), preferred that I didn't sit with the men, the other chauffeurs, and this was completely understood and sanctioned. From then on, if the servant girls were not dining with Princess Zaahira, as was usually the case, then I was permitted to wait in the car. The princess would always order food and have it sent out to me, and she'd even order extra for me to take to my husband waiting at home, presumably hungry. I've had some of the most expensive take-out food in the world but I preferred not to eat in the car, so it was always cold and soggy before I could enjoy it late at night in the quiet of my own house with my shoes off and my nightie on.

The job was so demanding that even in my downtime, when I was waiting for the little Princess Rajiya while she was in the movies, or stuck in a casino parking lot until the wee hours of the morning, I could never relax. I was unable to sleep or even close my eyes for a moment in the car as many other chauffeurs do easily and regularly, and I would have been terrified to do so even if I could.

There never was any real downtime anyway. My cell phone rang incessantly with calls from other members of the staff or entourage requesting this or that, even at two o'clock in the morning. I was constantly anxious about what I would be required to do the following day and whom I might have to drive and where. I was expected to know things, sometimes at the very last minute, that only a much more experienced driver or, better yet, a psychic could have known: the fastest surface route from West Los Angeles to Long Beach at rush hour in a convoy of ten cars, whether the Popcornopolis at Universal CityWalk serves caramel apples, and what time the In-N-Out in Westwood closes on a Sunday. How about the one in West LA? Wasn't the one near LAX open twenty-four hours? I didn't spend that much time eating In-N-Out burgers that I would know all the stores' hours by heart. If I whipped out my computer in public, then I was just asking for it. I was compelled to spend much of my alone time boning up on what I feared might be asked of me because I didn't know what might be expected or demanded at any given moment. Admitting ignorance was tantamount to saying, "I'm incompetent," and that was something I wanted to avoid at all costs.

I know that in part I put the pressure on myself. I prided myself on my competence and realize now that I would have been ashamed not to pony up and shine in as many ways as possible. But the potential for failure was immense, practically guaranteed, because there were just too many variables. And there was really no one I could ask for help besides Charles and Sami, and they were not supposed to answer their phones if they had their principals in their cars with them, which was usually the case. In the past, I'd been accustomed to a much more collaborative work environment that relied on shared information and effort; this was a harsh adjustment to make. I had to look out for *herself*.

Every now and then I had to talk myself down. I had to remind myself that I was only a chauffeur driving around a bunch of ridiculously rich people, and that was it. It was not essential work, it was not humanitarian work, and it really wasn't all that important if I didn't know if there was a Jamba Juice in Anaheim. There would be no Nobel Prize for me as a result of my ministrations to the Saudi royal family and their entourage. Stockholm didn't care.

In moments of extreme fatigue, however, I often daydreamed about what I would do if I had the money I needed to live the way I wanted. I used to play a game when I was a little girl, perhaps seven or eight years old, that involved furnishing my future dream house. I would allot myself a specific sum of money, say $5,000, and then I would go through all the furniture catalogues and magazines featuring weekly sale items that came with the Sunday paper. I'd choose a beautiful Oriental carpet from one store and a cushy sofa set from another, and then a coffee table and matching end tables, and lamps to go with them, and then maybe a dining room set if I had any money left over. I don't think I ever made it to any other rooms. I'd cut out the pictures and organize my chosen pieces in pleasing arrangements, as if making a paper dollhouse collage. I can't imagine where I learned this from, and I'm pretty sure I did it in secret. I didn't have any interior design ambitions either. It wasn't the aesthetics I was interested in; I just wanted to set up a house that was my very own with my own stuff in it.

For the first time in over thirty years, I began to play this game again when I had a few quiet moments to myself sitting in a restaurant parking lot waiting for the family to finish dinner, with a plastic container of prime rib, mashed potatoes, and sautéed green beans cooling on the seat next to me. I updated my childhood diversion by expanding it to include clothing, spa services, and career aspirations. I'd imagine that I'd just won $20 million in the lottery and had taken the cash option instead of the yearly payments. After taxes, I calculated that I might walk away with $8 million or so. I had a carefully culled list of worthies whom I'd bestow cash gifts on that included most (but not all) of my family members and several A+ rated charities. This left me with about $4 million to blow. That could go a long way.

I daydreamed that I would get monthly deep-cleansing and moisturizing facials that included light chemical peels to diminish fine lines and wrinkles. I would consider more invasive procedures after the age of sixty or so, allowing for advances in technology. I'd spend a year learning how to play the piano, focusing on nothing else as a sure way to guarantee my success and impressive proficiency. I'd pass out hundred-dollar bills on a regular basis to surprised baristas and gas station attendants and imagined smiling benevolently when they sputtered out their gratitude. I would throw away all my shoes except my very top favorites and purchase a tantalizing army of new ones with mucho toe cleavage. I would buy several sets of Pratesi egyptian cotton jacquard sheets and a new California king–sized bed for them to go on. I'd write and produce a short film that would win an Oscar and launch my fantastically successful producing career. In all my subsequent films, I would give myself cameo roles that demanded terrific artistic effort and expression. I would win accolades for these performances. I'd invest in real estate by buying a multilevel three-bedroom condominium at the beach that featured a very private and huge ozone-sanitized heated pool and several balconies on which to enjoy a gin and tonic. I'd swim naked in my pool every night, occasionally with an adoring man in attendance. I'd give my Midas brother about a half-million dollars and ask him to make some conservative investments on my behalf so that I could live on the interest, and I would give him 5 percent of the earnings—maybe 10 percent if he really did his homework. In support of my venture capitalist brother's epiphany that better business makes for a better society, I'd give him another half-million dollars to fund a socially responsible start-up that would benefit the world as a whole. I'd make yearly first-class trips to Provence, sometimes taking my mother and sisters, where I would stock up on lavender sachets for all my closets and drawers. I'd pay back all the money I owe people. (But not the $20,000 that one of my old boyfriends claims is due him for all the money he squandered on me. I figure that my time spent with him was worth at least twice that and I'm willing to call it even.) I'd take a trek to Antarctica. Why? I did not know. I just liked the idea of traveling in a vast whiteness completely alone, with the wind rushing around my ears, without a hairdresser interrupting my reverie screaming, "WHERE ARE YOU? WHY I WALK? WHY YOU MAKE ME WALK MYSELF?"

Actually I didn't need $4 million. The amount of money that one princess could burn through during two days of shopping on Rodeo Drive could change my life for the better in many ways.

18

"Yes, Janni. We Know This, Janni."

One evening I was particularly tired and sleep deprived, even more burned out than usual. It was week 5, day 35 of back-to-back shifts, and I'd been out driving the little princess for ten hours. Rajiya liked to walk up and down Rodeo Drive with her friends, just like Princess Zaahira and Princess Aamina did, but I had to follow her in the empty car with the radio turned up really loud so she and her friends could sing and dance to their favorite songs on Kiss FM. "Turn it up please, Janni!" Rajiya would yell to me from the sidewalk. *"It's like I've waited my whole life . . . Double your pleasure, double your fun.'* Janni! Please! Turn it up! I love this song! *'It's like I've waited my whole life.'"*

It was a strange sight: ten teenage Saudi girls scantily clad in thousands of dollars worth of Free City, Marc Jacobs, and Gucci gear dancing up and down Rodeo Drive followed by their *hijab*-covered nannies strolling several paces behind but always very near, flanked by several armed female bodyguards on Nextels and cell phones, tailed by a black convertible, windows and top down, blaring pop tunes, with nine other black SUVs and sedans slowly circling the block like a menacing cloud.

Occasionally Rajiya or one of her girlfriends would dance over to the car to quiz me. "Janni, do you know Paris Hilton? Do you know where she lives? Can we go to her house? Do you know David Beckham? Do you know Pharrell? Do you know Kanye West? Do you know any famous people, Janni?" Dissatisfied with my answers, they'd scowl and skip away. I did know where Paris lived but had no intention of telling them.

On the drive back to the hotel, Rajiya peppered me with questions as usual as she sang to the same mind-numbing songs on the radio turned up as loud as possible. The half-mile journey seemed like ten miles: " '*Cuz we only got one night. Double your pleasure, double your fun . . .* ' Janni, is the Juicy Couture at Century City nicer than the Juicy Couture on Rodeo Drive? Why is it called Juicy Couture? Have you been to Paris? Our house in Paris is next to the Tuileries. We go walking in the Tuileries every day when we are in Paris. It is beautiful. Do you know the Tuileries? Do you go to Aspen? We have many houses in Aspen where all the family stays. We go skiing in Switzerland too. Do you ski? I have three cars and my own driver at home in Riyadh, and my brother Momo has twenty-five cars and a Lamborghini and a Ferrari and a Maserati. I like the Maserati. Do you like the Maserati? My brother says that the future of all cars is electric. Do you think this is true? You said that you would take me to see the Tesla when the studio is open. I want to see this electric sports car that you talk about. I will ask my father to buy me this and then I will be only one in Riyadh with a Tesla. *'It's like I've waited my whole life, for this one night. It's gonna be me, you and the dance floor . . .* '"

Ten hours was a long day with little Princess Rajiya, and I couldn't help but think: *If the future of all cars really is electric then your family is in deep shit.* As I turned into the private back entrance of the hotel, going way too fast—much, much too fast I knew—I almost drove straight into Princess Zaahira's Mercedes as it was pulling out. It was a near head-on collision. Her driver looked at me and mouthed violently but silently, "What the fuck are you doing?" He had a big head and shook it at me so hard that it looked like he might come through the windshield.

I could see his hands were white and tight on the steering wheel. I threw my hands in the air as if to say, "I'm sorry. I didn't see you." The security in the seat next to him glared at me, a look of wild alarm on his face. They sped off. Princess Zaahira's chase car followed them, close behind, with their flashers on as if they were under assault. *I'm fucked,* I thought. *I am fired for sure.*

After I dropped off Rajiya and Malikah at the hotel entrance, I was shaking so uncontrollably that I almost couldn't park the car. I hurried to the ladies' room in the hotel lobby and tried to calm my breathing. I felt like I'd been punched in the stomach and couldn't catch my breath. The security command post had quickly heard about the near accident, called me on my cell phone, and bellowed at me to "WAKE UP FOR CRISSAKES!" *How can I wake up when I can barely even stand?* I thought. But they didn't fire me. *Okay, okay. I'm not fired. I'm not fired.*

I hid in an alcove and burst into tears. I couldn't stop crying; I was like an exhausted five-year-old who hadn't slept in weeks. Each time I thought I had finally collected myself and stemmed the tears, they'd come pouring out again. I must have gone in and out of the restroom at least five times. My nose was red and raw from blowing it. I couldn't go home, and I didn't want anybody to see me because I'd already been caught crying after Fausto chewed me out on the day, early on in the job, when I was demoted. I took the back elevator up to one of the servants' rooms. They knew I was the only female driver, and they invariably welcomed me. Their hotel room doors were always unlocked and usually ajar, as there was so much coming and going in all the rooms on the several hotel floors that the family occupied, and of course the security always patrolled the corridors and there were cameras all over. I eased open the room door. The double blackout curtains were drawn, and it was pitch dark. The room was warm and the air close. I heard the soft whispery sound of women snoring.

It took a moment for my eyes to adjust, and then I saw that there were three girls asleep on the one king bed and four more in little cots set up along the walls around the room. I had never seen the cots set up in the room before; they must have kept them in the walk-in closet most of the time. I had assumed that two girls shared each room, but I now saw that seven girls were asleep there, all in one room.

I knew that the family was paying for the princess's tea setup to have a whole hotel room to itself, and yet these girls were living like a little family of mice. Even if they were immensely fond of each other, that was a pretty tight living arrangement.

They were taking a nap while the princess was out shopping, and I had woken them up. Maysam jumped up to take care of me. "No cry, no cry, no cry, okay, Janni?"

"Oh, Maysam, I'm just so tired," I said. I could barely form my mouth around the words because I was crying so hard.

I'll never forget the expression on Maysam's face as she dried my tears with a tissue as if I were her child. It was almost chagrined but still kindly. She wrapped her arm around me and rested her head on my shoulder. "Yes, Janni, we know this, Janni. We know."

In an instant, my tears stopped.

They did know. By now, all the girls were awake, clutching the bedclothes around themselves and watching us with confused, sleepy frowns. I looked around at all these young girls blinking up at me and I realized they really did know how I felt: so tired and alone and beaten down. A shaft of hard light suddenly was shining deep into me, giving me a jolt, waking me up, fast and hard, and I was filled with shame. Their days were never their own, and they were making the best of it. And they even offered solace to me for my few measly weeks of hardship that barely matched their years of endless drudgery. But they lived like this every day, every week, every month, every year, maybe all their lives.

When the princess goes out to buy $5,000 worth of La Perla lingerie, the little servant girls get to take a short nap.

19

The Cool Driver Doesn't
Lose Her Nose

*L*ittle Princess Rajiya was out on the town again with her teenage buddies. It was 2:30 A.M., and she and her girlfriends
were cruising around Hollywood looking to get noticed. The
Pinkberry on Hollywood Boulevard was finally closed, but there was no
way they were ready to go home yet. They were too young to get into
any real nightclubs, and they certainly weren't allowed by their families
to go clubbing, so we were just driving up and down the Sunset Strip.
That was thrilling for them.

They did the same thing during the afternoons at the shopping malls,
sometimes spending four or five hours there every day. They preferred
the Grove on Fairfax and Third or the Century City mall because they're
both outdoor malls and the shops are the nicest in Los Angeles. Of
course, they did a phenomenal amount of shopping, but much of the
time they just walked in circles around the mall, around and around
and around, so that they could mix with everyone and feel as if they
were part of the social experience. It was their chance to see and be
seen. Malikah reminded me that Rajiya didn't have the same freedom
in Saudi Arabia, and that when she returned home to the Kingdom, "it
will all be just a beautiful memory, so we must let her enjoy herself as
much as possible now. This is our gift."

American kids do the same today when they're too young to drive but don't want to stay home with their parents. I often spent time traipsing around with my friends when I was growing up. Sometimes we moved as an exponentially expanding pack throughout the neighborhood and various backyards. This was normal. There was little danger of us compromising each other in some way; it was accepted that we were all just friends. There were occasional crushes or little romantic flare-ups, but most were pretty innocuous, at least before high school.

In the Kingdom, Saudis past the age of six or seven don't mix with the opposite sex at all unless they're close relations; any other mixing is forbidden. But Rajiya and her friends didn't talk to anybody even here, only to each other or to their nannies, who chaperoned them and were never more than six feet away. Boys were totally off-limits, and the nannies or security would quickly intervene if any males dared to approach them. The girls were allowed to go to the movies but the sanctioned selection (G or an occasional PG-13) was limited, so sometimes they saw the same movie four or five times. My idea of hell would be to sit through *Beverly Hills Chihuahua* over and over again, but they didn't seem to mind. For them, just the experience of being in a movie theater, and a mixed one at that with boys and girls together, was an exhilarating event in and of itself.

They would sometimes, however, walk out en masse if there was slightly objectionable behavior or content in a film. The princesses, not the nannies, usually made the decision to leave. Although accompanied by a posse of security and staff, it appeared they were also self-governing. One time I asked Rajiya why they had walked out of a particular movie, and she said, "Oh, we did not like it. It was boring." They often said this when something made them feel self-conscious or uncomfortable. I found out later that there was kissing in the movie; the girls became ill at ease and left.

Close to midnight one evening, they insisted on going to a late-night hot spot on Hollywood Boulevard that was owned and newly opened by a couple of celebrities. Even though it was a restaurant, after 10:00 P.M. it was hopping with people hoping to hook up after they'd had a bite to eat somewhere else less expensive. As soon as we dropped the girls off, I knew there was going to be trouble. A slew of young studs and starlets stood in line behind the restaurant's velvet ropes, smoking cigarettes and flirting coyly with each other. The crowd was stylish, with exposed belly buttons, bulging muscles, and sexy tattoos; I could tell by their boisterousness that some of them had already hit a few bars on the way there. The family's security had arranged dinner reservations for the teenagers, so they were quickly whisked to the front of the line and into the club, followed by their nannies, many of them in full cover dress with *hijabs* and long shawls. Within five minutes, the girls exited, looking unhappy. Rajiya said the food was "boring," but I knew the girls left because they felt so out of place among the Hollywood nightlifers, and they probably did not want to be in such close proximity to the young men who watched them with great interest.

The young girls weren't sneaking cigarettes or flirting with a cutie salesboy at Abercrombie & Fitch, or trying to sneak into an R-rated movie. Even so, they were chomping at the bit to make something, anything, happen to make their lives more exciting, but they always checked themselves at the last moment. I saw that a lot of this frustration was channeled into rudeness to the staff and the entourage, almost as if they were acting out to garner attention—and that this bad behavior was their only emotional outlet, however misdirected. I'm sure they were conflicted about this because I also knew that the girls were genuinely fond of and close to their caretakers, who might look after them their whole lives.

As on our other nights out on the town with the chickadees, I didn't have any security in the car while we cruised around; it was just Malikah and me as usual in the convertible tailing the group of teenagers. Rajiya and her friends were packed into one SUV ahead of us, followed by their female security and nannies in five other SUVs behind them. I usually brought up the rear because my car was only a four-cylinder; it had a lot of kick but not a lot of power so I was forced and also accustomed to playing chase with the big V8s.

Rajiya almost never had any security assigned to her, probably because her parents were more Westernized and didn't like to draw unnecessary attention to themselves. The best hotels and restaurants in Hollywood are filled with stars and their security, but many of the most famous don't surround themselves with bodyguards because they draw too much attention. I suspected, however, that Rajiya's parents knew that Malikah was the best security any teenager could have: she was fearsome and vigilant.

Only two of the girls had their own regular security, but the whole pack of spirited teenagers didn't need more than the chick duo working that night. One of the women was a former Los Angeles County sheriff who had obviously busted down a lot of doors. Even so, she was surprisingly feminine and immaculately groomed, with french-manicured fingernails and pin-straight bright copper hair pulled back in a tightly coiled perfect bun. She packed a Colt in her jacket, and another handgun strapped to her ankle, and she had three phones. She appeared to know everybody in town: every doorman, every maître d', every cop. If she didn't know them, she knew somebody who did. The other woman was an ex-marine and looked like a mixed martial arts welterweight fighter. She wore tight T-shirts revealing that she was seriously ripped, and she had better-looking guns than any gymhead in West Hollywood with HGH-fueled bulging biceps. I don't know when she had time to stay so buff because the security personnel were pulling the same hours as the rest of us, usually sixteen or eighteen hours a day, but she was superfit and looked as if she could break a brick without breaking a sweat. Both of them were attractive and sexy women in spite of, or maybe because of, their unusually masculine vigor. This was the first time I'd ever worked with them, but we ended up spending weeks together, and they were the only other American women I met on the job.

Suddenly all the SUVs ahead of us made a fast turn into the parking lot behind Chin Chin on the Strip. The Saudi girls quickly got out and moved toward my car as I pulled up next to the already-parked SUVs. Malikah left the vehicle to see what was going on, and when she did, several of the girls jumped into the backseat of the convertible; then Rajiya and another girl took over the front.

"Drive," ordered one of Rajiya's friends, another princess but slightly older and definitely the bossiest girl in the group. I pretended not to hear her.

"Drive!" she said again as she swung her hair at me. She had a carefully tressed long black mane that she used to punctuate her commands. She was astonishingly pretty; she knew it, and she already knew how to use it as a weapon. Her beauty made her powerful. She was also shockingly bold in her dress and usually wore very short skirts, halter tops, and high-heeled strappy sandals, as if she were going to a party at the Playboy Mansion. The other girls, including Rajiya, were still ultra-Hollywood chic in $200 Free City T-shirts and True Religion skinny jeans, but more modestly dressed than the bossy Princess TeenBee. It was strange to me that the girls led such carefully circumscribed lives but were allowed to dress as if they were twenty-something clubbers looking to get laid.

"Excuse me?" I asked. "You want me to drive all of you?"

"Now!" said Princess TeenBee and waved her hand dismissively for me to go.

What a nasty little creature, I thought, and decided to ignore her.

"Rajiya," I said. "I'm sorry but I cannot drive all of you in the car at once; there aren't enough seat belts."

"But we want to be in the convertible. We do it all of the time," said one of the other girls.

"Yes, many times," said another.

"We want to go now!" said another.

I'm sure that if I got to know them each better individually and not en masse, I would see that each girl was unique and interesting and complicated, just as I knew Rajiya to be, but in this pack, they blended together into a blur—a blur of brats.

"I don't know about your mothers," I said to them, "but I know Rajiya's mother would not be happy about this and would not let it happen." That quieted them down for a minute.

Rajiya's mother, Princess Aamina, had made a strong impression on me. On my first day of driving her daughter, she came out of the restaurant where the family was having lunch to meet the woman who would be chauffeuring her child. "Ah," she said taking both of my hands firmly in hers the same way Malikah had done, and holding my gaze for a long while. "I am so pleased to meet you, and I thank you for being available to drive my lovely Rajiya. I can see by looking in your eyes that you will take good care of her. Please do, I beg you. And I thank you. She is my only daughter, and I love her very much."

I couldn't help but stammer out, "Yes, yes, madam, of course I will do this," as if I were a medieval knight sworn to a high and noble service. I was moved by the fact that she took care to know who would be driving her daughter and to determine if I could be trusted. This was not typical of most of the parents I had met while working as a chauffeur. In my first few months of driving professionally, I was often assigned to drive the children of wealthy Los Angeles families who used a car service to escort their kids—which usually meant shuttling the kids of divorced couples from one parent's house in the Palisades to another parent's house in the Hollywood Hills. None of the parents would come out to meet me or to say a final good-bye to their children, or even wave from the door the way my mother still does when I leave her home. The kids were usually quiet on the drives and didn't talk even to each other. I found those trips unbearably sad.

Princess TeenBee jumped out of the convertible and announced, "It has to be all of us. Now! We want to ride together," and charged over to her female security on duty. The other girls started jabbering away in Arabic, and I had no idea what they were saying, but I could hear the ringleader complaining in English about me to Copperhead and the Welterweight. I figured out that Copperhead worked for her family, because Princess TeenBee was threatening to call her father. She was trying to have me overruled, and it was clear by their body language that the rest of the brats were endorsing this. The chick security duo were not pleased about the assault, and the shrill racket the teenagers were producing was making us all wince.

I looked at Malikah, who was closely watching the conflict, and saw that she was powerless to stop the onslaught. Normally she would have intervened. That was a bad sign and could only mean that TeenBee must have been from a very important family. I had seen the compound where her family was staying in Beverly Park, which they owned and visited several times a year. It had to be at least 20,000 square feet. It had two pools and a guesthouse the size of a bed-and-breakfast. It was faux Italian Renaissance and ugly as hell.

The other drivers were leaning against their cars watching with their heads down and one eye open. I could see that they were astonished by what was happening. They began to fidget and whisper among one another and then walked several steps away to distance themselves from any potential backlash. I didn't recognize any of them: they worked year-round for Saudi families who owned estates or rented compounds in Bel Air or Beverly Park. Most of them took great care in their appearance and dressed in Melrose Avenue hipster clothing, and two or three of them were sexy, in spite of their asshole demeanors, with sullen, smoldering good looks. Many were Romanian or Eastern European, and they made it clear to me early on that I was only a sexual object to them—and not a particularly desirable one at that. In spite of the fact that we ended up driving caravan-like together for weeks on end, I never became friends with any of them. In fact, they rarely spoke to me in the many hours we worked together, and if they did speak, they were invariably churlish. I wondered if they found me threatening because I was doing what they thought was a man's job. I was tempted to say, "Hey, asshole, I don't want your f'ing job. I can't wait until this f'ing job is over, so no need to be so nasty."

By now all the girls except Rajiya had gotten out of the car and were assailing Copperhead and the Welterweight. They had surrounded the two and were vigorously pleading their case. Every now and then one of them would snarl in my general direction.

I turned to Rajiya and said, "Listen, I'm sorry, but I absolutely cannot drive all of you in the car; it's completely illegal and dangerous. There aren't enough seat belts."

"But I told them we could do it," Rajiya said quietly into her hands, which she clenched together tightly in her lap. Her knuckles went white with the effort. "I already told them that we could all ride in the convertible." So that was it. Hers was the cool car, and she wanted to show it off. Rajiya kept glancing over at her friends working the security. Her face was flushed, and I could see she was trying with all her might not to cry. I understood that she just wanted to impress her friends and secure her standing.

"I told them we could do it," she whispered again.

"Okay, Rajiya. I can take three of you on one trip, and then I'll come back and get the others. Okay? And you can go both times because it's your car."

She looked at me plaintively: "But it has to be all of us at once, please. We want to be together. I told them we could do it." She looked so sad. She wasn't ordering me; she was asking me.

After a long noisy huddle with the blur, Copperhead walked over to the driver's side of the car and said in a low voice, "Just go up and down the Strip a few times. Drive slow. Don't worry about it. It's not going to be a problem." I didn't say anything. All the girls had jumped back into the convertible. Then Welterweight came near and said, "Just to shut them up. Make it quick, and it's gonna be fine." They walked several feet away and stood next to each other, hands on hips, and nodded to me as if everything was copacetic.

When I was a teenager, my mother warned me off riding on the back of a boyfriend's motorcycle by saying, "It would be one thing if you were killed, my dear, but what if you were to lose an arm . . . or your beautiful nose . . . or were horribly disfigured in some way? That would be truly ghastly." I never rode the bike again after that warning.

I got out of the car, walked over to Copperhead and Welterweight, and said, "Really? The bars and nightclubs just closed. You're going to guarantee me that some drunken loser is not going to hit us? And that these chickadees, with no seat belts on, aren't going to go flying out of the convertible? Maybe one of them loses a head, or an arm, or a nose? That'd be nice. I'm sure their daddies would like that. You sure that's not going to happen?" Both of them sighed deeply, as if I was making a big deal out of nothing, as if I was being difficult. I could see it was a show for the brats. They were the good cops, and I was the bad cop, but they were the ones with guns.

Princess TeenBee piped up again: "Do not make us wait any longer!"

Something in me just snapped. I almost slapped her, and I can't remember ever wanting to slap anybody ever—except one of my brother's friends who pushed me up against the wall when I was sixteen years old and alone with him in the Plaza Hotel elevator when he tried to kiss me. I slapped him hard but had lousy aim, so I hit his nose instead of his cheek, and that activated his tear ducts. When the elevator door opened and my brother saw me red-faced and gasping and the guy crying, he said, "What the hell happened in there?"

I leveled my eyes at the girls in the car and said nothing. There was no way I was going to let a spoiled little brat tell me what to do. I'd had enough. Weeks of watching entitled nincompoops spend hundreds of thousands of dollars on shoes and sweaters were taking their toll on me. I knew the right thing to do; I needed to exercise a little philotimia.

I opened the passenger door and said, "Get out, all of you."

Nobody moved. Princess TeenBee yelled, "You have to drive us!"

"Yes, you must. You must. We always do this!" chimed the others. Still, nobody moved. I took my hand off the door and put the car keys in my pocket.

"Out," I said evenly, "and you're lucky if I don't tell your parents what almost went down here tonight." My voice had dropped a full octave; this was the only way I could produce sound because I was so worked up. I was paralyzed with panic but my acting training came in handy at that moment. By lowering the pitch, I could force some air out, and a deep rumble emerged from my diaphragm. Even I was surprised by the timbre I was making; I could have been mistaken for a man.

The truth is, I had no idea what their parents would do or say; I didn't even know who their parents were. I only knew Rajiya's mother, and I hadn't seen her for days anyway. I was just saying what would have worked with an American kid even though I had already seen that no one said no to these girls ever, and certainly not a chauffeur. THEY WERE PRINCESSES! The tension was thick. The other drivers were looking at their feet whistling sotto voce or kicking at the gum on the concrete. One of them snickered. By this time, I'd been working over sixteen hours. I was fried. I was pretty damn sure I was going to lose my job, and I knew that a $20,000 tip was totally off the table if I did get fired, even if I was most likely saving these girls' lives and noses. But I had the moral high ground, and that would be just fine.

Finally Princess TeenBee said, "I want to go home. This is boring." She made for her SUV as her driver scrambled around to open the door for her. All of the other brats got out too and walked to their separate cars as if the whole thing hadn't happened.

Before she walked away, Copperhead turned to me and said, "Name's Cheyenne, and this is my partner, Cassie. Happy to meet you. Nice work. Sorry we put you through that. Hope to see you on the job again." She put her hand out for me to shake, and I took it. Cassie, the Welterweight, grinned at me and jogged over to pat me on the back and shake my hand too, "Yeah, man. Awesome. Kudos."

Malikah got back in the car, smiled at me, and said, "I am so glad you are here to protect us. For this, I am very happy." Rajiya was quiet on the way home, but I could tell by the way she looked at me that something had changed for her and that I had passed a test that neither of us had even known I was taking. I had stuck up for myself and what I thought was right in a way that she wasn't able to do because of her age and the pressure of her peers. For a brief moment, I saw myself through her eyes. She did have the cool car, and I had just shown everyone that she had the cool female driver too.

20

The Lockbox

*A*s I began to better understand the workings of the family and the job, I regularly learned disturbing information that confused or upset me and about which I felt I could do little. One afternoon, Malikah, Zeinab, and I were sitting at a café at the Grove mall while Rajiya and her princess friends had lunch a few tables away from us.

Zeinab was the cheery Egyptian nanny of one of Rajiya's friends. She was twenty years old and as pretty as a cherub. She wore brightly colored and comely *hijabs* and tunics, and long shawls that she flashed about as she moved, and always carried candy or lollipops in her pockets to share. I knew that Malikah was keeping her eyes peeled for a nice Arab American Muslim man for Zeinab to marry so that the young woman could stay in the States, which was her deep desire. Malikah told me that she'd already had several matchmaking successes over the years and was certain she could find an appropriate suitor. She spent time speaking with all the workers she met during her travels with the family in America, assessing the crop of potential husbands. "Someone kind and gentle," she said. "A calm man would be best for her. She has enough spark for two people, perhaps even three."

On most days Zeinab was as lively as a firecracker and sang and danced even when she was just chaperoning her charge while strolling around the mall, but today she wore an anxious expression on her face and I knew something was worrying her.

"Don't you feel well, Zeinab?" I asked her.

She looked at Malikah and me with tears in her eyes.

"Will you walk with me please, Janni?" she asked.

"Um, sure," I said, "if you want." It was an odd request but I agreed. We got up from the table and started to walk toward the bustling farmer's market just ahead of us. I looked back at Malikah and saw that she was staring out into space with a wistful expression on her face. I had now spent many weeks with Malikah, as well as many other nannies and servants; I sensed right away that there was big trouble afoot.

"Please, Janni, I must to tell you this," said Zeinab, clutching my arm as we walked. "I must. I had to say things at the American embassy, Janni, to obtain the visa to come to America. I do not want to lie. I do not lie." She kept an eye on her little princess while we walked in a wide arc; when we got more than 20 feet away she would guide me back nearer the tables where the girls were having lunch.

"Yes, Zeinab. I know. You consider it *haram* [forbidden] to lie."

"*Nam, nam.* There was a man who works for the embassy. My young princess's mother, Princess Nihad, she knows him, she tells me I must speak with him. He tells me what I must say to the questions for the visa with the American official the following day. He says I must say that I work only eight hours a day and that I am very happy with the family and things such as this so I am not . . . an escape risk? *Nam?* Otherwise they do not give me the visa to come to America with the family, and I must come! If this does not happen, Princess Nihad is very angry. I must to look after the little princess. And I want to be here! I want to stay! But you see how I work, Janni? How we all work? Sixteen or seventeen hours a day, and every day, and then one day after many years, the family they can say, 'Out!' And I must go, back to Egypt. There is no one there for me anymore. *Nam. Nam.* What will happen to me then, Janni? You see my employer holds the passports, Janni? You have seen the lockbox the security keeps? For me, and Malikah, and Maysam, and Zuhur—all of us. It is the same in the Kingdom. We cannot leave at the moment when we want; this is not possible. We have not a passport."

I *had* seen the lockbox in my first week on the job. At the end of each night, after our client released us, every driver had to check out with Alpha One Command Post on the twelfth floor to get cleared for the evening. Very late one night, I went upstairs in the elevator to the security room to receive permission to go home. I made a point of looking down and studying the marble rosette floor to avoid seeing my reflection in the mirrored four walls of the lift's compartment. It was only day 5 of the job, but I knew I was already looking haggard and I didn't want to scare myself.

Bill, an unsmiling ashen-faced twenty-five-year-old, was on duty. He always dressed in the poly/cotton short-sleeve white shirts and khaki pants that were standard security personnel attire, and had a "high and tight" buzz cut that never varied. He was standing in the middle of the room with two remote controls in his hands, staring at the multicamera monitors stacked on one of the long tables along the wall.

I knocked on the open door knowing that he had already seen me walking up the corridor on the monitor. "Hey, Bill. I'm clear for the night, okay?" I asked.

"Yeah. You're the last driver in again; that's three nights in a row. Better get used to these late nights; looks like it's your luck of the draw. Welcome to Riyadh," he said as he switched channels on the monitors with one of the remotes. I could see that there were camera views of several floors of the hotel, the bank of elevators, and various angles of the hotel entrances and underground parking garage.

I looked around the room. "You're on your own here?" Usually there were several security personnel working the computers or covering the phones.

"Yep, solo duty at night. That's all that's needed once the principals are in beddy-bye mode. I'm planning on it being nice and quiet, just the way I like it," he said. There were stacks of papers in front of him that he started sifting through to compile the daily command post reports. His eyes were puffy and swollen. He wheezed when he took a breath, and then exhaled slowly as if bracing himself for the long night ahead of him.

"I need a favor," I told him. "I can't remember anybody's name—the servants especially, and the cousins—and I'm driving a lot of different people. I never know how to address half of them, just to be polite. Is there a room list or something so I can get a visual?"

He opened up a small safe in the corner of the room and took out a silver Halliburton briefcase. He fiddled with it for a moment and then opened the lid. The case was filled with passports. As he rifled through them he said, "Yeah, here you go. These are just English transliterations, so don't worry about the spelling because it's always different. That's the Brits for you, Anglo-phying everything they can get their hands on. So here's Maysam, you're driving her, right? M-A-Y-S-A-M. Maysam. Here's another, F-A-H-I-M-A. Fahima. And Zuhur. Z-U-H-U-R. Okay, you covered? I've got stuff to do." He wiped his hand across his brow, closed the case, and put it back in the safe.

I stood there for a while. When Bill noticed I was still just standing there, he said, "You're cleared. Good night. You look like you need some sleep."

"Oh, oh, yeah, thanks," I said and walked out.

I had read that in the Kingdom, Saudi employers often kept the passports of their household employees, but I was shocked that this happened even here in the United States. And it wasn't the Saudis keeping the passports; it was the guys on the twelfth floor. A hired security team of mostly American retired cops, former marines, and other ex-military who had defended what America's founding fathers deemed inalienable rights (rights that challenged the "divine right of kings"): these same men complied with the feudal customs of the Saudi royal family who were paying them to lock up the passports of the household staff as if the Saudis owned the lot of them, as if they were chattel.

Royalty can mean whatever we want to imbue it with, whether it's English royalty, Washington insider royalty, Wall Street power broker royalty, Saudi royalty, or the Hollywood elite royalty, but ultimately it's about money and power, and our willingness to kowtow to it to gain access or to be rewarded. The "divine right of kings" was invented by ambitious men to justify power-mongering, oppression, and classism.

I was stunned when I saw the lockbox, but I was so tired that I convinced myself that maybe I had imagined it, and said to myself that perhaps it wasn't what I thought it was. *Maybe it was just easier for security to keep everyone's passport for traveling purposes?* But I knew that a passport isn't required to check in at an American hotel, especially when someone else is paying. I didn't say anything to anybody about what I'd seen and had even pushed it out of my head. It was easier not to think about it.

When I first saw the passports, I was just a distant observer, curious and somewhat disturbed by it, but still removed. Now that I knew Zeinab, Malikah, Maysam, and the other women working for the family and had grown to care for them, it was different. I was dismayed by the thought that they might be working against their wills or perhaps coerced by circumstances into taking jobs that offered them no hope of ever fulfilling any of their dreams.

I looked at Zeinab standing before me, shaking and struggling to tell me what was bothering her. I could see that she trusted me and relied on me; I was her friend. Zeinab was ashamed that she had lied to the man at the embassy, and as she spoke to me, I also felt shame. I struggled with the bitter truth that I had said nothing when I saw that lockbox; in fact, I had done nothing to act against what I knew was grievous wrongdoing. I struggle with this still today, and I am ashamed by my lack of action, then and even now. I'm not sure what I could have done exactly, but I know I kept my mouth shut because I was thinking about the money that I was making, and would make at the end of the job, and I didn't want to compromise that.

I didn't go to the California Labor Board, or the Immigration and Naturalization Service, or the Internal Revenue Service and tell them that the family was breaking the law by making everyone work night and day, nor did I report that many of the drivers were illegal immigrants, or that payment was in cash with no paperwork.

I kept my mouth shut—I was willing to work under those conditions for the money—and the security team was doing the same. We were all *mercenaries.*

I took the job knowing it was going to be arduous but with the promise that I might make a lot of cash; I was counting on that cash. I justified it as a means to an end and it was my *choice.* But the family's servants probably had no *choice,* they weren't free to leave when they wished. Most of them were most likely not free to change jobs, and couldn't even go back to their own homelands without the Saudis' permission.

Many of the other drivers, undocumented workers here in Los Angeles with no papers, were pulling fourteen-hour days with no overtime because they also had no *choice*; they had families to feed and couldn't complain to anyone. There's no recourse when you're illegal and afraid of being deported. And they had no advocate.

I can still hear Charles saying to me over and over again: "Take the money and run, girl, you gots to learn to take the money and run," and that's exactly what I had done. I had fully bought in and I was fully bought.

At the beginning of the seven weeks, I was awed by the immense wealth, power, and influence of the family and was perhaps even awestruck by their designation as "royal." But I know now that "royal" is no more than an ancestral designation inherited by the Saudi royal family because their distant progenitor conquered or killed neighboring tribes, annexed their women and lands, and thus proclaimed himself "royal," just as all other "royals" have done in some version or another throughout centuries.

I am left with a feeling of deep gratitude for the freedoms of this country—freedoms that I, and I am sure most of us, take so very much for granted. But I fear that I have contributed to the erosion of those freedoms through my complicity.

21

You Can Never Really
Know a Person

One afternoon, I was in the servants' hotel room as I waited for Maysam and the other girls to ready themselves for an afternoon outing. It was a pleasure to be in their company; they always made sure I was at ease and contented. Even though I worked for them, in a way, they made me feel as if I were tended to by a cluster of doting little sisters. They made tea for me, shared their Saudi chocolate candy bars and English digestive biscuits, and propped pillows up around me in an armchair so that I felt as if I was floating on a floral chintz–covered miniature throne.

They'd been cooped up for a few days, so this afternoon they were particularly jazzed because they were finally going out. They always got gussied up to leave the hotel even though I was only taking them for a ten-minute drive to the 99¢ Only store and then back again. The room was crowded with several ironing boards where they were busy freshly pressing their matching tunics and pants, and selecting which *hijabs* they wished to wear with their preferred outfit. They laid out the different combinations on the bed to compare each ensemble and conferred in Arabic as they swapped out various pieces to arrive at the most appealing selection. It reminded me of when I was a teenager and my friends and I would convene for hours in one girl's bedroom to get ready before a weekend party; we'd mix and match what each of us had contributed so that invariably we'd end up with a better outfit than the one we had brought.

Even inside the hotel room, the girls always wore *hijabs*. I had never seen any of them without a head cover, but the ones they wore daily were usually plain, pale blue, white, or beige in color and were somewhat uniform-like. For their afternoons on the town, the girls donned surprisingly colorful multilayered *hijabs* made of silk that were edged with embroidery, lace, or intricate beading.

The television was on, and every now and then, the girls would stop what they were doing, fix on the screen for a moment, and then explode into fits of laughter at what they saw, running around the room holding their sides as they roared with delight. They were watching a program that aired home videos of funny accidents—a snowboarder ran into a ski lift and took out a whole line of skiers like dominoes; a laughing baby spat food across the room, coating the camera lens and camera operator in mashed peas; a dog farted in his sleep and woke himself up, barking ferociously as if he'd heard an intruder in the house. They clucked with disappointment when it was over. They also loved the Spanish soap operas; they would turn the sound down and watch them with great attention, nodding sympathetically, understanding all the goings-on by the gestures and facial expressions of the actors.

The hotel's cable had special international channels that I had never seen before, many of them in Arabic, including Al Jazeera, Al-Arabiya, and MTV-Arabic. I started flipping around the news channels and watching coverage that was on all of them about recent incidents in Israel and the settlement building in the West Bank, with disturbing video that showed the troubles on both sides and the escalating violence of the conflict. I was interested in knowing the girls' views on what was happening in the Middle East, and by this time I felt I knew them well enough to ask that kind of question point-blank, but the communication was still somewhat challenging.

"Allah is great, Janni," said Maysam. "Praise be to Allah. Allah knows all."

"Yes, Maysam," I said. "But what do you think about what's going on over there?"

The room went quiet. Maysam didn't say anything, and none of the other girls spoke up either. This was strange because they usually had a lot of opinions on most topics, even if I couldn't quite comprehend all of what they said. We often had to go over the same material several times for me to better understand their unique perspectives, and sometimes even just to grasp what they were trying to say. Frequently we'd discuss something, and then I would ponder on what I thought it was that they were talking about or attempting to express, and then come back later with questions to put to them. One topic might continue in this way for several days, usually until we were both satisfied that we had reached a full understanding. This progressive round-robin of conversation became a regular and fruitful routine between us.

"Allah is great, and all the Jews is evil and all should be killed," Maysam said as she continued ironing the outfit that she had decided to wear for the day. Her long pants were a robin's egg blue poplin, and even though they'd just been dry-cleaned by the hotel, she liked to press a fresh crease in the legs before she wore them out. Her long-sleeved tunic was cream colored, with a blue and white floral brocade appliqué on the sleeves, hem, and bodice that matched the pants perfectly. Her *hijab* was navy blue and cream with tiny scarlet flowers. She smiled at me and then continued her ironing. As always, she hummed softly as she worked.

"I'm sorry?" I said, hoping with all my heart that I had misheard her.

"Yes, Janni. It is problems for the Arab peoples that the Jews must leave this place. They take the land; they must not keep it. This they must not. This land, it is not theirs to take; they must not, and many peoples suffers because of this."

"You don't think the Jews and Palestinians can figure out a way to live in peace together?" I asked.

"All the Jews is evil, and all should be killed," she said again. "Then there will be peace." I felt a rush of white noise around my ears and a hard pit growing in my throat. I realized that you can never really know a person in spite of the fact that most of us think we can or hope that

167

we do; and people often surprise you with another version of themselves when you least expect it.

"I don't understand. You mean, uh, what you're saying is that they should all die? That's what you're saying? I don't think that's what you mean."

"Then there will be peace," Maysam replied. She nodded her head several times to punctuate her conclusion.

"I do not think that's true, Maysam. I really do not agree with you," I said, raising my voice a little too loudly. I looked around for help from the other girls, but they had all resumed their tasks and weren't concerning themselves any further with our conversation, and it appeared Maysam was speaking for them all. Zuhur had chosen a tawny beige and gold ensemble made of damask cotton with a yellow and cream-colored polka-dotted *hijab* that complemented her coloring perfectly. Mouna was busy pressing two different outfits and was anxiously fretting over which was perfect for the day. The other girls were bustling in and out of the room, making sure that all their duties were taken care of before they left for their few hours off.

"This is as it must be, Janni. The Jews is all evil," Maysam said. She finished her ironing and placed her ensemble carefully on hangers. She liked to put them on at the very last moment just before we left so that they'd be as crisp as possible on the outing.

"No, Maysam. All Jews are not evil and besides . . . look around you here in Beverly Hills. Many Jews live here, and others, Christians, Muslims; we all live together. I mean we live together happily. There's no religious war here. The cell phone store where we get minutes to fill your phone, that's owned by a Persian Jew and he's a nice guy, right? You like him yourself, you said so. And remember when I took you to Westwood to get the pistachio and kataifi pastries that you like; many of those are Jewish shops. They like the same desserts as you. You eat the same food. No one here cares whether you're a Jew or a Muslim; we all shop, eat, and live together." I didn't even know how to argue with her; I was at a complete and total loss. I just kept talking about shared interest in desserts as if that was going to make a difference to her thinking.

"I am sorry for you, Janni, but Allah is great. Allah knows. When the Jews are dead all, then there will be peace in Middle East. This is Allah's will. *Insha'Allah.*"

The Quran specifically says that all people are created equal. Racism, sexism, and prejudice of any kind is abhorrent. And human life, all human life, Muslim or not, is sacred: "And whoever kills a soul . . . should be as though he has killed all humankind." (Quran 5:32)

Maysam was sixteen. She spoke to me so plainly, so calmly, so clearly, but it sounded rote, almost rehearsed.

I was at a wedding in the Southwest a few years ago when I overheard a young father talking to his ten-year-old son in the hotel where I was staying. As they walked past me in the lobby, the father leaned down as he spoke reassuringly to the boy, one arm wrapped protectively around him. "You need to forget about that goddamn faggot," he said. "You hear me? That kid's a faggot, so you just forget about him. He's not your friend. He should be dead." The boy looked up at his dad and said, "Yeah, he's a faggot. He should be dead." His voice was the same as Maysam's—flat and resigned, unquestioning.

Maysam and I round-robined on the Middle East issue a few times more. I kept on hoping that maybe if I could phrase things just right, somehow I might convince her that the obliteration of the Jewish people was not the only way to have peace in that troubled part of the world. But I never found the right words to get through to her, and it made me sad that I didn't make any headway. Hearing those terrible words coming from her is still distressing to me. I was reminded of a story that a friend told me about when he had traveled after college to France and had fallen in love with a Parisian beauty. After a few weeks, as his French improved and he began to comprehend more than just beguiling phrases of love, he woke up one day to understand that the magnificent woman in his arms was a raging white supremacist. He was so enamored of her that he worked hard to forget this very important detail for as long as he could, or rather until his visa ran out; then he returned home heartbroken but determined to forget her.

The first pillar of Islam is the profession of faith, or *shahada,* and in keeping with the Quran and the teachings of the Prophet Muhammad,

Maysam had to believe that I was going to burn in hell if I wasn't a Muslim. But my belief is that life is hell if one carries around that kind of bigotry and racism inside your head and heart. I didn't want to live my life that way, and I didn't wish that kind of hell on my young friend either, just as she didn't want me to suffer an eternity of damnation.

Maysam always ended our conversations with, "I will pray to Allah for you, Janni, and for the health of your husband who you love very much. *Alhamdulillah* [Praise be to God]. *Alhamdulillah.*"

22

Go, Nanny, Go! Run for
Your Life!

*I*n many ways, the job allowed me to witness or experience things that were startlingly new for me and that I am beginning to fully understand only now. I have traveled a little bit and have noticed that when I am away from my own country and immersed in a different culture, I often see and understand things in an unexpected way, perhaps because I am looking for and open to a new experience. The role of a chauffeur afforded me this opportunity here in my own homeland on a daily basis. All I had to do was watch and listen.

I regularly delivered goods to Princess Zaahira's hotel room, and two of her personal servants, who spent almost all of their time in the Presidential Suite, invariably answered the hotel room door. As I still knew only a handful of Arabic words and their English was equally limited, we'd never exchanged more than a word or two. But after weeks of deliveries, it was as if we knew each other well, and we commiserated with each other by our warm and tired smiles of greeting. They were both diminutive and delicate, like little doves, and I learned that they were from Eritrea. They rarely joined the other North African servants on outings, and I assumed this was because their workload was so great, but one day when I was in the hallway near the princess's suite, they timidly asked me to drive them downtown to the market. I had already taken some of the other girls to the Fashion District, where clothing and material are sold wholesale, so I knew this was the market that they meant. When they had a few hours off one afternoon, we headed there.

I tried to make conversation, but it was pretty rough going; they seemed happy just to be in the car and watched everything we passed with great interest. They did ask me about my ailing imaginary husband, and I said that he was feeling much better. Thank goodness, no one ever asked to see a picture of him because I didn't think to carry one. Also, whose picture would I have used? A brother's? That would be weird. An ex-boyfriend's? I wouldn't have wanted to do that. I have few pictures of ex-boyfriends anyway, and I wouldn't want to carry any of those men around with me, literally as well as figuratively. I made the mistake of dating an actor once, which I almost never do, and at the same time that I was trying to break up with him, he booked a commercial campaign. For months as I drove around Los Angeles, I was bombarded with 20- by 60-foot billboards of his face bearing down on me. It gave me the willies.

I decided to drive east on surface streets, avoiding the freeway in case there were any residual images of him darkening the skies. As we cruised along Pico Boulevard through what Angelenos call Little Ethiopia, we drove by an old Spanish-style mission when suddenly the two girls erupted in cheers and cries; I quickly pulled the car to the side of the road thinking something was amiss. They pointed at the building and exclaimed something like, "This church, this church!" They were ecstatic. I looked up at the mission and saw colorful mosaic tiling along one side and Amharic writing on the front with the words Ethiopian Christian Fellowship Church written in English just beneath it. In my ignorance, I had assumed all of the African girls were Muslim, but this wasn't true. And even though these girls wore head coverings, they were Christian. I pulled into the parking lot to see if we could go inside.

It was a weekday afternoon, and the place looked deserted, but I stood at the side door and rang the bell several times while the girls stayed in the car and watched eagerly. I glanced back at them as I waited at the door; they were so tiny that I could barely see the tops of their heads bobbing around in the backseat of the car. Just as I'd given up and was headed back to the car, the pastor came out of one of the buildings and walked toward us. I explained who we were and introduced the girls to him; they had now become very still, looking at him with fervent attention. The pastor leaned in the car window and smiled reasssuringly at them. He didn't speak any Arabic, but he did speak Amharic and a little Tigrinya, which they appeared to understand. He told them the service schedule, asked them to come back, and offered encouraging words to them. They looked like five-year-olds listening to a fairy tale being read out loud to them, eager but very relaxed at the same time. It was sweet to see him engage with them, although I couldn't understand most of what was said.

When we drove away, I promised to take them there the following Sunday morning, and their faces gleamed with pleasure. I knew that a morning service was early enough that it wouldn't interfere with my other duties, and even if it did, I would have asked a friend to drive them if I'd had to.

The following weekend, I reminded them of my offer, and they thanked me but were warily noncommittal, then shied away from the topic the following weeks whenever I saw them again. I assumed this must have been because they weren't able to get the time off, so I didn't press it. I thought back to when they were so delighted to see the church as we drove by it. They were as thrilled as children on Christmas morning.

I knew that they were forbidden by law to practice their own religion in Saudi Arabia and could be severely punished for doing so. They probably hadn't been home to their own countries in years, and perhaps for a moment they were caught up in the possibility of a happy communion with a community that they missed—one that wasn't even exactly their own but still close enough. It was comparable to my going into an English pub in China just to be near some people who might be a little like me, but not really, so that I would feel comforted in an unfamiliar place far from home. But they couldn't be comforted in this way because they weren't allowed a Sunday morning off.

One day soon after this, I was out driving Rajiya and Malikah, and we picked up Princess Aamina at the doctor's office after a checkup. She'd had several procedures a few days before, so she was strapped up with fierce white bandages holding everything tight in place. She was completely covered up in a long white diaphanous dress, a Hermès silk scarf tied around her face and neck making her look like a chic aviator, and a broad-brimmed white hat. Her steps were slow and careful, but otherwise you could barely tell that she'd just had surgery; she looked like she was stepping out to have lunch in Saint-Tropez after a lovely day at the beach. She handled it like a pro, and she never complained a bit even though she must have been in serious pain, because I knew that she had major work done, more than a few nips and tucks. Malikah told me Princess Aamina had various procedures done several times a year, all over the world, but Beverly Hills was her favorite place for the big stuff. Whatever she was doing was working for her and she looked fabulous, not at all like a surgery victim.

Princess Aamina preferred the front seat of the car, just as her daughter did; she always sat next to me and would chitchat during our rides together. I knew that she liked me and had come to count on my good judgment and assistance, and she relied on the fact that I was careful with my precious cargo, her daughter. She spoke with a refined continental accent and was a gracious woman who treated everyone around her with a great deal of warmth and respect. She was extremely agitated on this trip, however, because of family news that she had just received.

"Oh, my good heavens! I am just sick about it! How terrible, just terrible!" she said.

"What's happened? Are you okay? Are you hurt?" I asked as I helped her lower herself gently into the front seat.

"No, no, of course not, I am fine. This is nothing. Thank you. It is just that my beautiful friend, Princess Hadeel, has had terrible trouble. You see, she left Los Angeles early, before the family, to spend a few days to enjoy New York. It was agreed that she would take a flight from John F. Kennedy Airport to Geneva, and then she would wait for us to join her there. She has a beautiful baby girl, Badra. You have seen her, such a comely child, and a young nanny. I do not recall her name."

"Yes, I think I met them last week," I said. Princess Hadeel was lovely, tall, and graceful like a languid gazelle with a kindly and calm gaze. She had smiled genially at me when we passed each other in the hotel lobby. The nanny from Eritrea was tiny, painfully thin, and didn't appear to be more than sixteen years old. She looked as if she could have been a sister of one of Princess Zaahira's servants and had a high noble-looking forehead that is typical of that region, but she had a ghostly pallor in spite of her dark pecan-colored skin. She looked down always, her eyes combing the ground as if she were searching for something that she'd dropped.

"Last night," continued Princess Aamina, "Princess Hadeel was with the baby Badra and the nanny in line at the airport security—first class, of course. Princess Hadeel was ahead holding the baby Badra, and the nanny was behind them in line with the carry-on bags. Hadeel must give the nanny her passport to present to the official, and so they were in line and they are holding their passports. The official first speaks with Hadeel, and then he gives her the stamp, and then Hadeel turned to the nanny—and the nanny is gone! She has run away! Can you imagine? In the blink of an eye, she is gone. How terrible for Hadeel! How terrible! And the nanny took the nappy bag! Princess Hadeel had no nappies. Of course, she cannot possibly fly, so she has checked into the Pierre Hotel, and we will pick her up next week with the family plane, and then we will all go to Geneva together. How terrible! How terrible for Hadeel! The nanny just ran away!"

I had just heard that one of the Filipina servants had also escaped. She fled in the middle of the night by throwing her suitcases over the hotel balcony to a newly acquired American boyfriend waiting in the bushes below. Somehow she slipped away without being seen and met him down the street after he had secured her bags. The girl's disappearance wasn't discovered until the next morning, and by then she was long gone, secreted away by her boyfriend.

Princess Aamina turned to me, carefully and as best she could being bandaged from hips to ears, with tears in her eyes. "How could this happen?" she asked me.

I mumbled something to her about how inconvenient it all was, how unfortunate, how inconsiderate, but inside I was screaming, *GO, NANNY, GO! RUN FOR YOUR LIFE! You got your passport! Yeah! Go find your friends and family in Queens! Make yourself a new life! Maybe your other two friends from Eritrea can join you soon, and you can all go to church together whenever you want!*

And I was sure that Princess Hadeel and the baby Badra were fine. They were in a suite at the Pierre waiting for the family's private jet plane to pick them up, probably watching *Dancing with the Stars* and eating shrimp cocktail.

23

How Many Bras Are
Too Many?

*J*ust before the family was scheduled to leave, Princess Zaahira's secretary, Asra, summoned me and showed me a brassiere that the princess's cousin, Princess Basmah, had recently purchased and liked very much. It was sweet and sexy—the $500 kind of brassiere made of satin and lace with delicate detailing. Understandably, Basmah wanted more of them—a whole lot more. I presumed that she had some boob work done, and if I had new boobs, I know I'd want new bras too. Asra said Basmah wanted as many as I could get of the same bra but in all the colors available—baby pink, pale blue, black, nude, butterscotch, and ivory—and she needed them all before the family was scheduled to depart the following afternoon. *Great,* I thought. *Another last-minute all-important extra-special assignment: bra reconnaissance. For Basmah, no less.*

So far I'd had only a few encounters with Princess Basmah, and she did not wow me. She was very much like her younger cousin, Princess Anisa—petulant and sulking. I had decided to give her the benefit of the doubt and told myself that she was probably shy and that was why she appeared so standoffish. Basmah was in her late twenties and looked like many of the other Saudi women: truly full-figured, perfectly coiffed, and painstakingly made up at all times with heavily painted maroon lips, kohl-rimmed wide-set Arabian eyes, and carefully shaped high-arching eyebrows. She went through a lot of makeup. I'd already been on numerous runs to replenish her supply of lip and eyebrow pencils, and you could see that she was wearing in one day as much makeup as an average woman would wear in a year. Her face looked like a perfectly painted seductive mask, and she had very little facial movement or expression, perhaps so as not to disrupt her maquillage.

Basmah had bought the original bra at Neiman Marcus in Beverly Hills, so I started my search there. The very helpful lingerie saleslady, Sheila, sounded like she was from the Bronx. She had a big bouffant of back-combed frosted hair, enormous black Gucci eyeglasses, and blood-red lipstick applied in a thick, wet coat. Sheila immediately knew who I meant when I mentioned that a woman from a *family* (again I said this with great gravitas; while the thrill of being affiliated with one of the wealthiest families in the world was long gone, I knew that it could still garner results) had been in the store the previous day and had purchased some lingerie.

"Oh yeah," she said. "I couldn't forget her. That was a good day yesterday, lemme tell ya. She spent thousands of dollars. And she didn't even try anything on. Now she wants more bras? She already bought a lot. How many more does she want? I don't have much in stock. I'm gonna have to make some calls. When do you need them?" Her speech sounded like machine-gun fire.

"I need them now actually. And she wants as many as I can get of one particular bra in all the different colors," I said. Asra hadn't let me take the prototype on my bra search, probably just to make my job more difficult. I started to describe the $500 undergarment as best I could, wanting to provide as much detail as possible with the hope that Sheila could correctly identify the style without the bra in hand, but she stopped me almost right away.

"C'mon, I remember what she bought yesterday. How could I not? You're talking about the Chantilly. Did she want the one with the pearls at the cleavage?"

"Oh, yes," I said. "Yes, she wants the one with the pearls."

There were hundreds of bras on display, but Sheila turned toward one of the racks right near her and pulled out the exact one that Asra had shown me.

"This it?" she asked.

"Yes," I said. "That's it for sure. Wow, you really know your bras."

"Tell me about it. So whaddya mean as many as I can get? How many?" There was a flicker of movement on her forehead as if she had begun to raise her eyebrows at me but had then thought better of it. I studied her face for a moment and then remembered the *New Yorker* cartoon hanging in my dermatologist's office depicting the Grecian theater masks of Comedy and Tragedy: both the masks had flat nonexpressions, and above them was written "Theatre of Botox."

"Really, I think she'll take as many as you can get—at least five or six in every color if possible."

"You sure? That's a lot. What's she gonna do with all of them? Wear them on top of each other?"

"I don't know. Maybe she's afraid she won't be able to ever find them again."

"She's right. They're constantly changing styles. If you find a bra you like, buy a boatload of them because tomorrow they'll be gone, let me tell ya. Okay, we're looking for a size 44 DD, right? That's not gonna be easy. That's a big bra. We don't keep too many of that size in stock, especially not in the Chantilly. It's a little fragile for that big a load."

She pointed to a cushioned ottoman near her. "Sit down on that pouffe over there. You look like you could take a load off. I'll make some calls after I check the back. I'll see what I can get my hands on here. You sure you want as many as I can get?"

"Yes," I said. "Really. As many as you can get, please."

The lingerie department at Neiman's had soft lighting and a soothing atmosphere. I immediately sat down on one of the pouffes, as directed, and relaxed. I could tell that Sheila was going to hook me up. At eye level across from me was one of the most gorgeous negligees I had ever seen. It looked like something that only an ancient blind Italian seamstress could have sewn, and it would have taken her twelve years. It was a three-layered silk slip that fell just above the knee, with a softly structured embroidered bodice that would have been perfect for my figure. The innermost layer was a pale pink sheath, the second layer was even paler pink, and then the topmost layer was a finely woven lace brocade in ivory with a sheer ruffled skirt that started at mid-hip. All three of the layers met in the back with overlapping crisscrossed ties that secured the garment in a gentle three-layered corset. It was $2,500, and if I'd had the cash in my hot little hand at that moment, I would have had to cut off my arm not to buy it.

Sheila came out at that moment and saw me looking longingly at the negligee. I asked if it might ever go on sale. She looked at me, then at the garment, then looked at me again and said, "Fuggetaboutit."

She had several bras draped over her arms. "Listen, all I have are these. There's only eight. I'm gonna have to try our other stores. Newport Beach, Woodland Hills, and San Diego. You wanna go to San Diego?"

"San Diego? That's more than two hours away." I didn't want to drive to San Diego for a bunch of bras. The job was almost over, and I was so strung out that I couldn't trust myself to make the trip back and forth alone. I would've just FedExed the lot of them, but that's not the Saudi way. The Kingdom didn't abolish slavery until the 1960s, so maybe having limitless human resources at the royal family's beck and call was still too ingrained to do things any differently.

"I'm no fairy godmother. There's no way I can order them to have them by tomorrow. Maybe next week if you're lucky, but not tomorrow. There's no way. Not gonna happen. You're gonna have to drive," she said.

"Okay," I said. "If you can, please, then I guess we should check all the stores. I have no choice."

Sheila did end up being like a fairy godmother. She scored me over thirty bras at the various Neiman Marcus stores in the area, and with her help, I was able to locate many more from other luxury stores that carried the same line. "As many as I could get" turned out to be close to sixty, all exactly the same, but in different muted lingerie hues. It was trippy driving around in the car bursting with propagating bags of pale pink tissue and dozens of bras that weren't even mine and then hitting it in the Crown Victoria at 90 miles an hour driving back from Newport. I decided that if a cop—hopefully a beefcakey, sweet-natured one like the sergeant in Beverly Hills—stopped me, I would gesture sweepingly at all the sexy satchels around me, say that I was going to a bra parade in Hollywood and ask him if he cared to join me. Who could turn that down?

It took me a full day to get all the lingerie. And it had actually been quite pleasurable to be in so many lovely lingerie sections of luxury stores buying thousands of dollars' worth of sexy undergarments. Even the bags smelled nice—like perfumed money. For a moment, it was as if one of my little daydreams had come true. I noticed that the salespeople in the high-end stores made a quick assessment of me when I entered—their eyes quickly scanned me up and down to determine if I was capable of spending some real money—and their treatment of me was based on that estimation. After my hit at the first Neiman's, I made a point of carrying a few already purchased bras in their fancy bags on my arm, and my trips through each subsequent store were much more pleasant.

I had worked well into the evening the day Asra had asked for them, driving hundreds of miles, and had been at the last store as soon as it opened in the early morning securing as many bras as I could before the family's afternoon departure.

I was certain that none of the other drivers would have been able to get their hands on that many bras. I doubted that even the concierge at the Four Seasons or the Beverly Hills Hotel could have done it, and I was pleased with myself. I hoped that Basmah would notice and appreciate my hustle and that she would relay my efforts to Princess Zaahira. I knew Asra wasn't going to do it, and I wanted the family to know how diligently I had accomplished my assignment. It was important to me that they know this, and not just because I was banking on the chance it might be reflected in my tip. I wanted them to know that I was still doing a great job and that even though I was at my wit's end and weary beyond belief, I still had real staying power.

My sense of what was important was so skewed at this point that somehow I equated my undergarment treasure hunt with something of great significance—as if what I was doing was going to better the world in some way. I wasn't working on a cure for cancer or solving world peace issues, which would've been truly admirable. In actuality, I was simply procuring enough bras to outfit the entire Los Angeles Lakers cheerleading squad to satisfy a Saudi princess with a new boob job.

I went up to Basmah's hotel suite and tried to pass off the booty to her servant, Mouna, who took one look inside the bags and chirped with delight. She fingered them lovingly. These bras weren't nearly low-cut enough for her but she still marveled at them.

"You must to show to Princess Basmah," she said as she pushed me out the door. "She is asking, you must to show her." I left most of the bags with Mouna and went downstairs with a few bras in one bag in order to present them to Basmah. I spotted her SUV downstairs in the hotel driveway, parked in the shade, and went over to talk to her regular driver, my friend Charles.

The SUV was immaculate at all times, as if Charles owned the vehicle himself. He continuously cleaned and polished it with gentle adoring attention and a smile on his face; he looked as if he was bathing a woman he cherished. Because Princess Basmah chain-smoked, Charles had crafted an ashtray made of a highball glass filled with colored sand that he placed in the cup holder in the backseat next to where she sat, refreshing it regularly to make sure that the SUV always smelled inviting.

"How's my sunshiny girl?" he asked when he saw me approach the car. It was absurd that he called me "sunshiny girl" because I knew I was never even close to being sunshiny the whole seven weeks. I am sure I was much closer to morose, frazzled, and catatonic in varying and unpredictable spurts. He said it just to make me feel better, and I appreciated that; no one likes to be told they're unpleasant to be around even if it's true.

"We're almost done. I'm going to sleep for a week as soon as they leave." I slid into the backseat. It was cool in the idling SUV because he always had the air-conditioning cranked, ready for Basmah's arrival.

"Yep, it's almost over. Looks like we made it," he said.

Charles kept a constant supply of assorted snacks in the SUV that he'd share with everyone whenever our sugar levels dropped dangerously low. "You looking drawn, girl, like you could eat a cookie," he said as he passed me a bag of Oreo Bites. What he meant was that I was losing my feminine lines and he hated to see that happen. Both Charles and Sami had politely intimated to me that I looked better with a few more pounds. They didn't care for skinny chicks, bless their hearts. It wasn't lost on me that I was never offended when my two chauffeur friends expressed their unsolicited opinions about my looks. I knew that they were fond of me and cared about me as a person and not just as a piece of ass.

"Can I have the Fig Newtons instead, please?" I asked. I wolfed down a few cookies and chugged a frosty can of Red Bull that he kept in his cooler, probably just for me. He didn't drink Red Bull, Basmah didn't drink it, and her security didn't like it either, so he was possibly stocking it just to keep me hydrated and awake. Charles was considerate that way.

"I'm looking for Basmah," I said. "I have some goodies she wanted me to fetch for her, and she wasn't in her room." I didn't add that I had secured thousands of dollars worth of unmentionables for her, and he didn't ask what the goodies were in the bags that I was holding. We both knew to be discreet.

"My princess said she'd be ready to go out at noon, but you know how they is. I been waiting over two hours now," he said. He called her "my princess" affectionately, as if she were his baby daughter.

"They take care of you yet?" asked Charles.

"I'm sorry?"

"You know, they take care of you?" he said again. I remembered that this was chauffeur speak for a gratuity.

"Oh, you mean did they tip me yet? No, nothing. Did you get tipped already? I thought they were going to do it at the airport," I said.

Charles smiled and "My princess, she already took care of me."

"Nice!" I said. "Did you do all right?"

"I did just fine," he said.

I wanted to ask him how much "just fine" was worth, but I wasn't sure how to go about it without being rude. I'd never discussed money in this way with anyone before, so I wasn't clear on the protocol, but I did know that chauffeurs are notoriously secretive about their earnings.

"So you're happy?" I asked.

"Just fine," he said again.

"Fine but not happy?"

"Not unhappy," he said. Now I was confused. I couldn't crack the code. I needed a specific number. I had just worked seven weeks straight and I needed a dollar figure that would allow me to feel that it had all been worth it. Five thousand dollars would have been just fine with me.

Ten thousand dollars would have made me very happy. Twenty thousand would have made me hysterical with joy. But maybe his idea of happiness was different than mine.

"Was it way more than on your last Saudi job? The one that lasted a month?" I asked. I figured that maybe as long as I didn't name a number, he'd be more forthcoming.

"Let me think about that now . . . nope," Charles said. Perhaps he didn't remember that he had already told me how much he made on that job and I felt no need to remind him.

"Was it way less?"

"Nope," he said. Okay. I concluded that he received somewhere between an $8,000 and $12,000 tip. That was promising. Charles was a very senior chauffeur, however, and was also driving a princess who was quite high up in the entourage hierarchy; I am sure that was factored into his gratuity. As the afternoon wore on, I learned that many of the other drivers had already been tipped and most of them had received $5,000 and some even more, and most had received costly watches as well. I knew that I was going to be on the high end of the tip disbursement. That would be the only correct thing to do.

I started daydreaming about massages, mimosas, and movie marathons. My palms pulsed with excitement.

A short while later, I found Basmah and tried to show off the hard-won lingerie I had spent hours procuring for her. She dismissed me with a wave of her hand without even looking in the bag as if to say, "Do not trouble me with the details of your effort. It is of no consequence to me."

Well, goodie on you, I thought. *At least your new boobs will be happy encased in all that lovely silk even if you are a miserable wretch. And I am about to get a shitload of cash, so I forgive you for being the way you are. You probably can't help it.*

24

My Big Fat Envelope

On the last day of the job, the chauffeurs were again asked to wear black suits as we'd been required to do on the first day, when we'd picked up the group. I pinched in my suit pants with a safety pin to keep them on since I was now so much thinner than I had been at the beginning of the seven weeks, but they still hung off my hips like ghetto saggers. Even my fingers were smaller; I'd had to put masking tape around my grandmother's wedding band to keep it from slipping off my ring finger. A friend who hugged me good-bye one night just after the job ended pulled back in alarm saying, "I can feel your ribs! Gosh, you really need to take care of yourself." It wasn't just that I had lost weight. I had also aged considerably from the stress and massive sleep deprivation, and my friend was just too polite to say so.

The family was departing from a private airport in Long Beach, another cushy FBO with a VIP waiting lounge that served cocktails and hors d'oeuvres at all hours of the day. We had been told that we'd be driving in a caravan to the airport. The chauffeurs began assembling in the hotel breezeway close to the arranged time, and when I pulled my car up, I saw that there were drivers milling about and that the Saudi colonel was standing on the stairs passing out thick white envelopes. He looked completely spent. The black pouches under his eyes had grown to the size of ripe plums, and his face was caved in as if he had lost several teeth. He no longer had a soft round belly, and his shirt hung off him in loose folds. I wondered what it must be like to be a decorated military commander now acting as a travel agent, party planner, and babysitter for a princess and her children while they traveled the world shopping and undergoing plastic surgery. It was clear his job wasn't easy, or he wouldn't have looked so hellish.

I approached him and waited for him to acknowledge me. I didn't have to wait long. For the first time ever, he looked me in the eyes. I was so surprised that I almost tripped backward on the stairs. In all the seven weeks that I had worked for the family, we had never made eye contact. The colonel smiled wearily at me and then even spoke to me. He asked my name, and then confirmed that it was the same name on the envelope that he was holding for me.

"Thank you for your effort," he said as he handed me my tip envelope. I took it as a good sign that he had finally communicated with me in some way, and he obviously appreciated my work or he wouldn't have said so. He seemed like a man who meant what he said.

The envelope was fat and damp from the midday heat, with Arabic writing on it that I couldn't read. I knew it couldn't be a check. The envelope was too thick and, besides, the Saudis never wrote checks. I assumed my tip was in hundreds since they always paid in hundreds, and I concluded happily that there was undoubtedly a big stack of them. I quickly put the envelope in my pocket. I didn't want to open it then, not in front of the valets and other hotel staff, and I didn't want to be seen counting hundred-dollar bills to determine how much it was.

I wanted to ask the colonel something, anything really, so that we'd have some small version of a conversation, but he had already turned away to speak with another driver. I lingered for a few moments, the way people do when they are hoping to catch someone's eye, have a private word, or make contact with a celebrity ensnared by admiring fans. But he didn't look in my direction again. Eventually I felt silly just standing there near him and made my way to the hotel elevators.

As I waited to go upstairs, I watched the hotel guests and workers hustling and bustling around me. I could hear several languages being spoken, none of them English. Several guests smiled at me in recognition, and the lobby attendants wished me a good afternoon. They all presumed I was a regular guest or perhaps a hotel executive. I had now

185

been in steady attendance at the hotel for many weeks, in and out at all times of the day and night, so it did feel somewhat as if I were walking into my own marble-floored and crystal-chandeliered 600-square-foot front foyer. In the center of the lobby was a colossal exotic floral arrangement, with blooms that I did not recognize but whose intoxicating scent I could smell from 20 feet away. It was a lovely room, but even with the warm sunlight glinting off the chandelier's prisms and the perfume of the flowers, it had the cold feel of a mausoleum.

As the elevator doors opened, I glanced once more at the colonel and saw that he had been looking at me as I surveyed the lobby. His eyes swept over me once quickly when my eyes met his; he nodded tersely and then looked away again. I understood that he had known that I was waiting to speak with him but had not wanted me to do so.

25

The $300 Million Getaway

aysam had called me and asked me to come upstairs to say good-bye to her and the other servant girls. They were leaving the hotel earlier than the rest of the group in order to prepare the plane for Princess Zaahira and the family, and I wouldn't see them before I drove Malikah and Rajiya to join the group for the family's departure later in the day. Charles had told me that when he had worked for another Saudi prince, a flamboyant character, servants always went to the airport ahead of time to spread out a carpet of red rose petals for the prince's favorite wife to step on as she entered and exited the plane. The petals had to be fresh, completely unsullied, and she was to be the first to tread on them or he would become irate.

The servants' hotel room was in a flurry of activity, with a hum of orchestrated chaos pulsing the air. The ironing boards were out again, and there was a team working on clothing, a team working on final packing, and a team working on the family's last-minute demands. Huge boxes were set up around the room, piled on top of each other, which Maysam was filling with the remains of the incense, spices, and smaller accoutrements that had traveled with them from Saudi Arabia. The servants had spent most of the last few days packing away the more cumbersome items; they'd been doing a staggering amount of work, the job of twenty men really.

"Here, sit, sit, Janni," Maysam said as she pushed me into my little tufted throne armchair, plumping the pillows once I was settled. She placed a large blue and gold enamel tin covered in Arabic handwriting in my lap.

"Here, take, Janni. Is gift." The box was filled with aromatic tea leaves. "Oh, thank you, Maysam. I love this tea. *Shukran* [thank you]." The tea had helped me through many long, punishing days, and of course it could grow hair on your chest, as my dad would say.

It hadn't occurred to me that we might be exchanging gifts so I was empty-handed. Zuhur then passed me what looked like a book wrapped in thin gold tissue paper. I realized with dismay that they were all going to present me with gifts, and I had absolutely nothing to give in return. I had some aged and crumbly energy bars in the glove compartment of my car, and that was it.

"No, no," I said. "You have given me enough. No more. I will enjoy my tea and think of you all when I drink it." I pushed the book back at Zuhur; she pushed it again at me.

"Please," she said. "This gift for you to make the life peaceful and so cozy. Please to take." I had no choice but to take it and carefully unwrapped the package. The book had a soft Moroccan green leather cover stamped with gold lettering and ornamental motifs. Its pages were almost translucent, like onionskin, and were perfumed with sandalwood. The text was in Arabic with English translation on each facing page; the lettering was elegant and ornate. Zuhur watched me with pleasure as I fingered the book.

"Al Quran," she said. She touched the book, and then my chest above my heart, and then my temple. "To make you so cozy."

"Thank you, Zuhur," I said. "It's beautiful. I am sure it will make me so cozy."

Maysam pulled a small velvet pouch from her pocket and set it on my lap. It was maroon with raised gold lettering in Arabic, and I knew right away it contained a piece of jewelry. I untied it slowly and inside was a 24-carat-gold filigree ring with thin pieces of gold twisted, curled, and soldered to form a bas-relief crescent moon and star that is symbolic of Islam.

"For you, Janni," said Maysam. "We love you, Janni. We love you." I put the ring on my finger. It was delicate and tasteful, truly lovely, and a hugely generous gift. It was so precious I didn't know what to say. I knew these girls earned very little money, and I was humbled by their gift to me. They'd obviously planned and thought about this day, the day we would be saying good-bye, and had spent time considering what I would like and what would appropriately reflect their affection for me. I had done nothing. I had been thinking about the sleep I was going to get and what I was going to cook for dinner now that I would have the time to actually make a hot meal. And I had been thinking about the money that was burning a hole in my pocket, waiting to be counted when the family's plane was finally wheels up. I had been thinking about myself.

I kept my head bowed, pretending to look at my ring, not saying anything. Maysam saw that I couldn't speak. She leaned in close to me and softly pinched my cheek. Then she took my hand, patted it softly and smiled at me. "Yes, Janni, for you."

Mouna hurried into the room carrying an overstuffed hotel laundry bag bursting at the seams. Maysam and Zuhur extracted similar plastic bags from underneath the hotel bed, and the girls dropped the three heavy bags at my feet. I looked down and saw that the bags were filled with hundreds of the L'Occitane shampoo, cream, and soap amenities provided by the hotel. The girls knew that I loved them and had been squirreling them away for me. Even a few sewing kits and shower caps were thrown in for good measure.

"Here, Janni, take, take! For you, Janni. Then you smell so nice, be so soft!" they chanted, showering my lap with tiny bottles.

Many times in the preceding weeks, I had witnessed the girls shouting at the hotel maids, demanding something and then becoming livid if they weren't immediately given what they had requested. It was the only time I'd ever seen them angry, and I now realized that they'd been soliciting more toiletries for me. The hotel maids must have seen the huge stash the girls were stockpiling and wondered why the hell they needed more L'Occitane and had attempted to withhold it.

"I love L'Occitane," I said. "You know I love it. This is just wonderful."

I opened one of the verbena-scented creams right away and smoothed the silky lotion over my hands and elbows. The girls grinned triumphantly, looking satisfied with themselves, and then Zuhur double-layered each L'Occitane bomb in another plastic laundry bag so that I'd be able to carry them downstairs without mishap. Mouna procured a gargantuan Jimmy Choo boot bag from Basmah's room as camouflage for my booty so that the hotel security wouldn't think I was making off with a two-year supply of their amenities, which of course I was.

I carried the Quran around with me the rest of the day. I didn't want to stash it with all the soaps and creams, and I didn't want to leave it in the trunk of my car next to the spare tire and tool kit.

Just before the family's departure, the lobby of the hotel and the breezeway were maelstroms of frantic commotion, with people shouting in frustration, flying about this way and that hustling to get the group ready to leave. As I waited in the convertible for my passengers, every now and then I would finger the envelope in my pocket. I tried not to think about it.

I knew that Rajiya desperately did not want to leave and had been pleading with her mother to allow her to stay on for the rest of the summer with some cousins who had a home in Bel Air. I was afraid that they would expect me to continue being her driver if she stayed here, and I was simply not prepared for that. I was toast. Kaput. Totally done. Malikah said that the family wanted to be back in Saudi Arabia for Ramadan, which would commence in a few weeks. I was relieved when it looked as if Rajiya's appeal wasn't getting any traction.

The cars were lining up in the breezeway directed by one of the doormen, and when he saw me approach in my vehicle, he immediately waved me to the front of a lane near the lobby stairs since he knew I was driving Princess Rajiya. The lanes were cordoned off by four-foot-high green pillars bolted into the driveway, which the valets could reposition as they managed the traffic flow. Somehow I completely failed to see the last pillar in the lane, and as I pulled up, I scraped the whole side of the convertible along it—making a heart-stopping screeching racket as if the car was tearing open against a wall of metal sandpaper. All the action in the breezeway stopped. Now my car was stuck smack up on the pillar. I couldn't go forward or backward without scratching it further. I wanted to get out of the car and run.

Several of the valets hurried over to check out the damage and then with the help of several more jostled the car so they could unbolt the pillar and let the car loose. I couldn't muster up the courage to look at the destruction. One of the valets said, "Don't worry, *linda,* it's not so bad. It could have been worse." Another said, "No, it's baaaad." Another said, "*Si,* it's bad. Very bad." Luckily the ravaged side faced away from the lobby and as there was absolutely nothing I could do then, I decided to forget about it until later.

Most of the family had already come downstairs and gotten into their cars, ready for the drive to the FBO. No one except the hotel staff seemed to have noticed the debacle that just happened. Malikah and Rajiya were nowhere to be seen. *Oh no!* I thought. *Maybe Princess Aamina caved!* Just then I saw Malikah smiling at me from the top of the lobby stairs. Her eyes crinkled at me. "Don't worry. We are ready; we are leaving," they said. She said good-bye to all of the doormen and then got in the car. We had a few moments alone together before Rajiya and one of her servant girls joined us.

At first we were just quiet for a moment and smiled at one another.

"I am sure I will know you a long time," Malikah said as she took my hands in hers.

"It's been wonderful to meet you, Malikah," I said. "If it hadn't been for you, I don't think I would been able to get through this job. And I've learned so much. Thank you."

"I have learned much too," she said, "as I always do. In this way, we are very much alike, *nam?* And we shall see what Allah chooses for us and our futures. I know you have many dreams, and I pray to Allah that all of them will be realized."

She paused a moment then, as if she were remembering something she had forgotten. "I was a nurse in my country before I came to work for the family. When I go home now to Lebanon, it is hard to see my friends. One is the head nurse of the complete nursing department of the hospital, another has a big family with grandchildren even, and another is an author, with many books to her name . . . and I am a nanny."

191

I didn't know what to say at first, but I certainly understood how she felt. It was as if we were both a little bit behind and needed to catch up with the possibilities of our potential.

"Malikah, you know, here in America we can reinvent ourselves. My mom had ten kids, then she went to college and grad school in her fifties, then she had a career for twenty-five years, and now she is learning the tango. Anything is possible, and I'm counting on that. We can have one career at twenty, another at forty, and another even at seventy. That's why I'm doing this job . . . to take care of myself, *myself.* You are so smart, Malikah, and talented, and you can do anything you want, I'm sure. You could do that too. Anything is possible."

"*Nam,* Janni. *Insha'Allah.*"

"No, not if God is willing, if *you* are willing. I'm sorry but I don't think it's up to God; it's up to you."

Malikah smiled. "I am a nanny, and I am happy. I would not change what I have done. I had to help my family. And Allah sees us all, and I will be rewarded. *Nam, nam.*" I didn't know how to argue with that. She was at peace with who she was and how she lived. *Assalamu alaykum.*

I passed her a slip of paper with my e-mail and a different phone number from the one I was using for the job. "Take this," I said, "and please don't give it to anyone else? And please keep in touch with me?" She promised that she would safeguard it and that I would hear from her. I was relieved that she didn't present me with a parting gift.

"I will see you again, Janni. I will see you again, and Allah sees us both, and we will be rewarded," she said and gestured toward the sky with her palm open. I wasn't so sure that there was a God in the heavens who would reward us. But I hoped for Malikah's sake that there was an Allah who was watching her and that she would be rewarded.

Rajiya jumped in the car, and one of her servants, a young shy Filipina girl named Lilia, joined us. She smiled warmly at me when she got in the car. She was a new hire to the family and had rarely left the hotel, but whenever I saw her, she would slip me a treat—a pastry or a handful of truffles that she had salvaged from the family's rooms. The exchange of sweets had turned out to be common currency for all of us, of any nationality.

"Okay, looks like we're off like a prom dress," I said as I followed the family's caravan of cars out of the breezeway. Rajiya stifled a laugh. This group was a smaller line-up, only nine or ten cars, as most of the entourage and servants had already left for the airport. I was bringing up the caboose, and the drive was immediately harrowing. The cars ahead of me blew through stop signs and traffic lights, dead yellows and even dead reds; I didn't want to get left behind, so I ran through several lights too, my tires screeching as I made tight turns narrowly avoiding oncoming traffic. It dawned on me in the middle of one particularly hair-raising maneuver that what I was doing was just insane. It wasn't as if I had a freshly harvested live organ on board to rush to UCLA Hospital to save the life of a waiting donor recipient. I wasn't being pursued by a horde of bloodthirsty guerrillas trying to kidnap us. I wasn't even trying to catch a plane. The plane was *waiting for us* at the FBO and would leave only when everybody was comfortably onboard. But something happens when you get in a caravan of cars. An urgency kicks in that makes you want to stay on each other and travel together tight at fast speeds, as if your life depended on it. But actually my life depended on my not getting broadsided on the last day of the job because I ran a stop sign while trying to kiss the car ahead of me. I tried to slow down a little. Rajiya began to power down the convertible top at a stoplight, and I quickly removed her hand from the button. "Wait until we get closer to the airport, please," I said. "It's too dangerous right now." I was afraid the vehicle would roll at the speed and angles at which I was turning. She saw how hard I was working to keep up with the other cars and didn't question me. Her favorite song came on the radio, and then a few minutes later it played again, and then, unbelievably, again, and by that time we were all singing the lyrics: *"It's like I've waited my whole life for this one night . . ."* Rajiya was beyond happy.

When we got close to the FBO, I pulled over and powered down the top. Her special song came on again, and we all threw our hands in the air to celebrate. I gunned the engine, and we pulled up to the FBO gates just as the family was exiting their cars ahead of us on the tarmac. The FBO security buzzed us in, and I drove up to the plane. Rajiya jumped out without saying anything to me, but I knew she was just embarrassed to express any warm feelings for her chauffeur in public. Earlier she had shyly presented me with a piece of jewelry as a thank-you from her and her mother. It was an impressive gold antique reproduction cocktail ring with a large diamond flanked by two smaller stones. I'm betting it was a castoff that one of the princesses was tired of wearing. I had it appraised a short time ago just to see what it was worth, and was told that I could probably get several thousand dollars for it if I could find a buyer. The jeweler said that even though the stone was quite large, it had a shallow cut and was of inferior quality, or it would have been much more valuable. I much preferred the delicate one the servant girls had given me; I still wear it often and think of them fondly when I do. The gift from the royals was headed right for the back of my sock drawer in case I needed to hock it on a rainy day.

Lilia smiled at me and ducked her head as farewell as she struggled to follow Rajiya. Her arms were overloaded with last-minute purchases that hadn't yet been packed. The servant girls were busy carrying and arranging things as the family began to board the plane. They blew kisses and winked at me as they went about their work. Malikah lingered near the car to give me a final kiss good-bye.

When you board for travel at a regular airport via the airline's movable jetway attached to the door of the plane, you have very little sense of how big the plane is in relation to you because you're enclosed the whole time. But outside in the bright sunlight on the tarmac, I had driven up to and was now standing 50 feet from the family's 747 looking up at it.

The plane has a wingspan of almost 200 feet, it has three levels with over 4,000 square feet of space, and its tail is more than six stories high. It's truly immense.

Traveling in such a big bird is a nice way to fly, especially with only fifty people onboard instead of the usual four hundred. Air Force One is a 747, and no doubt the president of the United States, his staff, and the press corps fly pretty comfortably too.

The family had arrived seven weeks ago in a plane that bore the Saudi Arabian Airlines blue and gold logo on its tail, but this jet had no such markings, just the required FAA identifying numbers. The royal household would have many jets to choose from, which the extended family probably swapped out as needed. Maybe this one belonged specifically to Princess Zaahira's husband; that's why it had no logo. I didn't know, and I couldn't find out.

I assumed it was reconfigured for VIP accommodation, and I was dying to go in it to check it out. Maybe it was tropical themed and had a pool bar that you could loll around in while sipping virgin piña coladas.

"Is it nice inside?" I asked Malikah.

"Yes," she said smiling. "It is adequate."

"No doubt," I said.

"I will see you again," Malikah reminded me as she kissed me on both cheeks. "And Allah sees us all." I missed her before she even walked away. I can count on one hand the number of times I've become such fast friends with someone so quickly, and most of them I've never seen again in spite of our heartfelt promises to keep in touch. I hoped that this wouldn't be true with Malikah.

The servant girls blew more kisses at me. "We love you, Janni; we love you! We pray for you and your husband!" they cried from the plane stairs. They looked so trusting and full of affection for me.

I felt a pang of remorse—not a big one, just a little ouch. I am sure Malikah, Maysam, and all the girls would be aggrieved if they knew that I had lied to them about Michael, my imaginary husband. I invented him because it was easier for me than telling the truth and maybe, even more significant, I invented him to get what I wanted.

As a married lady, I got out of the casino torture because my ficti-tious husband's wishes were respected. I didn't have to explain over and over again why I was single, which I didn't think was anyone's business but my own and also made me extremely uncomfortable to answer, and in keeping with their social mores, my status was elevated because of my make-believe domestic bliss. I was welcomed into traditional adult female society with open arms, even though it was all based on a ruse. I have real married friends who use their husbands as an excuse as well, sometimes without even realizing it, to get out of things they don't want to do or to promote things they do want to do. Just last week I overheard a friend say, "I am so sorry, but I don't think we'll be able to be there. Although I'd positively love to, I cannot drag Bob to another school play against his will. They just bore him to tears, and I'll never hear the end of it. We have to pick our battles, don't we?" I knew the truth: school plays without her kids in them bore *her* to tears, and she'd rather pluck out her eyes than sit through a three-hour high school version of *Long Day's Journey into Night*.

There were many times during the course of the seven weeks, especially at the end, when I was tempted to confess to the girls. Often I could barely stop myself from blurting out: "I'm sorry, I made him up. There is no Michael. Please, don't waste your prayers anymore. He's not sick, so you can stop praying for him. He doesn't exist. I'm sorry. You can just pray for me if you have to pray for somebody. I'm the one who needs some divine intervention and attention."

I didn't say anything because it was better for me to keep the truth to myself. People lie because sometimes it's just plain easier, and they do it even when they know it will profoundly hurt the person to whom they're lying. Perhaps the girls would have chuckled about my mendacious act, but I doubt it. They might have felt that I had betrayed their trust, which of course I had and am perhaps even doing now as I write about them. I hope that they would forgive me.

The drivers were instructed to wait at attention until the plane was wheels-up. There were now far fewer of us than on the day we had started, and I didn't even recognize many of the others. I'd heard that there had been so many firings that Fausto had to recruit short-term reinforcements at the last minute. He had some difficulty doing so because word had gotten out that this was an unusually demanding family and the more professional drivers didn't want to leave their steady employment for a little extra cash. But Charles told me that this job was no worse than any other Saudi detail he'd done in the past. It was always the same. "All that money makes you wacky in the head," he said. "That's why they need to travel with a psychiatrist. They do some crazy shit." I didn't really see it that way. I think they traveled with a psychiatrist because many of the people in the group were lonely, unfulfilled, and depressed. That can make you crazy far more easily than too much or too little money.

We watched the plane ascend far into the sky, and then Fausto relayed to us the procedures for dealing with the cars, which all needed to be returned before the end of the day. I had parked my vehicle facing away from the plane and away from the other cars, so no one had yet seen the slash of green paint that ran along the side of the car. I couldn't tell what kind of structural damage was done because there was so much paint defacement. I pulled Sami aside and showed it to him.

"*Chica!* What did you do?"

"I know. On the last day too. It looks like I rubbed up against the Hulk. Do you think I can get this buffed out?" I asked. "I can't turn the car in this way. It could be thousands of dollars worth of damage. I don't even know what kind of coverage we have. I'll probably end up paying for this."

"Hold please," he said, throwing up his hand to stop my rant as he walked over to his SUV and popped the tailgate. Sami traveled with an astoundingly well-equipped vehicle in anticipation of any unforeseen emergency. He could have survived for two weeks just living off the edible contents in his car. He also had assorted power tools, several calculators, an electronic translator, and even a portable GPS satellite system separate from the car's system in case he was stuck in the desert with a dead phone and a dead car. You could've probably asked him for a chain saw and he would have been able to produce one. He put on surgical gloves that he pulled from an industrial-sized box (it was a little strange that he had such a huge box of them, but he was rather fastidious). Then he grabbed a chamois rag and a small can of liquid, doused the rag, and started working on the green gash. Within a few moments, some of the paint started to come away. He doused the rag again and worked on the gash a little more. It was definitely dissolving.

"What is that?" I asked.

"Gasoline, *chica.*"

"You're cleaning it with gas?"

"This is going to work but you're going to need a lot of it," he said. "Use this chamois and go easy. Here's some fresh gloves. Go get some more gasoline, and start scrubbing." With a few well-placed firm taps, he popped out the three-foot-long dent with a rounded hammer that he also kept with him. The car was going to be okay. I was so relieved that I grabbed him and hugged him. He didn't hug me back but instead turned away sheepishly when I let him go, just as my teenage nephew does when he's not sure how to respond to my affection. He's pleased that I've offered it, but he can't reciprocate.

"Did they take care of you?" he asked me.

"I sure hope so, but I haven't counted my tip yet. I wanted to wait until they were gone."

"Yeah, me too, but I couldn't wait."

"You do okay?" I asked. He didn't say anything but walked back to his car smiling.

"All right! Praise be to Allah!"

I knew that he really needed the cash to look after his mom, and a decent amount of tip money in addition to his pay could carry them through several months. She had recently been shot while coming home from the grocery store. It was a gang-related wild shot fired from a moving vehicle a couple of blocks away from where she was walking. Luckily, the bullet didn't hit any major organs; it just ran straight through the fleshy part of her upper arm. But she was severely traumatized by the incident and was now afraid to leave the house.

I spent the next hour rubbing off the paint at a nearby gas station. Sami's tricks worked like a charm. As I labored away at the green mess with the smell of fossil fuel filling my nostrils, I couldn't help but think: *Now I'm even cleaning with gasoline. Next thing you know I'll be bathing in it, maybe even drinking it. Thanks so much, I'll have a 93 octane please, up, bone dry. Lose the fruit.*

Before I turned the rental car in, I pulled into a shady Beverly Hills alley and parked. I was ready to count the tip money. I took the envelope out of my pocket and opened it.

Inside was a stack of hundred-dollar bills, as I knew there would be, and crisp as if they'd never been handled. They almost snapped as I counted them. But there were only ten.

One thousand dollars.

I suddenly couldn't hear anything except the beating of my heart and the distant sound of a leaf blower in one of the gardens off the alley. I paused for a moment to collect myself. Then I counted them again and again, hoping that I'd make a mistake, that the bills had somehow stuck together, praying that perhaps more were hidden somewhere in the envelope.

My tip was only one-fifth of what most of the other drivers had received, and yet I'd done at least ten times the work. *Do they not think I'm as valuable?* I wondered.

Later, I asked my friend to translate the envelope for me. It said *Maysam's Driver.* I thought that was odd. I was fond of Maysam, and I was happy to be associated with her, but only one name on the envelope implied that I had been assigned to one person when I had actually driven so many people, including Fahima, Princess Aamina, Princess Rajiya, Malikah, Asra, and of course the hairdresser as well as many of the servants. I drove to Palm Springs and back every night for almost three weeks straight. I was the go-to all-around girl. I scored twenty-seven bottles of Hair Off in a five-hour time frame. Who else could have done that?

My name wasn't written on it either, even though I thought the colonel had asked my name to confirm that he was giving me the correct envelope. But I am sure he must have known of most, if not all, of my duties and had probably even assigned some of them even if they were always conveyed via the security on the twelfth floor. *What the hell?* I thought. *Maybe they don't even know who I am or what I've done.*

To whom could I complain? The family was already 30,000 feet up in the air in a $300 million getaway vehicle. And even if I had mustered up enough courage to speak, what could I have said? *Listen here, missy princess, you should be ashamed of yourself. Hasn't all that beauty and privilege taught you something?*

Up until the very last moment, a little part of me was still holding onto the promise that the world is a meritocracy and that my hard work, conscientiousness, and dedication would be recognized. But I understand now that that was just crazy thinking. Nobody gave a shit.

Now as I track back through the experience, I see that it couldn't have turned out any other way. I was a woman, and I'm sure that they thought I didn't need or deserve the same money as a man who had the responsibility of taking care of his family. It didn't matter what the actual circumstances of my private life were. As a woman I would be taken care of; that is assumed. In fact, I had even invented a husband who was fast on the road to recovery, who no doubt would soon be able to provide for me again. I had told them Michael was on the mend when I should have killed him off. Maybe that would have generated some cash sympathy.

My head was spinning with fatigue and disappointment. I sat in the car in silence for over twenty minutes trying to get it up to turn on the ignition, drive away, and get on with my life. Several gardeners tending to the estates adjacent to the alley looked at me with curiosity as they emptied their refuse in the receptacles that lined the alley. One nice old man knocked on my window. "Miss, miss. You okay, miss? You need help?" I waved my hand at him in thanks.

In my angst, I had crumpled up the hundred-dollar bills and thrown them on the car floor, where they were now wedged between the back and front seats, the carpet and the console. It took me several minutes to find all ten of them, smooth them out, and put them back in the envelope.

Later I figured out that I had driven over 10,000 miles in seven weeks—sometimes 400 miles a day—on average eighteen hours a day, seven days a week for seven weeks straight. And I did it willingly. I thought I would be rewarded.

I did it for the money.

When I could finally see straight enough to drive, I turned in the rental car and was relieved when nobody said a peep about the condition of the vehicle. I asked the Regent courtesy car to drop me off at the Beverly Hills Hotel, a short distance up Rodeo Drive. My friend Lorelei was waiting there for me. She had won a load of gift certificates in a raffle and was having a full day of pummeling and buffing at the spa and wanted to treat me to a meal in the Polo Lounge her last evening in Los Angeles, before she moved back east to start a new life far away from the entertainment business. She'd had enough of the trials and tribulations. She'd come to Los Angeles just after I did and worked at her career with a diligence that would frighten a beaver. But she soon came to realize that she didn't have it in her to compete with talking dogs, singing puppets, and former Playboy models for the role of a twenty-one-year-old nuclear scientist.

The hostess seated us at the front part of the Polo Lounge, in a brushed velvet banquette near the piano, and I looked around the dark-green clubroom. The bar was jammed with lively and satisfied-looking people. All around me, well-dressed men and women were sipping from long-stemmed martini glasses, nibbling on spiced nuts and wasabi dried peas, and sucking down kumamoto oysters. The lights twinkled, and the shadows of the people bounced along the pictures of polo players lining the bar wall. A woman at the piano softly played smooth standards; an older couple was necking, ensconced in one of the comfy pale green banquettes, next to us. The man crooned into the woman's ear, "*Day and night, you are the one.*"

"Please have whatever you like; it's on me," Lorelei said. "We deserve it."

I shook my head in confusion. Only hours before I had been a lowly chauffeur, and now, in the same black Calvin Klein suit that I had worn all day pinned at the waist, I looked up at the debonair white-haired waiter wearing a white double-breasted jacket, an elegant little Five Star Award pin in his lapel, and ordered a forty-dollar Truffled Kobe Burger and a glass of Napa Valley cabernet, and watched him adjust the salt and pepper shakers on the table as a symbol to the rest of the staff that he had taken our order. Then I smiled at my friend and listened to her chime on about the endless possibilities of the new life ahead of her. She was rosy-cheeked and clear-eyed after her beautification treatments and said she couldn't wait to reinvent herself. "What the hell," she said. "That's what life is all about. Rebirth, re-creation, regeneration. And by the way, the burgers here are the best in the city! I'm so glad you ordered one. I want a bite."

From my seat on the banquette, I could see directly through the lounge doorway into the brightly lit hotel beyond. I watched uniformed hotel maids and housemen, pink-shirted valets, and black-suited chauffeurs trudge by, making their way silently down the long plushly carpeted hallway leading to the service elevators and the hotel's small private garage where the most expensive cars are housed: the million-dollar

Maybachs and Rolls-Royces. Periodically one of the workers would glance at the lounge door, his or her attention pulled by the music and clinking of glasses, listen for a moment, and then slowly look away while moving on. Occasionally I would catch someone's eye and smile.

As I brought my wineglass to my lips, I noticed that my hands still smelled like gasoline even though I had cleaned them several times since I'd polished the Hulk residue off the car. After a few minutes, I excused myself to go wash them again in the hotel's football field–sized ladies' room at the far end of the lobby. I used the soft terry towels to scrub my hands and face, and then freshened up my lipstick in the panoramic wall of gilded mirrors. From every angle, I was a fright. My parched hair had whipped up into a cotton candy mess at the top of my head from driving in the convertible without my cap. I knew it would be weeks before I'd be able to get a comb through it. My eyes were sunken and glassy, and my skin looked like an 8-ton truck had run over it after it had lost a few of its tires. I pinched my cheeks to brighten them up a bit, then quickly skedaddled.

The lobby entrance was jammed with women draped in satin, taffeta, and tulle and rushing tuxedoed men who almost ran me over as I exited the ladies' room. There was a wedding celebration in the hotel's grand Rodeo Ballroom, and I heard murmuring that the couple was about to arrive. I threaded my way through the beautiful people and sat down on one of the pink tufted lounge sofas to admire the hustle and bustle of the festivities, hoping to get a peek at the bride. The lobby air was heady with the powerful scent of the tiger lilies in the towering floral arrangements placed throughout the room, competing with the expensive French perfume and Italian cologne wafting from the wedding partyers. Soft diffused light glowed in the monumental gold-domed crystal chandeliers.

I watched a woman in a long gold lamé gown catch her heel in the carpet, stumble, and then drop her gold Chanel clutch purse as she hurried to the ballroom; the clutch bounced a few feet away along the thick green and pink carpet when a lobby attendant just behind her graciously retrieved and proffered it to her. She glared at him for a moment and then snatched it back without thanking him, as if he had tried to make off with it and she'd caught him. The attendant stood there for a second and then walked away, laughing to himself. I tried to let him know that I had seen what had happened, but he moved away too quickly to go about his work, and I was too tired to chase him.

I called Mr. Rumi from my cell phone.

"They're gone," I said.

"Wow, I thought they'd never leave. You okay?"

"I'm glad you answered."

"You want me to come get you?"

"No. But I'd like to see you later. I'm at the hotel with Lorelei, and I doubt I'm going to last long."

"Call me when you want to leave. I'll drive you home."

"That sounds really nice. It'll be nice to be driven," I said as I hung up. I had no idea whether I wanted to spend the rest of my life with Mr. Rumi, but I was more than happy to let him drive me around for a while.

More wedding partyers streamed by me, but there was still no sign of the bride. Lorelei came out to search for me and tell me that my forty-dollar burger was getting cold.

"Why are sitting out here? Are you all right?" she asked. "You look like you're lost."

I smiled. "No, I am fine. Thanks. I'm just taking it all in."

Epilogue

I hated being a chauffeur. The work was demeaning and exhausting, I felt trapped by the uniform and the confines of the car, was humiliated and disturbed by the unseemly behavior that seems to go with the job, and lost sight of any possible bright future when I was behind the wheel. The very place where I was supposed to be in control afforded me little autonomy or any comfort of command. Every now and then, though, something happened that restored my faith in life, my faith in mankind, and my faith in my future.

One morning, I had a pickup at the Hollywood Renaissance Hotel. The call was an A.D., which meant "as directed by the client" and could last all day or night, destinations and time frames unknown. If it were an evening call, that usually meant I'd be driving out-of-town businessmen to the Lakers' game and then to a slew of strip bars, maybe we'd hit a Koreatown massage joint around dawn, then I'd drop them off at a private plane for a 10:00 A.M. wheels-up. But I'd never been on a daytime A.D. before, so I had no idea what it might entail.

The Renaissance is not a luxury hotel; it's a 140,000-square-foot monstrosity behind the Kodak Theatre frequented by tourists who want to be close to the Hollywood Walk of Fame and Ripley's Believe It or Not! and who likely can't afford the Beverly Hills Hotel or even the Beverly Hilton but still want to feel as if they're part of the Hollywood elite. It was a pickup address that did not inspire hopeful anticipation. I only knew that it was going to be a long, probably achingly boring day, and I prayed that it wouldn't be awful.

As required, I arrived at the hotel fifteen minutes before the appointed pickup time, and my client was ready and waiting at the hotel entrance. I recognized him right away. Garrison Keillor climbed into the car without any fanfare, and we started off for Torrance, California, where he said he had a book signing. At first he was quiet on the long drive. He apologized for not conversing and said he was tired from his previous night's performance at the Hollywood Bowl, but after some time, he grew curious about me, and we talked about art, literature, and independent filmmaking. His voice was the same unusually deep baritone that I often heard on the radio as I waited in the LAX limo parking lot holding area for delayed planes on long, lonely Saturday afternoons.

He said he would have bet a hundred dollars that I belonged in the back of a limo and not the front, and that made me laugh out loud. I had ridden in a lot of limos and had even gotten the bright idea to be a chauffeur when I was sitting in the back of a limo. He was gentlemanly, almost courtly, and asked me many questions about who I was and what I thought about: How did a lady like me end up driving a limo, for God's sake? What did I do in my real, nonchauffeuring life? What did I dream of always doing but hadn't done yet? He seemed genuinely interested in me and my answers; I was so delighted that I almost drove off the freeway.

He mentioned the ancient Greek philosopher Heraclitus and his belief that the universe is in a constant state of change—that only by hitting rock bottom could an individual experience great change, and that all vital things come into being as a result of obstacle, strife, and effort. My ears perked up at this. Finally, he said, "Out of discord comes the fairest harmony." I found this strangely comforting, and as he spoke, I could feel my body relax, in a small quiet way, as if every cell stilled itself for an instant and then exhaled a soft little sigh. His voice lulled me into a happy and alert repose. And in that very moment, a tiny glimmer of hope sparked in my heart that things might get better.

We arrived at a mall bookstore in Torrance, and he went in to give a lecture. I stood in the back and listened and laughed along with the crowd of hundreds to see him; he winked at me when he saw I was there. He spoke for an hour or more and then began to sign books and converse with people. I saw that he really spent time with each person; many were fans who just wanted to fawn, but many wanted to share their personal stories with him, and he listened patiently and attentively. He was never abrupt. Sometimes he even consoled people. From a distance, it looked like an older man wept on his shoulder for a short while, but maybe they were just sharing a memory. After several hours, I hunted down the store manager and got some tea and a muffin for him. I set them on a table near where he was standing. "Oh, my dear, thank you so much," he said. "I am famished and parched." He continued to sign books throughout the rest of the afternoon, standing all the while, until no one was left in line; many fans had been waiting for hours with stacks of books for him to sign. I wandered around the bookstore and saw that there were titles by him in the children's section, the nonfiction section, the fiction section, and the poetry section. He even had a book of jokes. "What's green and hangs from trees?" (Giraffe snot.) I hadn't realized he was so prolific.

As it neared dusk, I pulled the car up to the bookstore entrance to wait for him to finish. Again he got in without letting me open the door for him, and we started on the journey back to the hotel. He was pale and tired. "I am delirious with fatigue," he said before he fell asleep on the long ride home. Every now and then he sighed or snored softly.

An hour or so later, he awoke with a start and looked around in confusion, craning his neck to see where he was; then he asked me to take him to an ATM. I told him that we were close to the hotel, moments away, but he asked me to find one anyway. I spotted a bank in a strip mall on Hollywood Boulevard, and we stopped there briefly while he used the cash machine, and then I dropped him at his hotel. As he exited the car, he handed me $300 and said, "Thank you for your most pleasant company; this is but a small token of my gratitude. You are a remarkable lady, and I am sure you will succeed."

As chance would have it, on my drive home, I listened to an evening rerun of his show on the radio. It was as if he were in the car with me again. Even now when I hear his voice on the radio, I feel buoyed by that same tiny glimmer of hope . . . hope that out of discord comes the fairest harmony.

Acknowledgments

I have always wondered why the acknowledgment pages in some books are so ludicrously long, and now I know why: At least in my case, it took a battalion to write this book. Luckily I know a lot of ridiculously generous and able soldiers who were willing to perform prodigious acts of tireless effort on my behalf, including the following:

wining and dining me; extreme and reckless encouragement; occasional coddling; general good nature and advice that cheered me up countless times, or infrequent unsolicited advice that turned out to be invaluable; gifts of computers, cell phones, paper, printer, printer ink, pages printed, airline miles, and salon services; last-minute and sometimes life-saving accommodations; more wining and dining; a substantial amount of cash flow over many years, starting at my birth; producerial assistance and directorial assistance; reading my pages RUSH, even overnight; allowing me to delude myself regularly, often without comment; helping me to secure one-of-a-kind keys lost down an elevator shaft by magically wielding a hockey stick taped with magnets (three hours!); even more wining and dining; scouring libraries and bookstores for material to assist me in research, and helping with my understanding of that research; and other kindnesses too embarrassing to name.

Most of the people and institutions named below participated in several of the above assists, some in almost all. You know who you are and what you did. In no particular order: Khaled Gabriel Tolba, Robert Knott, Julie Rose, Carol Beggy, Mike Rose, Annie Gwathmey, Emily Margolin Gwathmey, Buzz Kinninmont, Jared Moses, Richard Krevolin, Monique Vescia, Barbara Gubelman, Helena Gubelman, John Pappas,

Acknowledgments

Jennifer London, Zeinab Oumais, Alberto Ortiz, Tim Sullivan, Elissa Scrafano, Amy Schmidt, Kerry Schmidt, Annie Biggs, John Haslett, Charlie Stratton, Patrick Terry, Gerold Wunstel, Dalia Mogahed and the Gallup Center for Muslim Studies, Dr. Eleanor Abdella Doumato, Dr. Jan Morgan, Lisa Bishop, Lisa Cantor, Jeanne Darst, Giti Khajehnouri, Peter Gethers, Kate Warren, Yanni Kotsonis, Professor Bruce Levitt, Dr. David Feldshuh, and the Cornell University Department of Theatre, Film and Dance, Jackie Nichols and the Memphis Playhouse, Ernie Zulia and Hollins University, August Holler and the Vienna Einfahrt Café, Naked Angels, Galapagos Art Space, the 92nd Street Y-Tribeca, the staff and librarians of the Los Angeles Public Library and the Santa Monica Public Library, and Jim Krusoe and the Santa Monica College Writing Workshop.

My family—Sandy, Michela and Eddie, Marthe and Charles, Gus and Nancy, Robbie, Bitty and John, Margo, George and Ramona, Jon and Meghan, and my mother, Francesca Nadalini.

My editor Leah Miller (with her gracious and winning ways), Edith Lewis (copyeditor nonpareil), Jennifer Weidman, Dominick Anfuso, Meg Cassidy, Nick Greene, Karyn Marcus, and all the talented and patient people at Free Press and Simon & Schuster.

The dedicated, passionate, and tireless booksellers all over the world—without you, the printed book wouldn't exist.

Lindsay Edgecombe (aka L'Edge, aka The Velvet Hammer), agent extraordinaire, who spent a Friday afternoon in mid-August in a Manhattan theater with no air conditioning and still had the powerhouse vision to see a book in my play.

I am indebted to you all.

About the Author

© AMY J. SCHMIDT

Jayne Amelia Larson is an actress and independent film producer based in Los Angeles, and has also been an occasional chauffeur between gigs. She has degrees from Cornell University and from Harvard University's American Repertory Theatre Institute and is a regular at Jim Krusoe's writing workshop at Santa Monica College. Her one-woman show, *Driving the Saudis,* has been performed throughout the country, and won Best Solo Show at the 2010 New York Fringe Festival. She is an excellent driver.